"We, and all others
who believe in freedom
as deeply as we do, would
rather die on our feet
than live on our knees."

Franklin Delano Roosevelt

EYEWITNESS
★ ★ ★ ★ ★ ★ ★ TO ★ ★ ★ ★ ★ ★ ★
WORLD WAR II

UNFORGETTABLE STORIES FROM
HISTORY'S GREATEST CONFLICT

READER'S EDITION

NEIL KAGAN ★ STEPHEN G. HYSLOP

NATIONAL
GEOGRAPHIC

WASHINGTON, D.C.

Since 1888, the National Geographic Society has funded more than 12,000 research, exploration, and preservation projects around the world. National Geographic Partners distributes a portion of the funds it receives from your purchase to National Geographic Society to support programs including the conservation of animals and their habitats.

National Geographic Partners
1145 17th Street NW
Washington, DC 20036-4688 USA

Get closer to National Geographic explorers and photographers, and connect with our global community. Join us today at nationalgeographic.com/join

For information about special discounts for bulk purchases, please contact National Geographic Books Special Sales: specialsales@natgeo.com

For rights or permissions inquiries, please contact National Geographic Books Subsidiary Rights: bookrights@natgeo.com

Library of Congress Cataloging-in-Publication Data
Names: Kagan, Neil, editor. | Hyslop, Stephen G. (Stephen Garrison), 1950-
Title: Eyewitness to World War II : unforgettable stories
    from history's greatest conflict / Neil Kagan, Stephen G. Hyslop.
Other titles: Eyewitness to World War Two
Description: Reader's edition. | Washington, D.C. : National Geographic,
    2018. | Includes index. |
Identifiers: LCCN 2017038741 (print) | LCCN 2017039117 (ebook) | ISBN
    9781426218897 () | ISBN 9781426218880
Subjects: LCSH: World War, 1939-1945--United States. | World War,
    1939-1945--Personal narratives, American. | World War,
    1939-1945--Pictorial works.
Classification: LCC D769 (ebook) | LCC D769 .E94 2018 (print) | DDC
    940.540973--dc23
LC record available at https:// lccn.loc.gov_2017038741

Special thanks to Linda Dudik, creator of the website WWII Experience *(www.wwiiexperience .com),* for her invaluable assistance finding first-person accounts by those who experienced World War II, both in the military and on the home front.

Interior design: Nicole Miller

Printed in the United States of America

18/QGF-PCML/1

"Secure this lousy piece of real estate
so we can get the hell off it."

Lt. Col. Charles Shepard
28th Marine Regiment, Iwo Jima

★ ★ ★ ★ ★ ★ ★ ★ ★ ★

Page 2: *A battle-weary GI smokes a cigarette during the invasion of Saipan in 1944,
which brought U.S. bombers within range of Tokyo.*

THE MIGHTIEST CONFLICT OF ALL TIME

"Almost everyone directly involved in the war
is gone now, but their stories
still resonate in history."

World War II was the greatest calamity ever to befall humanity. An estimated 75 million people died—3 percent of Earth's population—including 25 million soldiers, sailors, and airmen. Entire cities were destroyed, leveled almost to the ground, while others were so seriously bombed it took 30 years to repair the damage. Whole races of people were nearly wiped out in attempts at "ethnic cleansing." The carnage was finally brought to an end with nuclear weapons so powerful they could annihilate large metropolises in a single flash and bang.

We are now at the 80th year since the war's outbreak in 1937 when imperial Japan invaded the Republic of China. Subsequently, Nazi Germany began taking countries in Europe before finally facing a declaration of war by France and Great Britain after invading Poland in 1939. Germany went on to conquer Denmark, Norway, Belgium, the Netherlands, and France. For nearly a year, Great Britain stood alone against Hitler's vast armies while they turned on the Balkan states and

A wounded GI awaits evacuation on Okinawa, where nearly 50,000 U.S. soldiers and sailors were killed or wounded in the spring of 1945.

North Africa. Then the Japanese conducted a surprise attack on the United States at Pearl Harbor, Hawaii, and the entire world was at war.

Eyewitness to World War II follows the action across both Atlantic and Pacific fronts, in the air, on the sea, under the sea, and on land, where infantry grapples with infantry from the steaming jungles of the South Pacific to the Italian Alps. This book portrays all the major theaters of war in North Africa, Russia, and the Allied invasion and victory in Europe, along with the mostly American push up the Pacific from New Guinea to the home islands of Japan.

The war produced great deeds of heroism as well as cowardly acts like the mass execution of unarmed civilians, including women and children, because they belonged to a particular race or ethnic group. In the end, the Allied nations prevailed. The Nazi leader, Adolf Hitler, committed suicide and the Japanese leader, Hideki Tojo, was executed for war crimes. Peace returned to the world. But none who lived through it could ever forget it, no matter where they were.

The war touched almost everyone, from the disruption of traffic and the rationing of food and other desirable goods in many countries to the ravages of war in mainland Europe, the Soviet Union, and, ultimately, Japan. For generations, people defined themselves and their lives as "before the war," or "during the war," or "after the war."

Almost everyone directly involved in the war is gone now, but their stories still resonate in history, and some of the finest are reproduced in these pages. Louise Whatley, now of Cedar Rapids, Iowa, for instance, lived near Pearl Harbor and vividly describes the day of the attack. It was 7:30 on a Sunday morning, December 7, 1942, she remembered, and "I was still asleep when all at once the sky was full of planes and a million guns going off." She threw on her red robe and rushed outside with "all the other crazy people," standing in the streets to watch what they all thought was "the army's latest battle practice," when "just then a plane went down in flames and flew over our heads, spitting bullets from a machine gun, so low we could see the Jap pilot and the markings of the rising sun on its wings."

Lt. Cmdr. Wade McClusky describes being chased by two Japanese fighter aircraft Zeros after dropping the bombs that sank enemy carriers *Akagi* and *Kaga* during the desperate Battle of Midway in late 1942. He was skimming the water about 20 feet above the waves when "a sudden burst seemed to envelop the whole plane. The left side of the cockpit was shattered, and my left shoulder felt like it had been hit by a sledgehammer. It seemed like the end." Then for a few seconds there came an "unusual quietness." He turned painfully to see if his tail gunner had been hit. "He was facing aft, guns at the ready and unharmed," McClusky said. "He had shot down one Zero and the other one decided to call it quits."

In these pages, you'll also find the diary of a Japanese sergeant starving to death during the last days of the Battle of Guadalcanal. All he's had to eat in the past week is a portion of maggoty meat and ant nests; he's so weak he's afraid he can't carry his equipment. Suddenly the Americans begin broadcasting from a loudspeaker, telling him to surrender. "What fools the enemy are!" he writes. "The Japanese army will stick it out to the end. This position must be defended with our lives."

Each of these moving vignettes is a dramatic eyewitness account of the human participation in the war; they enliven the main narrative, which follows the course of the action. The descriptions of battles here are breathtaking, and the heartrending story of the conflict is both illustrious and perceptive. Distinguished readers of history will cherish this account of the mightiest conflict of all time.

—Winston Groom
Point Clear, Alabama

A WORLD GONE MAD

The people of the United States feel strong ownership of World War II and for good reason. Our homeland was bombed, our young men fought and died, our civilians worked and sacrificed to ensure a successful outcome, and our entry into the war was key to driving back vicious and aggressive dictators from the world's stage. But the seeds of this war were sown far from home, in Europe and Asia, and long before the fateful day when America woke from its isolationism, shocked into action by bombs raining down on Pearl Harbor.

In 1939, a quarter century after enlisting to fight for Germany in calamitous World War I, Adolf Hitler invaded Poland. For millions who had endured that earlier conflict, World War II came much too soon. But for Hitler, warfare was welcome. Any peace lasting "more than 25 years is harmful to a nation," he insisted. "Peoples, like individuals, sometimes need regenerating by a little bloodletting." He was prepared to spill more than a little blood to regenerate the German Reich, an empire of medieval origins that rose anew in 1871 but collapsed in 1918 while Hitler was recuperating after being blinded in battle. When he was told of Germany's defeat, Hitler wrote, "Everything went black before my eyes again."

Flanked by Nazi storm troopers holding swastika banners, Adolf Hitler ascends to the podium during a rally at Bückeburg, Germany, in October 1934.

Hitler regained his eyesight but emerged with a warped view of the world. Although German commanders bore responsibility for losing World War I, Hitler blamed communists and Jews and vowed to purge them from the Third Reich, which he forged by promising to restore order to a nation convulsed by the Great Depression. Appointed chancellor in 1933, Hitler assumed emergency powers, crushed opposition to his Nazi Party, and became Germany's unchallenged führer (leader), backed by an expansive new Wehrmacht (armed forces). He was "our savior, bringing light into darkness," said a devotee at one of the mass rallies where Hitler whipped followers into a frenzy. His incendiary words and deeds sparked conflagrations at home and abroad as like-minded dictators joined him in fanning the flames.

ROME'S NEW CAESAR

Benito Mussolini was Hitler's paragon and precursor, hailed by Italians as Il Duce ("the Leader") a decade before Germany's führer seized power. Rising to prominence in the chaotic aftermath of World War I when Italy's democratic system was unraveling, Mussolini posed as a modern-day Caesar. Like Roman rulers of old, he received stiff-arm salutes from his adoring Blackshirts, known as Fascists (for fasces, bundles of rods with ax heads attached that symbolized Roman authority). Granted emergency powers temporarily in 1922, Mussolini became Italy's permanent strongman. "We have buried the putrid corpse of liberty!" he declared in 1934 after abolishing elections, banning labor unions, and crushing dissent.

In 1935, Rome's new Caesar invaded Ethiopia. Great Britain threatened action and the League of Nations imposed sanctions, but Mussolini remained defiant, accusing the British and other imperial rivals of denying Italians "their place in the sun." He touted his campaign as a "war of civilization and liberation," but his forces brutally overpowered the lightly armed Ethiopians by bombing, strafing, and gassing them. With victory in his grasp, the British backed down and the League caved in, despite an impassioned plea from Ethiopian ruler Haile Selassie, who foresaw further aggression if Italy went unpunished. "It is us today," he warned. "It will be you tomorrow."

> "It is us today," he warned. "It will be you tomorrow."
>
> Ethiopian ruler Haile Selassie, warning of the dangers of allowing fascist aggression to go unchecked

Hitler, who had withdrawn from the League of Nations in 1933, was glad to see it discredited as a peacekeeping body. He was gearing up for war, and Nazi Germany had much greater military and industrial potential than Fascist Italy did. By 1939, when he forged his Pact of Steel with Mussolini, Il Duce was very much the junior partner in that alliance. He would continue to seek victories over vulnerable opponents, but as one Italian official said, his posturing as a great Roman conqueror was "a bluff, a fraud."

SHOWDOWN IN SPAIN

War returned to Europe in 1936 when Spanish Nationalists led by Gen. Francisco Franco assailed Republicans and their democratically elected government. Both sides in the Spanish Civil War had extremists within their ranks, including communists among the Republicans and fascists among the Nationalists. The struggle intensified when Hitler and Mussolini backed Franco and Soviet dictator Joseph Stalin aided the Republicans.

Britain, France, and the United States remained neutral, but thousands from those countries volunteered to fight Franco. Among them was British author George Orwell, who found

"Bullets hurt, corpses stink, men under fire are often so frightened that they wet their trousers."
George Orwell

that war for a lofty cause was still a nasty business. "Here we are, soldiers of a revolutionary army, defending Democracy against Fascism," he wrote, "but the details of our life are just as sordid and degrading as it could be in prison . . . Bullets hurt, corpses stink, men under fire are often so frightened that they wet their trousers."

For Hitler and his commanders, Spain was a proving ground for new weapons and tactics. In April 1937, warplanes of Germany's Condor Legion demonstrated the fearsome impact of strategic bombing by blasting the town of Guernica in Republican-held territory and killing more than 1,500 people. Such attacks drew fervent protests, but moral indignation did not halt Hitler's forceful intervention on behalf of the Nationalists, who took Madrid in 1939 and installed Franco as Spain's dictator.

Orwell emerged from the struggle contemptuous of communism, which tainted the Republican cause, but convinced that Western democracies were inviting disaster if they failed to oppose Hitler. "When one thinks of the cruelty, squalor, and futility of war," he wrote, "there is always the temptation to say, 'One side is as bad as the other: I am neutral.' " In this war, Orwell concluded, neutrality weakened the democracies and left his complacent homeland "sleeping the deep, deep sleep of England, from which I sometimes fear that we shall never awake till we are jerked out of it by the roar of bombs."

MAYHEM IN CHINA

While fighting in Spain intensified, the Japanese invaded China in 1937 and set the stage for further convulsions in the Far East that would eventually draw the United States into the conflict. Like Germany, Japan was hit hard by the Great Depression, which undermined its constitutional government. Parliamentary leaders who favored peace were attacked, and commanders intent on expanding the Japanese Empire gained the upper hand. In 1931, Japan seized Manchuria, from which its troops began infiltrating China. In July 1937, fighting erupted near Peking (Beijing) between Japanese soldiers and Chinese Nationalists, whose leader,

This shocking photo, showing a wounded infant abandoned in a bomb-blasted railroad station in Shanghai in 1937, drew international attention to Japan's devastating assault on China.

Chiang Kai-shek, vowed not to yield "one more inch of our territory." Military chiefs in Tokyo then authorized a punitive expedition "to chastise the outrageous Chinese" for acts "derogatory to the prestige of the Empire of Japan."

In December, Japan attacked Nanking (Nanjing), Chiang's capital. He and his officials fled, but many Chinese soldiers were trapped there and removed their uniforms to avoid detection by Japanese troops, who had been told to take no prisoners. The invaders began killing men indiscriminately, and soon they were assaulting women, thousands of whom were raped, and attacking children. Japanese officers failed to restrain their soldiers, some of whom used bayonets on civilians. This provided a "finishing touch to training for the men and a trial of courage for the officer," one commander said. "After that, a man could do anything easily." More than 200,000 people may have died in the Nanking massacre.

The atrocity alarmed Americans, as did the Japanese bombing of a U.S. gunboat in Chinese waters. President Franklin Roosevelt proposed a "quarantine" on foreign aggressors. Not until Japan joined Germany and Italy to form the Axis and expanded its offensive, however, would he impose tough sanctions and force Tokyo to choose between renouncing its imperial ambitions or defying America.

"PEACE FOR OUR TIME"

Before Hitler went to war in 1939, he won territorial concessions in Europe and the loyalty of his skeptical generals by exploiting the desire of the French and British to avoid conflict. His first bloodless victory was in March 1936, when he sent troops into the Rhineland, an industrial zone bordering France that had been demilitarized at the end of World War I. Hitler's forces were not yet overpowering and had orders to withdraw if French troops opposed their advance. But France would not act alone and could not get Britain to join in a military

> "Today we own Germany and tomorrow the entire world."
> Nazi storm trooper parade chant

response. Hitler's gamble succeeded, and Nazi storm troopers celebrated by parading in Berlin and chanting: "Today we own Germany and tomorrow the entire world." German generals who were plotting to overthrow Hitler changed their plans.

Hitler went on to annex Austria, an ethnically German country, where his troops were greeted in March 1938 with banners proclaiming "One People, One Reich, One Führer!" When leaders in London and Paris let that provocation pass unchallenged, Hitler threatened Czechoslovakia, where ethnic Germans were a minority, concentrated in the Sudetenland along Germany's border. Hitler's growing military strength made France and Britain all the more cautious. British prime minister Neville Chamberlain was so intent on avoiding war that he ended up encouraging German aggression.

Meeting with Hitler at Munich in September 1938, Chamberlain and French premier Édouard Daladier agreed to let German troops occupy the Sudetenland, placing all of Czechoslovakia at risk. Hitler's one concession was to sign what the führer deemed a meaningless "scrap of paper," stating that the Munich accord signaled the desire of Germany and Britain "never to go to war again." Chamberlain returned home touting the deal as "peace with honor . . . peace for our time." Hitler doubted his resolve and soon broke the peace by overrunning the rest of Czechoslovakia. Britain and France then

An overwrought woman raises her arm dutifully as German occupation forces enter the Sudetenland in October 1938.

pledged to fight if Germany invaded Poland. Appeasement had failed, and war was imminent.

BLITZING POLAND

Poland's fate was sealed on August 24, 1939, when Germany and the Soviet Union concluded their Nonaggression Pact. A temporary truce between Hitler and Stalin, the pact allowed those two ruthless dictators from opposite ends of the ideological spectrum to pursue the one goal they had in common: wiping Poland off the map. Hitler could now expand his Reich by seizing central and western Poland, including the capital, Warsaw, and the Polish Corridor separating East Prussia from the rest of Germany. Stalin would then enlarge his empire by occupying eastern Poland. With the Soviet leader as his new comrade in arms, Hitler had Poland cornered and doubted that Britain and France would intervene to save that country. "Our enemies are little worms," he told his generals. "I got to know them at Munich."

On September 1, German ground forces swept into Poland while siren-equipped Stuka dive-bombers and other warplanes of their formidable Luftwaffe struck military as well as civilian targets. Britain and France declared war two days later and began mobilizing to fight, but they could do little to prevent Poland from being overrun by Hitler's army, which advanced so rapidly in tanks, trucks, and other vehicles that reporters coined the term *blitzkrieg* ("lightning war") to describe the campaign. "The Germans have proceeded not only with might and speed, but with method," wrote *New York Times* war correspondent Otto Tolischus, "and this bids fair to be the first war decided not by infantry, 'the queen of all arms,' but by fast motorized divisions and, especially, by the air force." By month's end, the Germans had captured Warsaw and seized the bulk of Poland, while Soviet forces claimed their share to the east. Hitler's quick victory did not bode well for his opponents in western Europe. In upcoming campaigns, German forces would refine their blitzkrieg tactics and combine swift armored thrusts with precise air strikes to achieve stunning breakthroughs.

BREAKTHROUGH IN THE WEST

After conquering Poland, Hitler prepared to settle scores with France and Britain. He was surprised but not dismayed when they declared war as promised. Now that the battle lines were drawn, he saw an opportunity to use his highly effective new blitzkrieg strategy to defeat France "in one gigantic knockout blow" that would leave the British isolated and force them to come to terms. Before launching that strike, Hitler secured his northern flank by invading Denmark and Norway in April 1940 and ensuring Sweden's neutrality. By May, he was ready to slug it out with the western powers.

The path of least resistance for German forces invading France, whose border with Germany was shielded by the formidable Maginot Line, lay through the vulnerable Low Countries to the north. On May 10, one German army group invaded Holland, luring French troops and the British Expeditionary Force (BEF) northward into Belgium to meet that threat. Meanwhile, the armored divisions of a second army group were moving furtively through Luxembourg and the forested Ardennes, mistakenly considered impenetrable by tanks. On May 13, they stunned French forces at Sedan, crossed the Meuse River, and raced toward the English Channel, driving a wedge between Allied forces in Belgium and those still in France. When one French general learned of that devastating breakthrough, he "burst into tears," an aide recalled. "He was the first man I had seen weep during this campaign. Alas, there were to be others."

On May 24, fearing that his fast-advancing panzers (German tanks and armored units) were overextended and vulnerable to a counterattack, Hitler halted them near the French port of Dunkirk, just south of the Belgian border, until infantry could catch up. The pause allowed the imperiled BEF to fortify Dunkirk and hold out long enough for an improvised fleet to ferry nearly 340,000 troops across the English Channel to safety. That "miracle at Dunkirk" encouraged the British to defy Hitler and keep fighting. But many Allied soldiers were cut off and captured when Dunkirk fell in early June, leaving France vulnerable to the Germans, who began bearing down on Paris. "The new advance will not be very arduous," wrote Maj. Gen. Erwin Rommel as his panzers turned southward. "The sooner we get on with it, the better."

THE FALL OF FRANCE

The climactic battle for France began on June 5, 1940, when German forces crossed the Somme River, the site of prolonged trench warfare during World War I. The French commander, Gen. Maxime Weygand, urged his countrymen to stand fast as they did in 1914 when they stopped the Germans short of Paris.

> "All officers . . . must be filled with the grim desire to fight to the death."
>
> French commander Gen. Maxime Weygand, urging his citizenry to resist German invaders

"The battle on which the fate of the country depends will be fought, without thought of withdrawal, from the position that we now occupy," Weygand declared. "All officers . . . must be filled with the grim desire to fight to the death."

This time, there would be no holding back the German invaders, whose mobile forces were primed to wage blitzkrieg and avoid the deadlock that had exhausted their country in the previous war. General Rommel's tanks were among the first to punch through Weygand's static defenses. "All quiet forward," he reported that evening, "enemy in shreds." French officials abandoned Paris on June 10 and declared the city open, or undefended, to spare the populace. A week later, 84-year-old Marshal Philippe Pétain took charge of the government and announced to the nation: "With a heavy heart, I tell you today that it is necessary to stop the fighting." Gen. Charles de Gaulle denounced Pétain for yielding and fled to London as the self-proclaimed leader of the Free French.

On June 21, Hitler imposed an armistice on French commanders in the same railway car where German officers had conceded defeat in 1918. His terms confined Pétain's compliant Vichy-based administration to southern France and placed the rest of the country under German occupation. Afterward, Hitler toured Paris with his chief architect, Albert Speer, and told him that he had been considering destroying that majestic capital. Instead, he had decided to transform Berlin into the world's greatest city. "Paris will be only a shadow," he said. "So why should we destroy it?"

THE BATTLE OF BRITAIN

Winston Churchill succeeded Neville Chamberlain as prime minister on May 10, 1940, the same day Hitler launched the offensive that defeated France and left Britain alone to oppose Nazi Germany. A fervent critic of appeasement, Churchill ruled out coming to terms with Hitler and pledged continued defiance. "We shall fight on the seas and oceans," he vowed in June, "we shall fight with growing confidence and

"We shall fight on the seas and oceans, we shall fight with growing confidence and growing strength in the air, we shall defend our island, whatever the cost may be, we shall fight on the beaches . . . we shall fight in the hills; we shall never surrender."

Winston Churchill, in a speech to the House of Commons, June 4, 1940

Londoners huddle in the Underground, whose stations became bomb shelters at night.

growing strength in the air, we shall defend our island, whatever the cost may be, we shall fight on the beaches . . . we shall fight in the hills; we shall never surrender."

Churchill's confidence in British airpower was well founded, for the Royal Air Force (RAF) possessed an unrivaled radar network to detect attacks and superb warplanes, flown by skilled pilots. Hitler could not risk crossing the Channel and fighting the British on their beaches without first defeating the RAF. The numerically superior Luftwaffe launched the Battle of Britain in July and came close to victory by pounding RAF bases and depleting its corps of trained pilots. Goaded by the British bombing of Berlin, Hitler then vowed to "eradicate their cities."

Axis occupation forces in the Balkans responded to assaults by rounding up civilians indiscriminately and executing them by firing squad or by hanging.

That aerial blitz was appalling for civilians—more than 100,000 dead or wounded—but allowed the RAF to repair its airfields and replenish its squadrons. Strategic bombing "makes headlines, kills people, and smashes property," radio correspondent Edward R. Murrow reported from London in September. "But it doesn't win wars," he concluded, and "will not cause this country to collapse." Hitler scrapped plans to invade Britain as winter approached. For the first time, an opponent had withstood his threats and assaults by resolving, in Churchill's words, never to give in, never to yield "to the apparently overwhelming might of the enemy."

WAR IN THE BALKANS

Hitler was drawn into the treacherous Balkans—a region of forbidding terrain and fierce ethnic rivalries—by his faltering Axis partner, Mussolini. In October 1940, seeking to rival Hitler's conquests, Mussolini ordered troops in Albania, occupied by Italy in 1939, to invade Greece. The Greeks, however, routed the Italians and strengthened ties with Britain, which sent troops to bolster Greece and urged Yugoslavia to resist Germany and its allies in the region, including oil-rich Romania. When Yugoslav officers hostile to the Axis took charge in Belgrade in April 1941, Hitler invaded their country and ordered the Luftwaffe to "destroy the city." At least 17,000 people died in that attack, described by one German general as "a matter of Hitler's vanity, his personal revenge." By month's end, Axis forces had overrun both Yugoslavia and Greece, and British troops had withdrawn to Crete. In May, the Germans launched a paratrooper-intensive airborne assault on that island, killing or capturing some 15,000 British soldiers.

Conquering the Balkans proved easier than pacifying that fractious region. Serbs in Yugoslavia had long been at odds with Croats, a rift the Germans exploited by setting up a puppet Croatian state, led by fascists called Ustaše. Opposing them were partisans led by Josip Broz, a communist who took the name Tito. A Croat himself, Tito forged a multiethnic resistance movement that incorporated many Serbs but clashed with Serbian monarchists called Chetniks, who began collaborating with occupation forces. Churchill set aside his aversion to communism and aided Tito's partisans because they were doing the "most harm to the Germans." Hitler responded by boosting his forces in the Balkans to 100,000 and ordering the execution of 100 Yugoslavs for every German killed. That vicious conflict was an added burden for his Wehrmacht, already severely strained by the huge task he undertook in late June 1941: the invasion of the Soviet Union, delayed for several weeks by the distracting Balkans campaign.

TAKING ON THE SOVIET UNION

In deciding to break his pact with Stalin and invade the Soviet Union in June 1941, Hitler threw caution aside and exacerbated an ongoing conflict by challenging a nation far larger than his own. A safer course for Germany would have been to go all out to defeat British forces around the Mediterranean, seizing the Suez Canal and other vital links between Britain and its colonies while subjecting that island nation to relentless submarine warfare. But Hitler had always considered fighting the British to be of secondary importance—a mere prelude to his grand scheme, which was to advance eastward against the Soviets and fulfill his twin obsessions: living space for Germans and degradation or death for Slavs, Jews, and others defined as subhuman by Nazi zealots, who had a method to their madness that made them all the more dangerous. This would be a "war of extermination," warned Hitler, who told his generals to ignore international law and act with "unprecedented, unmerciful, and unrelenting harshness."

Beginning on June 22, three million German troops invaded the Soviet Union in a blistering offensive code-named Operation Barbarossa that caught Stalin and his Red Army off guard. One-fourth of the Soviet Air Force was destroyed that first day, much of it on the ground. Nazi officials didn't neglect the ethnic cleansing they had been sent to do either, dispatching death squads to murder Jews by the thousands and inciting the incidents of orchestrated mob violence against Jews known as pogroms.

Huge gains by German armored columns in the opening weeks seemingly confirmed Hitler's prediction that Stalin's regime would soon collapse under attack. The Soviet dictator had deep reserves, however. If the Germans smashed a dozen divisions, "the Russians simply put up another dozen," wrote Gen. Franz Halder in August. "We have underestimated the Russian colossus," he concluded. Hitler's Japanese allies would soon make the same miscalculation in taking on the American colossus.

Japanese emperor Hirohito upheld the policies of the militarist faction that dominated the government and armed forces.

CHRONOLOGY

DECEMBER 1, 1941 Emperor Hirohito approves Japanese attacks on the United States and its allies.

DECEMBER 6, 1941 President Franklin D. Roosevelt sends a message to Hirohito seeking peace.

DAY OF DESTINY

THE ATTACK ON PEARL HARBOR

On Monday, December 1, 1941, Japan's military and political leaders gathered at the Imperial Palace in Tokyo for a war conference presided over by Emperor Hirohito, who sat above them on a platform in front of a golden screen. A slight, unassuming figure with thick glasses, the 40-year-old Hirohito did not look like a man who held Japan's destiny in his hands. Yet he was in fact the nation's commander in chief. He was being asked to approve an offensive that would set Japan against the United States—which was still at peace—and its embattled ally Great Britain. He did not seek that conflict, but he bore ultimate responsibility for exposing his people to the huge risks it entailed. Hirohito, whose constitutional duties as emperor included appointing Japan's prime minister, had recently entrusted that high office to Gen. Hideki Tojo. A staunch advocate of imperial

DECEMBER 7, 1941 Japanese attack Pearl Harbor and launch a far-reaching offensive in Asia and the Pacific.

DECEMBER 11, 1941 Adolf Hitler declares Germany at war with the United States.

DECEMBER 8, 1941 Japanese attack American bases in the Philippines. U.S. Congress declares war on Japan.

expansion, Tojo expected to continue on the aggressive course he and other Japanese officers had set when they invaded China in 1937 and maneuvered their country into the Axis alliance with Germany and Italy through a series of agreements culminating in 1940 with the signing of the Tripartite Pact. That defensive pact did not require Japan to join its Axis partners in their war against Britain. But Tojo and his fellow militants, who dominated the government, hoped to exploit the fact that many European countries were now under German occupation or attack by seizing vulnerable British, French, and Dutch colonies in Asia—lands rich in oil, rubber, and other militarily vital resources that Japan lacked.

The urge to grab those assets increased when the United States responded to the Japanese occupation of French Indochina in July 1941 by imposing an oil embargo on Tokyo. Japan shelved plans to join Germany in its ongoing invasion of the Soviet Union, a traditional enemy, and settled instead on a sweeping offensive that included attacks on British Malaya and Singapore and the Dutch East Indies, as well as American bases in the Philippines and Hawaii, where the U.S. Pacific Fleet lay sheltered at Pearl Harbor.

Tojo could not launch those attacks without the consent of Hirohito, who served not just as commander in chief but as Japan's national idol, revered as a living god who watched kindly over his people. As such, the emperor tried to remain above the fray and hold out hope for peace even as his officers prepared for war. Shortly before appointing Tojo prime minister, Hirohito had prompted one last effort to resolve the crisis diplomatically by quoting a poem composed by his grandfather, Emperor Meiji: "Across the four seas all are brothers. / In such a world why do the waves rage, the winds roar?" Japanese envoys in Washington, D.C., entered into talks with Secretary of State Cordell Hull that contin- ued into late November. By then, however, Tojo had set the offensive in motion, with the understanding that forces on their way to battle would be recalled if a diplomatic breakthrough occurred. Prospects for peace dwindled when American officials learned that a Japanese convoy was carrying tens of thousands of troops toward Malaya, an invasion the United States would not tolerate. Secretary Hull, who doubted that a government headed by Tojo could be trusted, saw no point in negotiating under the threat of immi- nent hostilities and made a final offer to Tokyo: Washington would lift the embargo and offer Japan economic incentives if it nullified the Tripartite Pact and withdrew its forces from China and Indochina.

> "Across the four seas all are brothers./In such a world why do the waves rage, the winds roar?"
>
> Emperor Hirohito, quoting a poem composed by his grandfather, Emperor Meiji

Whether to retreat and make peace or press ahead and wage war was the great issue facing the imperial conference on Decem- ber 1. Hirohito hosted the meeting but did not speak. He left it to the head of his privy council, Yoshimichi Hara, to question Tojo and other officials and deliver the verdict. To yield to the American demands, Hara concluded, would threaten the "exis- tence of our empire." Tojo understood that this was Hirohito's conclusion as well. "Once His Majesty decides to commence hostilities," he stated, "we will all strive to meet our obligations to him, bring the government and the military ever closer together, resolve that the nation united will go on to victory, make an all-out effort to achieve our war aims, and set His Majesty's mind at ease."

Hirohito, accompanied by senior military officers, inspects massive acoustic locators used by Japan in the 1930s to defend against air raids. Resembling giant tubas, the passive listening devices pivoted to locate the engine noise of approaching planes and direct the fire of the antiaircraft guns in the background.

Throughout the conference, Hirohito "displayed not the slightest anxiety," one witness reported. "He seemed to be in a good mood. We were filled with awe." He may have taken comfort in the thought that he had exhausted the possibilities for peace before embarking on war. But by appointing the militant General Tojo as prime minister—and by allowing warships and troop transports to be launched menacingly while negotiations in Washington were under way—Japan's commander in chief had undermined those talks. Soon after the conference ended, Hirohito affixed his seal to a document approving the offensive. To bow to Washington, he remarked, would be humiliating.

Hirohito and his officers, already embroiled in a punishing conflict with China, were taking a big gamble by widening their war to include the United States. Japanese forces were far better prepared for conflict in Asia and the Pacific than their European and American foes and saw an excellent opportunity to achieve supremacy there, yet there were those who worried that their country was biting off more than it could chew. Among those who harbored doubts was Adm. Isoroku Yamamoto, commander of the Combined Fleet (incorporating most of Japan's naval forces), who planned the assault on Pearl Harbor by a formidable naval task force, including six aircraft carriers of his First Air Fleet. Yamamoto had spent several years in the United States as a student and naval attaché and marveled at its industrial might. He knew that Japan could not match American war production if the conflict lasted long. But he was a gambler by nature who loved poker and other games of chance, and he was prepared to risk all on a surprise attack on Pearl Harbor.

On December 2, when Yamamoto learned that Hirohito had approved the offensive, he signaled Vice Adm. Chuichi Nagumo, commanding the task force destined for Pearl Harbor, to attack there as planned early on Sunday morning, December 7. If the plan succeeded as Yamamoto hoped, America might be left without the will or means to wage a costly war in the Pacific while also defending its allies against Germany in the Atlantic. If his bid failed, however, and the United States retained the strength and determination to strike back, he had little hope of prevailing in the long run. "I shall run wild for the first six months or a year," he remarked, "but I have utterly no confidence for the second or third year."

WARNINGS IN WASHINGTON

While Hirohito was settling on war, President Franklin D. Roosevelt was returning to the White House from his retreat at Warm Springs, Georgia, where he had shared Thanksgiving dinner with children at a rehabilitation center he had founded for those afflicted with polio as he was. Paralyzed from the waist down in 1921 at the age of 39, he had overcome that setback to become the only American ever elected to three terms as president. Roosevelt had faced many trials since his first inauguration in the depths of the Great Depression in January 1933, but nothing as dire as the crisis that confronted him now in Washington. On his desk when he got back was a message broadcast in code by radio from Tokyo to Lt. Gen. Hiroshi Oshima, the Japanese ambassador in Berlin. Intercepted and deciphered by the U.S. Army's Signal Intelligence Service (SIS), the dispatch warned that "there is extreme danger that war may suddenly break out between the Anglo-Saxon nations and Japan through some clash of arms and that the time of the breaking out of this war may come quicker than anyone dreams."

This was the latest of many alarming messages decoded by an SIS team led by William Friedman, a brilliant cryptanalyst who had succeeded in reproducing the electronic circuitry of a machine known as Purple, which the Japanese used to encode and decipher their diplomatic communications. The machine "spewed sparks and made loud whirring noises," recalled one officer, but the treasure trove of intelligence—code-named Magic—that Friedman's team produced allowed Roosevelt and others in high positions in Washington to read the minds of their counterparts in Tokyo. A recent Magic intercept had revealed that if the talks with

Secretary of State Hull did not yield a settlement by November 29, "things are automatically going to happen." That hostilities were imminent was confirmed by the message to Oshima, indicating that one or both of the "Anglo-Saxon nations," meaning the United States and Great Britain, might be attacked by Japan at any time.

No one in Washington knew of the impending assault on Pearl Harbor, though, because Tokyo did not inform diplomats of its specific war plans, and the Japanese navy had its own code for radio signals. That code was changed shortly before the attack on Pearl Harbor, and the strike force approaching Hawaii observed radio silence, leaving U.S. Navy cryptanalysts with no clue as to its whereabouts or intentions. The SIS did gather intelligence suggesting that Pearl Harbor was a likely target, but those clues were overlooked. One message sent from Tokyo to the Japanese consul in Honolulu on December 2 requested daily reports on the presence in Pearl Harbor of aircraft carriers and other warships and asked whether they were "provided with antitorpedo nets." A reply sent to Tokyo on December 3 contained a report on the Pacific Fleet by a naval intelligence officer at the consulate, Ensign Takeo Yoshikawa. The SIS passed those messages along to the U.S. Navy's cryptographic bureau, where a linguist new to the staff, Dorothy Edgers, translated the Japanese text into English. She was alarmed by the dispatches and brought them to the attention of her chief, but he set them aside until the following week, when he would have more time to review her work. "We'll get back to this on Monday," he told her.

Takeo Yoshikawa, the sender of the report Edgers translated, was a gifted intelligence agent undercover at the Japanese consulate in Honolulu as a diplomat named Tadashi Morimura. Yoshikawa, who had graduated from the Imperial Naval Academy at the top of his class, had trained on surface ships and submarines before joining the Intelligence Division of the Navy General Staff, where he became an expert on the U.S. Pacific Fleet and its bases. His mission was to collect "legal intelligence" on Pearl Harbor and the Pacific Fleet, which meant conducting surveillance without breaking any laws to avoid being apprehended as a spy. He chose to operate alone. "My superiors in Tokyo had cautioned me severely as to the vital nature of the mission," Yoshikawa recalled, "and I was never to find anyone whom I could trust sufficiently to assist me in its accomplishment." Although not told the exact purpose of his assignment, he understood that he was paving the way for an attack on U.S. naval facilities.

The young consular official had rented a second-story apartment in Honolulu overlooking the harbor and worked tirelessly, gleaning information about the military bases around Pearl Harbor and their security procedures, taking photographs of ships, and recording their movements. Posing as a carefree diplomat with few duties and plenty of leisure time, he took rides on tugboats, listened to gossip in bars and restaurants, and rented small aircraft for sightseeing flights over Honolulu to observe the military airfields. A strong swimmer, Yoshikawa joined tourists on Oahu's beaches to examine underwater obstructions, time the tides, and examine beach gradients. He made almost daily strolls through Pearl City with its clear view of the Ford Island airfield and Battleship Row and hiked up slopes overlooking Pearl Harbor to observe the comings and goings of the fleet.

Yoshikawa's favorite observation point provided excellent cover. He frequented the Shuncho-ro tearoom, a traditional Japanese geisha establishment perched above Pearl Harbor's East Loch. Yoshikawa always requested a table with a view from which he could observe ships in the harbor. He occasionally questioned the restaurant's geisha, who often entertained U.S. naval personnel, but he never took them into his confidence, aware that most of Hawaii's Japanese population was loyal to America.

Yoshikawa sent a steady stream of intelligence reports to Tokyo, detailing the number and types of ships present, the location of fuel and ammunition depots, and fleet dispositions within the anchorage. His messages were enciphered using the Japanese Foreign Ministry's J-19 diplomatic, or "Purple," code, the same one Ambassador Oshima used. Though the code had been broken, U.S. intelligence officers gave communications from the consulate in Hawaii low priority and overlooked Yoshikawa's reports.

On September 24, Yoshikawa's superiors requested that all intelligence he provide be of "immediate tactical significance." Then in late November, Lt. Cmdr. Suguru Suzuki arrived in Honolulu aboard the Japanese liner *Taiyo Maru,* disguised as a steward. Suzuki delivered a list of detailed questions concerning Pearl Harbor, to which Yoshikawa replied that same day. He knew that an attack was imminent when he was ordered to submit daily reports placing all ships in a grid system and was asked whether they were protected by antiaircraft defenses or antitorpedo nets. Yoshikawa sent his final message on December 6, reporting that the aircraft carriers "Enterprise and Lexington have sailed from Pearl Harbor."

On December 7, as the attack drew to a close, Yoshikawa and others in the consulate would be arrested by FBI agents, who would find no evidence of espionage. Eight months later, he would be quietly repatriated to Japan in a diplomatic prisoner exchange. American officials did not know that they were releasing a spy who had proudly contributed to the attack. "For a moment, at least," he wrote afterward, "I held history in the palm of my hand."

Certain that Japan would soon attack, but unsure when or where the blow would fall, Roosevelt found himself in an unenviable position as commander in chief. To win the war he knew was coming, he felt compelled to let the nation's enemies strike the first blow. A preemptive attack on Japan would cast the United States as the aggressor and upset American isolationists, who would support war only if their country was forced into it. Furthermore, Army and Navy chiefs hoped to avoid conflict with Japan long enough to allow them to build up strength in the Pacific. There was little they could do now that war appeared likely except place American bases on alert. Army chief Gen. George Marshall stated the government's position in a warning sent to commanders in the Pacific after negotiations ended: "Japanese future action unpredictable but hostile action possible at any moment. If hostilities cannot, repeat cannot, be avoided the United States desires that Japan commit the first overt act. This policy should not, repeat not, be construed as restricting you to a course of action that might jeopardize your defense." The last thing Marshall or Roosevelt wanted was for U.S. forces to be caught napping and suffer heavy losses. A Japanese attack rebuffed by alert defenders would be ample justification for war—and far better for American morale than a costly defeat.

> "Japanese future action unpredictable but hostile action possible at any moment. If hostilities cannot, repeat cannot, be avoided the United States desires that Japan commit the first overt act."
>
> Army chief George Marshall in a warning sent to American commanders in the Pacific

In choosing not to initiate hostilities with Japan, Roosevelt was supported not just by his military chiefs but also by British prime minister Winston Churchill. Roosevelt was aiding Britain against Germany and shared Churchill's conviction that war in Europe should have priority over war in the Pacific if a showdown with Tokyo could not be avoided. "It seems to me that one important method remains unused in averting war between Japan and our two countries," Churchill wrote to Roosevelt, "namely a plain declaration, secret or public as may be thought best, that any further act of aggression by Japan will lead to the gravest consequence." The British would make a similar declaration, added Churchill, who closed on a personal note: "Forgive me, my dear friend, for presuming to press such a course upon you, but I am convinced that it might make all the difference and prevent a melancholy extension of the war."

A Japanese naval officer briefs pilots before the attack on Pearl Harbor in a scene recorded by a motion picture cameraman. The Imperial Navy was eager to document the historic operation. With more than 420 aircraft on its decks, Vice Adm. Chuichi Nagumo's First Air Fleet was the most powerful carrier task force that had ever been assembled.

Roosevelt responded by issuing a private appeal to Hirohito. On Saturday, December 6, he sent a radiogram urging the emperor to withdraw his forces from Indochina, a gesture that might preserve "peace throughout the whole of the South Pacific area." Roosevelt invited Hirohito to join him in seeking "ways of dispelling the dark clouds. I am confident that both of us, for the sake of the peoples not only of our own great countries but for the sake of humanity in neighboring territories, have a sacred duty to restore traditional amity and prevent further death and destruction."

Roosevelt doubted that this message would sway Hirohito. He had good reason to believe that Japan was now firmly set on a destructive course. Even in the darkest hours, however, he retained his innate optimism and keen sense of humor. After dispatching his last-ditch appeal to the exalted emperor, Roosevelt remarked to his wife, Eleanor, and guests who had joined her that evening at the White House: "Well, this son of man has just sent his final message to the Son of God."

That same day, officials in Tokyo began transmitting a long message in code to the Japanese ambassador in Washington, Adm. Kichisaburo Nomura, to be delivered to Secretary Hull at 1 p.m. on Sunday, December 7—a time chosen by the Japanese to coincide with the onset of the attack on Pearl Harbor. The dispatch, which constituted Tokyo's official response to Hull's final offer in the recent peace talks, was in 14 parts, but transmission of the last part was held back until Sunday. The SIS deciphered the first 13 parts and delivered the transcript to the White House around 9:30 p.m. on Saturday. Roosevelt and his trusted adviser Harry Hopkins read the harsh statement with deep concern. They feared that the delayed 14th part of the message would mean war. If so, Hopkins asked, why not strike the Japanese first? "No, we can't do that," Roosevelt replied. "We are a democracy and a peaceful people."

DAY OF DESTINY

Up well before dawn on Sunday, December 7, naval aviators aboard the aircraft carriers of Admiral Nagumo's task force sat down to a ceremonial breakfast of rice and red beans and took sips of sake before setting out to attack the U.S. Pacific Fleet at Pearl Harbor. These warriors did not have to wait until they had achieved victory to celebrate their mission. They believed that a man who entered battle for his beloved country and its divine emperor was blessed, whether he prevailed or perished. "I shall die only for the emperor," sang

"I shall die only for the emperor."
Japanese naval academy song

cadets at Japan's naval academy. "I shall never look back." Cmdr. Mitsuo Fuchida, chosen to lead the attack, spoke for many in the strike force when he recalled his feelings that morning. "Who could be luckier than I?" he asked himself. In risking his life for what he held sacred, he remarked, "I fulfilled my duty as a warrior."

Fuchida and his men felt no qualms about carrying out a surprise attack on Americans. Their great military icon was Adm. Heihachiro Togo, who launched Japan's triumphant war against imperial Russia in 1904 with a surprise attack and secured victory a year later by smashing the Russian fleet at Tsushima. The idea of knocking out a larger but less agile opponent with a sudden, stunning blow was cherished by those who practiced Japanese martial arts such as kendo, among them the architect of the Pearl Harbor assault, Admiral Yamamoto, who hoped to match Admiral Togo's success against the Russians by catching the Americans off guard. What many Americans found contemptible—a sneak attack—was viewed by the Japanese as heroic when used against great powers that tried to thwart their imperial ambitions.

As dawn approached around 6 a.m., the first wave of 183 fighters, bombers, and torpedo planes took off from Nagumo's six carriers, 230 miles north of Pearl Harbor. A second wave of nearly equal strength followed a short time later. Storm clouds had helped Nagumo's ships evade detection as they crossed the North Pacific, but rough seas made conditions hazardous now for Fuchida and his aviators, whose heavily laden planes came perilously close to the wave tops before gaining altitude.

On board those planes alongside their fighting colleagues were photographers and motion-picture cameramen assigned to document the action. Vice Adm. Chuichi Nagumo's First Air Fleet was the most powerful carrier task force that had ever been assembled, and the Japanese Imperial Navy was eager to record the historic attack. The aerial observers were equipped with bulky F-8 oblique cameras with glass plates or smaller handheld Type 99 aerial cameras with rolls of film. Their assignment was to record the damage done to American ships and port facilities for naval intelligence analysts.

Ascending above the clouds, they saw golden light glimmering on the eastern horizon—a good omen for men whose imperial emblem was the rising sun. Fuchida worried that cloud cover would obscure their target but was reassured when his radio picked up a Honolulu weather forecast promising clear skies. He understood English and used the broadcast to home in on Honolulu.

Residents there were waking to what looked like another placid Sunday in paradise. They had less than two hours of peace left.

Japanese forces carried out several attacks on American and British targets on what was December 7 in Hawaii and the continental United States and December 8 in Asia. But none of those assaults came as more of a shock than the raid on Pearl Harbor, thought to be safely beyond Japan's reach. Despite warnings that Tokyo was preparing for hostilities, many American officers believed that their base on the island of Oahu and their country at large remained secure against attack. "The Japanese will not go to war with the United States," insisted Vice Adm. William Pye on December 6. "We are too big, too powerful, and too strong." Pye's superior, Adm. Husband Kimmel, commander in chief of the Pacific Fleet, assured a reporter that same day that the Japanese would not risk conflict with the United States as long as their old enemy, Russia, now the Soviet Union, remained undefeated by Germany and capable of attacking them. "I don't think they'd be such damned fools," Kimmel was quoted as saying.

If Japan did strike, Kimmel assumed that the first blow would fall elsewhere. Neither he nor Lt. Gen. William Short, the U.S. Army commander in Hawaii, had received intelligence indicating that Pearl Harbor was a likely target. Like their chiefs in Washington, they thought that the main threat was to American forces stationed closer to Japan at bases in the Philippines and on sparsely defended Wake and Midway Islands. Accordingly, Kimmel had recently dispatched the aircraft carriers U.S.S. *Enterprise* and U.S.S. *Lexington* to deliver fighter planes to Wake and Midway. The Pacific Fleet's only other carrier, the U.S.S. *Saratoga,* was in San Diego Harbor on December 7 after being overhauled. Aircraft carriers were the greatest assets that modern navies possessed, and

Japanese commanders were deeply disappointed to learn from agents in Honolulu that Kimmel's flattops were not at Pearl Harbor as the attack loomed. But they were consoled by reports that the fleet's eight battleships were now docked there, along with dozens of cruisers and destroyers. Pearl Harbor's defenses included antiaircraft batteries and squadrons of fighters and bombers at several surrounding air bases. Aerial reconnaissance was intermittent, however, and no pilots, soldiers, or sailors were placed on high alert. The one threat they were actively guarding against was sabotage by Japanese residents of Honolulu. Warplanes were parked close together on runways, which made them easier to protect against saboteurs but more vulnerable to air strikes.

So ill prepared were Pearl Harbor's defenders for war that two clear warnings of an imminent attack failed to reach Kimmel and Short between the time Fuchida and his men took off and when they reached their target shortly before 8 a.m. At 6:45, Lt. William Outerbridge, captain of the destroyer U.S.S. *Ward*, dropped depth charges on an odd-looking submarine lurking near the narrow entrance to Pearl Harbor. Operated by a two-man crew and armed with a single torpedo, the midget Japanese sub was one of five assigned to slip furtively into the shallow harbor—where the larger submarines that hauled and released them could not safely go— and target American warships. (All five midget subs were lost in those missions.) Outerbridge promptly reported the startling incident, but communications were slow on a Sunday morning. It took an hour for his report to work its way up the chain of command to Kimmel, by which time Fuchida and his men had Pearl Harbor in sight.

The second warning came around 7:15 a.m. when Pvt. Joseph Lockard, operating a mobile radar station near Kahuku Point at the northern end of Oahu, reported an "unusually large flight" of aircraft approaching the island at a distance of less than 100 miles. "Don't worry about it," replied Lt. Kermit Tyler, the watch officer of the Army Air Forces' 78th Pursuit Squadron. Tyler assumed that the planes were friendly B-17 bombers, expected in from California that morning for a stopover at Pearl before they continued on to the Philippines. No fighters were dispatched, and no word of Lockard's report reached General Short before the attack began.

At 7:40 a.m., Fuchida was looking anxiously through breaks in the clouds for sight of land. "Suddenly a long white line of breaking surf appeared directly beneath my plane," he recalled. "It was the northern shore of Oahu." As he approached Pearl Harbor on the island's south shore, the skies cleared as forecast. He saw "ships riding peacefully at anchor. One by one I counted them. Yes, the battleships were there all right—eight of them!" At 7:49, he signaled for the attack. "No enemy fighters were in the air," he noted, "nor were there any gun flashes from the ground." Breaking radio silence, which was no longer necessary, he informed Admiral Nagumo that surprise was complete by repeating three times the code word "*Tora!*" (Tiger!). Born in the Year of the Tiger, Fuchida was now fulfilling his destiny by pouncing like a cat on the unsuspecting Americans.

> *"Tora! Tora! Tora!"*
>
> Cmdr. Mitsuo Fuchida, signaling a successful surprise attack on Pearl Harbor

SURPRISE ATTACK

In the early hours of December 7, 1941, diplomat-spy Takeo Yoshikawa was eating breakfast at the Japanese consulate in Honolulu when the first bomb fell on Pearl Harbor. Upon hearing the explosion, he switched on a shortwave set tuned to Radio

A photographer captured the first wave of attack on Pearl Harbor from his warplane.

Tokyo. As more explosions rocked the area, Yoshikawa listened attentively to a news broadcast for the repetition of a seemingly innocuous phrase, "east wind, rain," inserted into a weather report. It was a coded message that the Imperial Japanese Navy had attacked Pearl Harbor. Outside, Yoshikawa recalled, "bombs were falling and black smoke was clearly visible, hanging in a pall over the harbor."

The attackers' first objective was to pound airfields around Pearl Harbor and destroy U.S. warplanes on the ground. Japanese commanders had studied the blitzkrieg tactics of Germany's Luftwaffe, whose preemptive strikes had shattered opposing air forces by destroying hundreds of planes before they could take off. Within minutes of Fuchida's signal launching the attack, the naval air station on Ford Island, in Pearl Harbor, and the army air bases at nearby Hickam and Wheeler Fields were engulfed in smoke and flames as dive-bombers blasted hangars, barracks, and scores of aircraft parked wingtip to wingtip. The initial reaction of most men on the ground was disbelief. Harry Mead, a radio operator on Ford Island, assumed that the air raid was a training exercise. When he saw the first explosion, he figured that someone was going to catch hell "for putting live bombs on those planes." Moments later, a petty officer standing near Mead recognized the distinctive Japanese rising sun emblem on the dive-bombers and let loose a burst of profanity echoed by many men at Pearl Harbor when the truth hit them: "Them [expletive deleted] bastards are bombing us!"

> "Them [expletive deleted] bastards are bombing us!"
>
> Harry Mead, radio operator on Ford Island

Smoke was billowing from Ford Island when Lt. Cmdr. Shigeharu Murata led a squadron of 40 Japanese torpedo planes against the big ships on Battleship Row. On the battleship U.S.S. *Nevada*, a Navy band had assembled on deck to play the national anthem as the flag went up. Like Mead, bandleader Oden McMillan figured that the explosions on Ford Island were part of a drill, so he launched into the anthem at eight o'clock sharp—just as the first torpedo planes swooped in. Standing watch on the *Nevada* was Ensign Joseph Taussig, who thought the approaching aircraft must be U.S. Navy planes practicing torpedo runs. Pearl Harbor is only about 40 feet deep, and any torpedoes dropped by the incoming planes would, he assumed, sink harmlessly to the harbor floor. To his astonishment, the planes dropped torpedoes that were equipped with stabilizers to run in shallow waters. One of them struck the battleship U.S.S. *Oklahoma*, docked near the *Nevada*, which was strafed by the attackers as they flew over. McMillan and his band

Louise Milke Moats Whatley
A Letter to the Folks Back Home

Whatley, the wife of a civilian employee of the military, lived only blocks from the Army air base at Hickam Field, and so had a front-row seat to the Japanese attack on Pearl Harbor. Two days later, she wrote to her family in Cedar Rapids, Iowa, about the experience.

December 9, Tuesday
1:00 P.M.

Dear Mom and all:
Well it finally happened, the thing that everyone over here said and thought couldn't happen. You should have my wire by now. Scoop and I are both all right except we are so worn-out from lack of sleep and nervous strain. He is working 13½ hrs from 4:45 P.M. till 6:45 A.M. Our house and car weren't touched, we have plenty to eat. There is no use of anyone at home there worrying. There can't possibly be another surprise attack now.

Now to tell you of the attack. We live about two blocks from Hickam Field and then a little further is Pearl Harbor where the heaviest bombing occurred. So we are right in the midst of

With Hawaii under martial law, Louise Whatley's letter was read by censors to make sure no details of military significance were shared.

all of it. Scoop had just got up Sunday morning at 7:30 and I was still asleep when all at once the sky was full of planes and a million guns going off. We both rushed into the street in front of the house, me in my night gown & red robe, to watch the Army having their latest battle practice (what we thought) all of us crazy people standing out in the streets watching. When someone said Pearl Harbor was being bombed too, everyone laughed. Just then a plane went down in flames and flew over our heads spitting shells from a machine gun, so low we could see the Jap pilot and the markings of the "rising sun" on its wings. Then we finally all came to—we were really being attacked. Then a call came from the Harbor for all the men to respond to fight fire, so Scoop left. I took some workers over in our car and just as we got near the second attack came. How I drove the car back with all the shells flying around me I don't know. Most everyone left their houses out here right after the second attack but are slowly coming back now. I didn't leave as I figured it just as safe here as anywheres in town. The first attack lasted about ½ hr, the second about 15 min. That night the guns fired at planes 3 or 4 times but they (Japs) didn't get to do much.

"Well it finally happened, the thing that everyone over here said and thought couldn't happen."

Today is the first we've had our electricity on all day. As soon as it starts getting dark we have blackout. I'm sure getting good at doing things in the dark. Cars run around on the streets with no lights. There's soldiers with guns all over the place. If the cars won't put out their lights they shoot their lights out for them

Call Scoop's mother and tell her you heard. There's no use for her to look for mail, any of you in fact till you get it as we don't know if the Clipper is taking any out as they might not even let us send letters out. Don't worry for it won't do any good.

Our love to all of you

Louise and Scoop ∎

dutifully stood their ground long enough to finish the anthem, then scrambled for cover as Taussig sounded the general alarm and shouted over the loudspeaker: "This is no drill!" A short time later, a torpedo slammed into the *Nevada*. During the attack, Taussig was severely wounded in his left leg, which was later amputated, but he remained at his post directing anti-aircraft fire until the burning ship was abandoned. As he recalled: "I was placed in a cab and driven to the harbor hospital, bleeding all over this poor man's taxi."

The damage done by the torpedoes was compounded by bombs dropped at high levels that crashed through the decks of warships before exploding. Around 8:20 a.m., a bomb penetrated the forward magazine of the battleship U.S.S. *Arizona* where gunpowder was stored, triggering a volcanic blast that killed hun-

A sailor standing near the wreckage of a PBY Catalina flying boat and other seaplanes on Ford Island watches a violent explosion on the destroyer U.S.S. Shaw *in Pearl Harbor.*

dreds of men instantaneously and knocked sailors off the decks of neighboring vessels. Fuchida, who was directing bombers at an altitude of nearly 10,000 feet, felt the shock wave buffet his plane and looked down to see smoke and flames leaping skyward. "It was a hateful, mean-looking red flame," he remarked, "the kind that powder produces, and I knew at once that a magazine had exploded." Of the nearly 1,400 men aboard the *Arizona* that morning, fewer than 300 survived. Among them was John Rampley, a gunner's mate in the only turret that remained intact. "We felt a tremendous jolt, as if the ship had been lifted up and slammed back down," he recalled. "Rivets popped from the steel walls and flew about." When the call came to abandon ship, he climbed down from the turret onto a deck strewn with charred and shattered bodies: "They lay crumpled like broken dolls who had been picked up in the air and slammed against the structures of the ship . . . All around, the air was filled with the smell of burning oil and burning flesh." Menacing patches of flaming oil coated the water into which Rampley and others leaped. He managed to swim to Ford Island, but many wounded men who abandoned the *Arizona* and other stricken ships were too weak to save themselves and drowned or were burned to death.

"They lay crumpled like broken dolls who had been picked up in the air and slammed against the structures of the ship."

John Rampley, gunner's mate, U.S.S. *Arizona*

For those at Pearl Harbor who remained unscathed, shock and disbelief gave way to the urge to strike back at the enemy with any weapon at hand. U.S. Marines camped near the harbor rushed from their tents when the attack began and shot at low-flying warplanes. Among them was Cpl. James Jenkins. "Most of us were in our underwear," he recollected, "and had our old World War I helmets on." Their outdated bolt-action rifles posed little threat to the attackers. One Marine grabbed a machine gun and began firing wildly, doing more harm to his own side than to the Japanese, who flew so close that Jenkins "could see the goggles on the pilots' heads." When the shooting stopped, he was sent to stand guard at the docks, where Navy boats began "bringing in burned bodies and throwing them at my feet." He could see the smoldering hulks of several battleships, including the *Oklahoma,* which had capsized.

By the time the last wave of Japanese bombers departed around 9:45 a.m., all eight battleships and a dozen other warships had gone down or been severely damaged. Most would eventually be salvaged, but the *Arizona* and *Oklahoma* were shattered beyond repair and accounted for nearly three-fourths of the Navy's casualties on this bloody Sunday. Losses among members of the other services and civilians brought the day's toll to just over 2,400 killed and nearly 1,200 wounded. Pvt. Melvin Faulkner, who helped bury the dead at the Army's Schofield Barracks, where some 200 soldiers were laid to rest,

> "I wondered how many more Americans would lose their lives before the war was over and prayed that I wouldn't be one of those buried so far from home."
>
> Pvt. Melvin Faulkner

never forgot that solemn ceremony: "I wondered how many more Americans would lose their lives before the war was over and prayed that I wouldn't be one of those buried so far from home."

As Fuchida and his men returned to their carriers, the elation they felt at catching their foes off guard drained away. Their losses were lower than many of them had feared: 29 planes downed by antiaircraft batteries or American fighters, few of which made it into the air. That was a small figure compared with the more than 250 U.S. warplanes destroyed in the attack. For all the harm done at Pearl Harbor, however, the Pacific Fleet had not been incapacitated. The oil depots and repair yards on which it depended had suffered little damage, and officers urged Admiral Nagumo to launch another strike against those vital facilities and the undamaged warships. But the cautious Nagumo would not risk sending his warplanes out again while carriers of the Pacific Fleet were somewhere at sea and posed a potential risk to his own vessels. "The attack is terminated," his chief of staff announced that afternoon. "We are withdrawing." When Admiral Yamamoto learned of the results at his headquarters, he saw little reason for celebration. There was no glory, he wrote, in mauling "a sleeping enemy" who was now wide awake and capable of striking back. "Angered and outraged, he will soon launch a determined counterattack," warned Yamamoto, who understood that the tide might turn against him if he did not complete the task his forces left unfinished on December 7.

A WORLDWIDE CONFLICT

Within hours of the attack on Pearl Harbor, Japanese forces hit several other targets up to 6,000 miles away. It was the broadest offensive ever launched at one time by a single nation, and it transformed World War II into the first genuinely worldwide conflict—far bigger in scope than World War I, which had left most of Asia unscathed. As bombs fell at Pearl Harbor, Japanese troops landed on the Malay Peninsula and began advancing southward toward the British stronghold of Singapore. Elsewhere in Southeast Asia and the western Pacific, Japanese warplanes pounded Allied defenses to clear the way for invasions that would follow in the days and weeks to come. Among the American

GEORGE D. PHRANER
SURVIVOR, U.S.S. *ARIZONA*

Machinist's Mate 1st Class Phraner, a member of a five-inch gun crew on the U.S.S. Arizona, *was at breakfast aboard his ship on December 7, 1941, when the Japanese struck.*

The U.S.S. Arizona *smolders in the aftermath of the attack on Pearl Harbor, which claimed the lives of most of the battleship's crew.*

I looked across the bow of the ship and could see large plumes of smoke coming up from Ford Island. At first, we didn't realize it was a bombing. It didn't mean anything to us until a large group of planes came near the ship and we could see for the first time the rising sun emblem on the plane wings. The bombing was becoming heavier all around us and we knew this was REALLY IT! . . .

It was then that general quarters sounded over the speaker and everything became automatic. My battle station was on a forward 5-inch gun and it was standard practice to keep only a limited amount of ammunition at the guns . . . the gun captain pointed at me and said, "You go aft and start bringing up the ammunition out of the magazines." The aft magazines were five decks below.

A few moments later I found myself deep below the water line in a part of the ship I normally would never be in. I remember getting these cases of ammo powder and shells weighing about 90 pounds each. I had begun lifting shells into the hoist when a deafening roar filled the room and the entire ship shuddered. It was the forward magazine. One and a half million pounds of gunpowder exploding in a massive fireball disintegrating the whole forward part of the ship. Only moments before I stood with my gun crew just a few feet from the center of the explosion. Admiral Kidd, Captain Van Velkenburg, my whole gun crew was killed . . .

Seconds after the explosion the lights went out and it was pitch black. Almost immediately a thick acrid smoke filled the magazine locker and the metal walls began to get hot. In the dark and not being able to breathe, we made our way to the door hatch, only to find it shut and locked. Somehow we were able to open the hatch and start to make our way up the ladder. I was nauseated by the smell of burning flesh, which turned out to be my own as I climbed up the hot ladder . . .

After a while I began to get weak and light-headed. I could feel myself losing the battle to save my own life. I hung to the ladder, feeling good. I felt that it was all right for me to let go. At that moment I looked up and could see a small point of light . . . It gave me the strength to go on. After what seemed to me like an eternity, I reached the deck gasping and choking. ■

> "I could feel myself losing the battle to save my own life. I hung to the ladder, feeling good. I felt that it was all right for me to let go."

targets bombed on the first day of the offensive and later seized by Japanese troops were bases on Guam, Wake Island, and the Philippines, where 18 B-17 bombers and dozens of fighters were destroyed on runways at Clark Field around noon on December 8 (11 p.m. on December 7 in Washington). Gen. Douglas MacArthur and his officers in the Philippines knew by then that Japan was waging war on the United States, but they were no better prepared for the onslaught than the commanders at Pearl Harbor had been. For Filipinos, who had been promised independence by the United States within five years, the prospect of Japanese occupation was appalling. In Manila, young Antonio Quintos was sent home from school early when news of war broke on December 8. He and his brother came upon two distraught American soldiers in the street. "They were crying like kids," he recalled. "We were too scared to cry."

Back in Washington, President Roosevelt got little sleep that night. He spoke by phone with Prime Minister Churchill, who promised to seek a declaration of war against Japan in London the next day as Roosevelt did the same in Washington. Churchill told the president: "We're all in the same boat now." Then in the early hours of December 8, Roosevelt met with correspondent Edward R. Murrow at the White House. Their talk was not broadcast, and Roosevelt felt free to speak his mind. Like many other Americans, he was angry and ashamed that U.S. forces had been caught by surprise. Speaking of how American warplanes were blasted like sitting ducks, he pounded his fist on the table and exclaimed: "On the ground, by God, on the ground!" When he went before Congress at noon that day, however, he set aside any misgivings he had about America's readiness to fight and focused his anger on the Japanese and their "unprovoked and dastardly attack." He famously declared, "Yesterday, December 7, 1941—a date which will live in infamy—the United States of America was suddenly and deliberately attacked by naval and air forces of the Empire of Japan." He expressed "confidence in our

> "Yesterday, December 7, 1941—a date which will live in infamy—the United States of America was suddenly and deliberately attacked by naval and air forces of the Empire of Japan."
>
> President Franklin D. Roosevelt, December 8, 1941

armed forces" and promptly received the congressional declaration of war he requested.

To secure America and its place in the world, Roosevelt knew that he would have to join Churchill in opposing not just Japan but the Axis as a whole. But there was little support in Congress or the country at large for widening the war against Japan to include Germany and Italy. How to rally reluctant Americans against those European belligerents was a vexing problem for the president.

On December 11, 1941, Hitler solved it for him by declaring war on the United States, a step that Germany's defensive pact with Japan did not require. In a rambling speech before the Reichstag—the powerless parliament from which he had eliminated all opponents of his regime—Hitler portrayed Roosevelt as a warmonger who sought "unlimited world dictatorship." Under no circumstances, he vowed, would he allow such an enemy "the opportunity to strike first." True to his aggressive principles, Hitler struck first by joining Japan in its war on the United States.

Germany's impulsive führer was trying to assure his listeners that he was still in command of events. For the past two years, this had been essentially Hitler's war—a conflict he instigated and expanded until it embraced much of Europe and the

In Roosevelt's hand-edited draft of his message to Congress, he altered his description of December 7 from "a date which will live in world history" to "a date which will live in infamy," a memorable term that branded the attack as shameful and intolerable.

Mediterranean. Now, however, he was caught up in something larger: a global struggle over which he had limited control. Instead of calling the shots as he did before, he would spend much time and energy responding to the initiatives of his foes in Washington, London, and Moscow, whose collective resources were greater than those of the Axis. "Today I stand at the head of the mightiest army in the world, the most powerful air force, and a proud navy," Hitler boasted on December 11. Within the past week, however, Soviet forces had pushed his vaunted army back from Moscow. And now he was taking on America, a colossus that he and his Axis partners antagonized at their peril.

ОТСТОИМ МОСКВУ!

*A Red Army propaganda poster from January 1941 exhorts
Soviet citizens with the message "Let's Fight for Moscow!"*

CHRONOLOGY

SEPTEMBER 1940 U.S. Congress
passes the Selective Training
and Service Act.

JUNE 22, 1941 Germany
invades the Soviet Union.

MAY 1, 1941 President Roosevelt purchases the
first of a new series of U.S. Savings Bonds to begin
the process of funding a war as yet undeclared.

SEPTEMBER 8, 1941 The
Siege of Leningrad begins.

AWAKENING SUPERPOWERS

DEFENSE OF THE SOVIET UNION
AND WARTIME ON THE U.S. HOME FRONT

By the time the winter of 1941-42 descended on the Wolf's Lair, Hitler's headquarters in East Prussia, it had become painfully clear that his all-out war on the Soviet Union, which he had hoped to win before the first snow fell, was far from over. So confident had he and his aides been of quick victory when Operation Barbarossa began on June 22, 1941, that few German troops were furnished with wool overcoats and other winter gear. Having conquered France in six weeks, Hitler figured that Soviet resistance would crumble within three months. The Slavs of the Soviet Union were an inferior race, he believed, and Joseph Stalin had weakened the Red Army by purging thousands of its most experienced officers. "Just kick in the door," Hitler assured one general before the invasion began, "and the whole rotten structure will collapse."

DECEMBER 5, 1941 Soviet forces counterattack German troops near Moscow.

MARCH 1, 1942 United States begins food rationing.

JANUARY 31, 1943 Soviets retake Stalingrad and begin pushing the Nazis back toward Berlin.

DECEMBER 11, 1941 Germany declares war on the United States after the United States declares war on Japan.

MAY 27, 1942 U.S. Women's Army Auxiliary Corps (WAAC) begins recruitment.

Despite inflicting massive casualties on the ill-prepared Soviets—nearly six million of whom were killed or captured by the end of 1941—German troops faced mounting opposition as the year wore on. Having rejected an advance on Moscow in late August in favor of operations in Ukraine, the Soviet breadbasket, Hitler belatedly unleashed the armored divisions of Army Group Center against the Soviet capital in October. By then, the dazzling German blitzkrieg he had envisioned earlier was reduced to a painstaking slog along muddy roads, which froze hard in November, briefly allowing vehicles to make headway before snow began falling in drifts and the nights grew so cold that tank crews had to light fires under their engines in the morning to get them started.

With nighttime temperatures falling as low as minus 49°F, exposure took a steep toll on the Germans. By the end of that terrible winter of 1941-42, the number of frostbite victims in their ranks exceeded a quarter of a million. Thousands more were stricken by pneumonia, influenza, and trench foot. The "infernal cold," stated Field Marshal Wilhelm Keitel, had "catastrophic results for our troops, clad as they were only in improvised winter clothing." Many obtained warmer clothing eventually, but some men had suffered lasting damage by then. One German soldier wrote in his diary that winter: "My hands are done for, and have been ever since the beginning of December. The little finger of my left hand is missing and—what's even worse—the three middle fingers of my right one are frozen . . .The best thing I can do with the little finger is to shoot with it."

Soldiers slept huddled close together in huts or dugouts and risked death by exposure if they went out to relieve themselves. More than a few men perished "while performing their bodily functions," noted Maj. Gen. Heinz Guderian, a pioneer of blitz-krieg tactics. His armored columns had punctured Allied defenses in Belgium and France with startling speed in 1940 but were stalled now by the arctic weather and Soviet forces far better equipped for winter warfare. As Guderian recalled: "Only he who saw the endless expanse of Russian snow during this winter of our misery, and felt the icy wind that blew across it . . . who drove for hour after hour through that no-man's land only at last to find too thin shelter, with insufficiently clothed half-starved men; and who also saw by contrast the well-fed, warmly clad and fresh Siberians, fully equipped for winter fighting; only a man who knew all that can truly judge the events which now occurred."

> "Only he who saw the endless expanse of Russian snow during this winter of our misery, and felt the icy wind that blew across it . . . can truly judge the events which now occurred."
>
> Maj. Gen. Heinz Guderian

Hitler was in a poor position to understand what his forces were up against. He seldom left the Wolf's Lair, a dreary command post ringed by barbed wire and minefields. One visitor likened the place to a concentration camp—whose inmates were not foes of the Third Reich but its top generals, subject to the whims of their overbearing führer, a former corporal who considered himself a military genius. By imposing his will on his chiefs, he flouted the proud traditions of the German General Staff, which had once been the envy of the world. Critical thinking and vigorous debate at headquarters gave way to the führer principle—the idea that Germans of all ranks must bow to Hitler's superior judgment and follow their leader. Officers who defied that principle and questioned his assumptions and pronouncements risked being fired like the army's chief, Field Marshal Walther von Brauchitsch, who opposed Hitler's August decision to postpone the drive on Moscow and became a scapegoat when troops failed to take the city in December. Hitler relieved him and assumed personal command of the army. "Anyone can do the little job of directing operations in war," claimed the führer, who would no longer have someone else to blame when those operations went awry.

As late as December 4, Hitler thought that he might still be able to lash the faltering Army Group Center into taking Moscow. German forces had advanced to the north and south of the city in pincers that threatened to close around the capital. Some units were within a dozen miles of Moscow, and their commander, Field Marshal Fedor von Bock, reportedly got close enough to see the spires of the Kremlin through his field glasses. But his troops were now dangerously overextended and vulnerable to a counterattack. Guderian and other officers took it upon themselves to pull back to more defensible positions. Hitler's view of the situation at the front "does not correspond in any way with reality," wrote Guderian's chief of staff, who added, "We are too weak to defend ourselves."

In rare moments of candor, Hitler conceded that things were not going well. "We started a month too late," he confided to an aide. The grim precedent of Napoleon's disastrous invasion of Russia in 1812, when the icy blasts of "General Winter" doomed the French army, was too obvious for him to ignore. But he never considered turning back, for this was a war of annihilation that would bring terrible retribution on Hitler and Germany if his army was repelled. He had violated the cardinal rule of military conduct by committing systematic atrocities against civilians, using not only the dreaded Schutzstaffel—the black-shirted SS security forces who carried out his murderous racial policies—but also regular German troops.

The invasion of the Soviet Union unleashed the Holocaust, whose victims included millions of Jews as well as members of other groups defined by Nazis as subhuman or enemies of the Reich, including communists—lumped together with Jews by Nazis as part of a supposed "Jewish-Bolshevist" conspiracy—and Slavs in occupied areas like Ukraine, who starved when the Germans instituted a policy of feeding their own troops and civilians at the local people's expense. The ultimate goal of the invasion, remarked SS chief Heinrich Himmler, was to "decimate the Slavic population by thirty millions" and make room for German settlers.

SS death squads, which rounded up Jews and other victims in the Soviet Union and shot them by the thousands, were abetted by some German generals, including Field Marshal Erich von Manstein, who wrote that the "Jewish-Bolshevist system must now and forever be destroyed." Manstein's one concern was that his subordinates not be present when civilians were massacred, for he considered that spectacle "unworthy of a German officer." Death squads excavated trenches to serve as mass graves for their victims, who were often forced "to lie face down inside the trench and were then shot in the side of the head," testified one SS executioner. "The next batch of victims always had to lie down on the corpses of those who had just been killed before," he added. Even when those "corpses had been covered with sand and chalk, the next victims often saw them, because body parts would frequently be jutting out of the thin layer of sand or earth." German soldiers and police sometimes assisted the SS in carrying out such massacres and also shot suspected partisans or communists. In many cases, the mere suspicion that a detainee was Jewish was considered grounds for

An SS noncommissioned officer, watched by German police and Wehrmacht personnel, prepares to shoot a Jewish man kneeling before a mass grave near the Ukrainian town of Vinnytsya in 1942.

execution. By December, an SS report stated, Army Group Center had put to death 19,000 "partisans and criminals, that is, in the majority, Jews."

If Hitler's war of annihilation faltered, those and other atrocities would be exposed, including the brutal neglect of Soviet prisoners of war, more than half of whom died in captivity. Defeat or retreat would subject German soldiers and civilians to similar abuse at the hands of vengeful Soviets and reveal Hitler's war for what it was: a monumental crime that claimed countless lives on both sides. Only by holding the line and demanding more sacrifices from German soldiers could he achieve a victory large enough to cover that crime—a triumph he believed would vindicate all the destruction wrought to achieve it. "This land, which we have conquered with the blood of German sons, will never be surrendered," he said of the Soviet Union. "Millions of German peasant families will be settled here in order to carry the thrust of the Reich far to the east." That conquest was far from complete, however, and Soviet troops were about to parry Hitler's thrust with a strength and determination he did not know they possessed.

CRISIS IN MOSCOW

Comrade Joseph Stalin was a changed man. Since the invasion of his country had begun in June, this brutal tyrant long dreaded by his own citizens had himself lived in mortal fear of defeat and destruction. Having ignored warnings that Hitler was about to turn on him and violate their cynical Nonaggression Pact—which set World War II in motion in 1939 by allowing the two dictators to carve up eastern Europe and terrorize its inhabitants—Stalin was aghast when three million German troops crossed the frontier and shattered Soviet defenses. He retreated from the Kremlin to his dacha outside Moscow, where he paced the floor at night, unable to sleep. A week after the invasion began, he was visited there by officials of the Politburo, the

Major Roesler
Holocaust by Bullets

*In July 1941, a German officer identified as Major Roesler
of the 52nd Reserve Infantry encountered an SS death squad,
assisted by German police, in action near Zhitomir in Ukraine
and reported the massacre to superiors.*

The notification from the Infantry Reserve Regiment 52 concerning "Conduct with regard to the Civilian Population in the East" causes me to submit the following report: Towards the end of July 1941, I.R. 52, of which I was in command, was on its way from the West to Zhitomir, where it was to move into a rest camp. On the day of our arrival, in the afternoon, when I had moved into the Staff Quarters together with my Staff, we heard salvoes of rifle fire at regular intervals, fired at no great distance, and followed by pistol shots after a little while.

I decided to investigate this matter and with my Adjutant and Ordnance Officer (1st Lt. v. Bassewitz and Lt. Mueller-Brodmann) set out in the direction of the rifle fire. We soon received the impression that some cruel show must be taking place here because after a while we saw numerous soldiers and civilians streaming towards a railway embankment in front of us; we were informed that executions were being carried out continu-

A woman is overcome with grief in a killing field near Kerch in Crimea.

ously behind it. Throughout this time we were unable to see across the railway embankment to the other side, but at regular intervals we heard the sound of a trilling whistle and then a salvo of about 10 rifle shots, followed after a certain interval by pistol shots.

When we finally climbed up the railway embankment a sight was revealed to us on the other side of a horrible cruelty that was bound to shake and disgust anyone who came face to face with it unprepared. A pit had been cut in the ground, about 4 m. wide and 7-8 m. long, and the excavated earth had been piled up on one side. This mound and the side of the pit beneath it were stained all over with streams of blood. The pit itself was filled with human corpses of all kinds and both sexes in such numbers that it was difficult to estimate them; it was not possible to judge the depth of the pit.

Behind the mound of excavated earth a Police Commando was lined up with a Police Officer in command. The uniforms of the commandos were stained with blood. In a wide circle stood countless soldiers of troop units already stationed there, some as spectators, dressed in swimming trunks, as well as many civilians with women and children . . .

I stepped right up to the pit to obtain a picture that I have not been able to forget until this day. Among others there was an old man with a long white beard lying in the grave, with a little walking stick still hooked over his left arm. As this man still gave signs of life by his stertorous breathing, I requested one of the policemen to kill him off, but he answered with a laugh: "I fired seven shots into his belly, he'll croak on his own." The persons who had been shot were not placed in the grave in any order, but stayed there lying as they had fallen from the wall of the pit after they were shot. All these persons had been killed by shots in the back of the neck and then finished off with pistol shots from the top. I did not acquire any excessive sensitivity of the emotions during my service in the World War and in the French and Russian campaigns of this war; and experienced much that was more than unpleasant when I was active in the volunteer units in 1919, but I cannot recall ever having witnessed a scene such as that I have described here. ∎

Communist Party's ruling council, which Stalin had dominated since the death of Vladimir Lenin in 1924. "Why have you come?" he asked nervously, suspecting that they intended to arrest him. Instead, they asked him to take charge of a newly formed national defense committee.

Three days later, Stalin broadcast his first speech to the nation since it was thrust into war, urging Soviets to lay waste to their country rather than surrender anything of value to the advancing Germans: "The enemy must not be left a single engine, a single railway car, a single pound of grain or a gallon of fuel." At first, Soviets at the front were overrun too quickly to carry out that policy, but in time they made good on Stalin's stratagem. Entire factories were disassembled and shipped eastward by rail to sustain the production of guns, tanks, and aircraft on which the war effort depended. What could not be moved was destroyed.

Despite Stalin's defiant tone, he and his commissars feared that Soviet resistance might collapse under the German onslaught, and they stopped at nothing to make their men fight to the death. Commanders who faltered and soldiers who fled were shot. Officers who surrendered or let themselves be captured alive brought down official punishment on their wives, who were subject to arrest. Stalin's eldest son, Yakov, was taken prisoner by the Germans in 1941—a "crime" for which his wife spent two years in a Soviet labor camp while he languished and then died in enemy hands. Stalin, of course, was exempt from the harsh rules he imposed to keep others from retreating. He made plans to abandon Moscow before deciding to remain at the Kremlin as winter closed in. Addressing the public on

"If they want a war of extermination they shall have it!"

Joseph Stalin

November 9, the anniversary of the Bolshevik Revolution, he set aside the usual communist rhetoric and appealed instead to Russian patriotism and hatred of the invaders. "If they want a war of extermination they shall have it!" he vowed. "Our task now will be to destroy every German, to the very last man!" By shifting his deadly aim from domestic foes to foreign enemies, Stalin emerged as a grimly effective war leader.

He was strengthened in his determination to hold Moscow by one of the few Soviet commanders bold enough to stand up to him—Gen. Georgi Zhukov. Despite long and faithful service in the Red Army and Communist Party, Zhukov had narrowly escaped the fate of other officers who were liquidated in the mid-1930s by the morbidly suspicious Stalin. Those purges had left many survivors cowed by their dictator, but Zhukov remained self-assured and outspoken. When Stalin angrily rejected his recommendation that the doomed Ukrainian capital of Kiev be abandoned to the Germans, he asked to be relieved. Such defiance might have cost him his freedom or his life in earlier times, but Stalin desperately needed the strong-willed Zhukov. He was sent to organize the defenses of Leningrad (St. Petersburg), which would withstand a long and punishing siege by the Germans. Then as winter approached, he was summoned to the capital. "Are you certain we can hold Moscow?" Stalin asked him in mid-November. "Speak the truth, like a Communist." Zhukov was not yet sure that his troops could save the city, but steadied the anxious Stalin by exuding confidence: "We'll hold Moscow without a doubt," he promised.

By month's end, the German advance on the capital had stalled, and Zhukov came to the Kremlin to offer his plan for a counter-attack. Accompanying him was Maj. Gen. Pavel Belov, who had not seen Stalin since 1933 and found the 61-year-old dictator much altered. "In eight years, he seemed to have aged 20," Belov noted. "His eyes had lost their old steadiness; his voice lacked assurance." Hitler's stunning offensive had shaken Stalin and forced him to lean on a proven commander like Zhukov and trust in his judgment. It was a lesson that Germany's 52-year-old führer had yet to learn and would never entirely absorb. Stalin quickly approved Zhukov's plan and sent him on his way.

The counterattack began on December 5 and intensified the next day. Elusive Soviet ski troops cloaked in white found gaps in the enemy lines and slipped behind their startled foes, who were immobilized by the bitter cold while the Soviets advanced in winterized tanks that kept churning in the deepest of freezes. Soon the Germans were falling back and in danger of being cut off by their swarming opponents. Some units lost cohesion and retreated in disarray. As one German officer observed, it was every

Ice-encrusted horses haul German supply wagons through a driving blizzard.

man for himself: "More and more soldiers were making their own way west, without weapons, leading a calf on a rope, or drawing a sledge with potatoes behind them—just trudging westward with no one in command. Men killed by aerial bombardment were no longer buried." As Hitler's troops fled Moscow, Stalin ordered General Zhukov to step up the pressure.

The rugged Siberian troops that drove Germany back from Moscow had been an inadvertent gift from Japan, whose focus on attacking British and American bases in the Pacific had allowed Stalin to move the defenders of his eastern front west to protect Moscow. That Stalin knew Japanese plans far enough in advance to have Siberian troops in place in time to defend his capital was the doing of a master spy in Tokyo named Richard Sorge, one of the most successful secret agents of World War II. Born in 1895 in Baku, in what is now Azerbaijan, to a Russian mother and a German mining engineer father, he served in the German army during World War I, suffered severe wounds in 1916, and recuperated in Berlin, where he studied economics and became a Marxist. After the war, Sorge joined the German Communist Party and spent several years in the Soviet Union, where he was recruited by the GRU (Soviet military intelligence).

In 1929, Sorge returned as a spy to Germany with instructions to join the Nazi Party. Traveling abroad as a reporter, he settled in Japan in 1933 and assembled an extensive network of agents and informants, including German diplomats—who confided in him, believing that he was indeed a Nazi—and journalist Hotsumi Ozaki, an adviser to Japan's prime minister. In May 1941, Sorge signaled Moscow that Hitler would soon invade the Soviet Union—a warning that Stalin refused to believe. In fall 1941, Sorge again secured vital intelligence, reporting to his superiors that Japan was planning to wage war on the United States and had no intention of attacking the Soviet Union in the Far East. This time, Stalin trusted his master spy and shifted nearly 40 divisions from Siberia to reinforce battered Soviet forces defending Moscow. Japanese authorities arrested Sorge on October 18, 1941, and later offered to return him to Moscow in a prisoner exchange, but the Soviets declined. "The man named Richard Sorge is unknown to us," they claimed. After three years in prison, he was hanged on November 7, 1944.

Hitler averted disaster in the weeks after the retreat from Moscow by forbidding any further withdrawals and insisting that his officers stand fast at all costs. German troops paid heavily in blood, but the price would have been even higher had they continued to give way. As they dug in and held out, Stalin's hopes for a smashing victory faded. As German troops of Army Group Center retreated from Moscow, Soviet forces swept around their flanks and tried to trap the invaders near Smolensk. But the Germans heeded Hitler's stand-fast order and rallied, preventing Soviet pincers from closing around them. In spring 1942, Soviet troops counterattacked Army Group South and advanced 60 miles with deceptive ease before they were stopped below Kharkov and cut off by the German Sixth Army, losing over 300,000 men killed or captured.

THE SIEGE OF LENINGRAD

In September 1941, when the siege began, German troops of Army Group North had outflanked Soviet defenders and encircled Leningrad. In addition to the soldiers manning its fortifica-

A truck with its door open to allow the driver to escape if the vehicle breaks through the ice crosses slushy Lake Ladoga on the "Road of Life" in the spring of 1942.

tions, the besieged city had nearly 2.5 million residents and was harboring more than 100,000 refugees. Their only link to the outside world was a fragile lifeline that opened when winter set in—a 200-mile-long track called the "Road of Life" that crossed the frozen surface of Lake Ladoga to the east of the city and remained open only as long as the ice was thick enough to support vehicles. Truck convoys brought in a mere hundred tons of fuel and food a day—not enough to provide for all those in need. As the siege continued, food was strictly rationed, with small daily allotments for soldiers and factory workers. Office workers, dependents, and children received even less; by January 1942, they were limited to a quarter of a pound of bread per day. To stretch short stocks of flour, they mixed it with cottonseed or cellulose.

German air raids destroyed public transport and damaged the city's water system. Oil and coal supplies dwindled, and the use of electricity in private homes was banned to provide power to industry and the armed forces. People used wood to heat their homes, burning furniture and scraps of lumber scrounged from bombed-out buildings. By March 1942, more than 200,000 people were dead of cold and starvation. Frozen corpses piled up in the city streets and parks, left there by people too exhausted to bury them. "Many a time I saw a man suddenly collapse on the snow," a staff officer in the Leningrad garrison recalled. "There was nothing I could do. One just walked on." Leningrad held out against the Germans, but the ordeal took a terrible toll on its populace and defenders. More than 640,000 would die there before the siege was finally broken in January 1943.

In spring 1942, the Germans had also surrounded Sevastopol, which would fall to them in mid-1942 after Soviet efforts to relieve that Black Sea port failed. By then, Hitler was back on the offensive, but his forces had suffered so many losses to the enemy and the elements over the winter that he could no longer attack along the entire front.

DEFENDING THE MOTHERLAND

Despite harsh conditions and horrendous loss of life, the struggle that Soviets called the "Great Patriotic War" united their country and filled people with nationalist fervor. Soviet propaganda downplayed communism and stressed patriotism, calling on their people to defend their motherland against the brutal German invaders. Authorities reached deep into Russia's past to inspire resistance, offering the medieval prince Alexander Nevsky, the Napoleonic-era general Aleksandr Suvorov, and the Red Army hero Vasily Chapayev as models of heroism. Religion, which had been suppressed under Stalin before the war, was now officially embraced to rally the faithful behind the war effort. Posters and newspaper articles extolled ordinary citizens who risked death or gave their lives to save the Soviet Union from defeat and destruction.

Soviet women shouldered their share of the war effort by driving trucks, operating railroads, and toiling in munitions plants, shipyards, and aircraft factories, filling jobs vacated when men joined the Red Army. Many women replaced men on collective farms and worked the fields, feeding more than 11 million soldiers and 80 million civilians. Still others enlisted and joined the fight. As many as 800,000 women entered the Soviet armed forces during the war, serving not just as nurses or clerks but as combatants, including snipers, machine-gun teams, tank crew members, and partisans fighting in German-occupied territory. Red Army sniper Natasha Kovshove described her motivation in a letter to her family: "My hatred for the cursed fascist beast grows stronger every day, with every battle . . . I will shoot the vermin point blank. I will pump bullet after bullet into their foul skulls, stuffed with insane thoughts about our Moscow and of ruling over us, a free, proud, and bold people." The Soviet Union was the first nation to allow women pilots to fly combat missions. Three regiments of women aviators flew a combined total of more than 30,000 combat sorties, and two of those pilots became fighter aces.

> "My hatred for the cursed fascist beast grows stronger every day, with every battle . . . I will shoot the vermin point blank. I will pump bullet after bullet into their foul skulls, stuffed with insane thoughts about our Moscow and of ruling over us, a free, proud, and bold people."
>
> Natasha Kovshove, Soviet army sniper

THE BATTLE OF STALINGRAD

In 1942, unable to advance along the entire front, Hitler resolved to seize oil fields in the southern Soviet Union. Designated

Operation Blue, the German offensive was launched on June 28 by Army Group South, which pushed east toward the Volga River to secure its flank before advancing southward through the Caucasus Mountains to oil-rich Baku on the Caspian Sea. In mid-July, an overconfident Hitler decided to expand the offensive and split Army Group South in two. Army Group A was assigned to capture Baku while Army Group B attacked Stalingrad, a sprawling industrial city on the Volga crucial to Stalin and the Soviet war effort.

Hitler assigned armored forces and Luftwaffe squadrons to bolster Gen. Friedrich Paulus's Sixth Army at Stalingrad. That buildup came at the expense of Army Group A, which stalled in the Caucasus in September as the battle for Stalingrad intensified. Ordered by Stalin to stand fast, Gen. Vasily Chuikov's Soviet 62nd

Russian soldiers fight amid the rubble of Stalingrad, where Hitler's renewed offensive in 1942 came to a grinding halt.

Army fought desperately as German artillery and bombers blasted the city. "We moved back, occupying one building after another, turning them into strongholds," a Soviet officer recalled. "A soldier would crawl out of an occupied position only when the ground was on fire under him and his clothes were on fire."

On November 19, the Soviets launched a massive counteroffensive and drew a noose around Stalingrad, trapping the Sixth Army and other German and Axis troops, who suffered from hunger and exposure as the winter deepened. By January 1943, the Stuka dive-bombers above were flying over a city largely reduced to rubble. "Animals flee this hell," one German soldier there wrote; "the hardest stones cannot bear it for long; only men endure." Efforts to supply them by air failed, as did an attempt

> "Animals flee this hell; the hardest stones cannot bear it for long; only men endure."
>
> A German soldier on the battle for Stalingrad

by Field Marshal Erich von Manstein to break the siege. On January 22, 1943, General Paulus sought permission to surrender, but Hitler refused, ordering him to fight "to the last soldier and the last bullet." To discourage Paulus from yielding, Hitler promoted him to field marshal on January 30. When Soviet forces closed in on his headquarters the next day, however, Paulus gave up. The defeat left 91,000 Axis prisoners in Soviet hands, few of whom survived.

Following their victory at Stalingrad, Soviet forces advanced in February 1943 and liberated Kharkov, one of Ukraine's largest cities. Field Marshal Manstein then bolstered his Army Group South with German forces withdrawn from the Caucasus and recaptured Kharkov in March. North of the city, however, Soviets gouged a 90-mile-long bulge in the front and held out there. To eliminate that menacing Soviet salient, Hitler authorized

Operation Citadel, which called for armored pincers to advance from north and south and close on the enemy near Kursk, in the middle of the bulge.

In preparation for that attack, the Germans massed 900,000 men, 10,000 big guns, and 2,700 tanks, including hefty new Panzer V Panthers and Panzer VIB King Tigers, built to contend with sturdy Soviet tanks like the T-34. Awaiting them in the bulge were more than a million Soviet troops and 3,600 tanks, shielded by minefields, tank traps, and other forbidding defenses. The stage was set for the greatest battle ever waged between armored forces.

The attack opened at dawn on July 5 as Gen. Hermann Hoth's Fourth Panzer Army, supported by the Luftwaffe, struggled forward in the south under intense Soviet artillery fire. Hoth's battle-weary forces paused on July 10 after advancing only 20 miles. In the north, armored units of the German Ninth Army advanced only eight miles. On July 12, Hoth unleashed the powerful II SS Panzer Corps, which collided near the village of Prokhorovka with Gen. Pavel Rotmistrov's Fifth Guards Tank Army. For eight hours, German and Soviet tanks—more than a thousand in all—fought each other to a standstill, leaving the battlefield littered with broken and blazing vehicles.

On July 13, Hitler called off Operation Citadel. As German forces began withdrawing from the Kursk salient, the Soviets counterattacked, reclaiming Kharkov permanently in August. Soviet casualties in the titanic Battle of Kursk—which involved more than two million men, 6,000 armored vehicles, and 4,000 aircraft—were far higher than German losses. But the Soviets had deeper reserves and prevailed, and Hitler faced a longer and increasingly desperate struggle against foes whose ranks had swelled enormously since 1941, with both sleeping giants—the Soviet Union and the United States—now wide awake.

PREPARING A NATION FOR WAR

Although the U.S. mainland was never invaded as the Soviet Union had been, the sense of outrage at the Japanese attack on Pearl Harbor united Americans against their foes in much the way the invasion of the Soviet Union had rallied its citizens. Never before in the history of the nation had the United States so swiftly and vigorously mobilized its human and material resources for a single purpose. Building support for a foreign war that might have felt far away to many Americans, President Roosevelt declared, "There is one front and one battle where everyone in the United States—every man, woman, and child—is in action. That front is right here at home, in our daily lives, and in our daily tasks."

> "There is one front and one battle where everyone in the United States—every man, woman, and child—is in action. That front is right here at home, in our daily lives, and in our daily tasks."
>
> President Franklin Roosevelt building support for the war on the home front

The first and foremost task on the home front was transforming millions of civilians into soldiers at induction centers and training camps. In September 1940, as Germany attacked America's close ally Great Britain, Congress had passed the Selective Training and Service Act, instituting the nation's first peacetime draft. The act required all men between ages 21 and 35 to register for the draft and authorized conscription of 900,000 to serve for one year. After Pearl Harbor, men as young as 18 were drafted to serve for the duration of the war plus six months. More than 10 million men were called up by 1945. Another six million Americans volunteered for service.

Wearing his hat and little else, an Army draftee is inoculated for smallpox and typhoid simultaneously by medical officers during his induction at Fort Dix in December 1940.

Nearly one million African Americans entered the armed forces. Segregated in the Army throughout the war and accepted only as mess attendants in the Navy when the conflict began, blacks had to overcome prejudice at home before they could fight enemies abroad. Maj. Gen. George S. Patton doubted that they were ready for combat until he saw the African-American 761st Tank Battalion excel at training maneuvers. "I would never have asked for you if you weren't good," he told them when they joined his forces in France. "I have nothing but the best in my army."

At induction centers, recruits were poked, prodded, and inoculated for smallpox, typhoid, and other illnesses they might encounter overseas. Some induction centers, like Fort Dix in New Jersey, also served as training camps, where soft enlisted men were hounded and hardened by drill sergeants. "He roared at us from the moment we appeared until the moment we left," one Marine wrote of his boot camp sergeant. "Our bare existence, for which we were humbly apologetic, plagued him, and sent him into spasms of rage." Not until they faced far worse ordeals in combat did men fully appreciate the lessons drilled into them in camp: the necessity of obeying orders, working as a team, and practicing skills needed to survive in battle repeatedly until they became automatic.

Not just men answered the call. On May 27, 1942, more than 10,000 volunteers jammed recruiting centers to become the first to enroll in the new Women's Army Auxiliary Corps (WAAC). In New York City, the line stretched for blocks, and women waited up to eight

"If the guys can take it, so can I."
Volunteer for the Women's Army Auxiliary Corps on women in boot camp

hours to enlist. Although destined for noncombat duty, they underwent basic training that included running obstacle courses under a tear-gas barrage and other trials similar to those that men faced in boot camps. "If the guys can take it," one woman said, "so can I."

Initially most WAACs worked as typists and clerks. But as more men were sent overseas, women in uniform took on a broader range of duties at bases in the United States, where they served as mechanics, cryptographers, radio operators, and air traffic controllers. In November 1942, WAACs went overseas to serve in North Africa, where they faced new hazards. Five women on their way to join Lt. Gen. Dwight Eisenhower's staff in Algiers were rescued after their ship was torpedoed and were later commended by Ike for their "skill, spirit, and determination." In July 1943, they and other auxiliaries officially became WACs in the newly designated Women's Army Corps, which was now an integral part of the U.S. Army.

Pfc. Buddy Howe
Recruit Reporting for Duty

William L. "Buddy" Howe, Jr., became a radio operator with the Battery B 29th Field Artillery Battalion, part of the famous Fourth Division that figured so prominently in the D-Day landings and the defeat of Nazi Germany. By the time the war was over, he had been awarded a Bronze Star and a Purple Heart. But in summer and fall 1943, he was a raw recruit one month out of high school.

After reporting to the Induction Center in Watertown [Massachusetts], I was sent via troop bus to Fort Devens, MA, where I reported for duty in July, 1943. When we left Watertown lots of people turned out to say good-bye to all their young sons off to war. I left my Mom, Dad, sister, Grandma and Grandpa Packard and never suspected that I would not see my father alive again. I was given a New Testament when I left home and carried it with me in my fatigue pocket all during the war. Included in it was the Ten Commandments scripture, selected Psalms and prayers as well as the words to Christian hymns and America the Beautiful, My Country 'Tis of Thee, and all three verses to The National Anthem. I still

Buddy Howe proudly poses in his uniform.

have this NT and cherish it to this day.

Fort Devens was the true beginning. I was 6-ft tall and weighed 139 pounds. (When I returned home after the war, I was still 6-feet tall and weighed 139 pounds.) At Fort Devens, I stood in line for everything I did, including chow line, physicals, indoctrination, clothing, and haircuts. It was the typical Army "hurry-up and wait."

From Fort Devens, I was shipped by troop train to Fort Bragg, for my basic training.

Buddy sent the following letter home, probably in late September 1943:

Dear Folks:

Well today we went over the infiltration course. It was really a wow. We have to stand up at one end of the course and when they throw a charge of dynamite at us we have to dive on our bellies and crawl on our bellies until we reach some barbed wire. We turn over on our backs and use our rifle to hold it up because it is lying on the ground. When we get out of the barbed wire we go over on our stomachs again. We do this until we have gone under three layers of barbed wire then we roll into a trench. Then they throw a grenade in the trench and we have to get out, but quick!!!!! All the time we are going over the course they are shooting a machine gun over our heads. They are also throwing dynamite right next to us, within a foot of us and every time a stick of dynamite goes off the concussion makes the whole ground shake and we rise right off the ground. We also have to hug that ground or get hit by machine gun bullets. When I got through, my pants were so ripped that really all I had left was a pair of shorts. I had to walk home 2½ miles like that. It was really a swell experience.

I wonder if you would get me a photograph album so I can paste the photos I have in it. Not too big a one. Also would you get some of those black things that you put in the four corners of the picture to hold it in. I also wish you would buy me a cigarette case. If you can get one with a lighter on the end get that. If not just a case. I can't get one here. Take the money out of my account and if I go easy this month I will send some money home.

Love to all,
Bud ∎

> "Then they throw a grenade in the trench and we have to get out, but quick!!!!!"

In September 1942, the U.S. Army Air Forces formed a separate unit for pilots, the Women's Auxiliary Ferrying Squadron, whose duties included shuttling military aircraft around the country and transporting cargo. Known later as WASPs (Women Air Force Service Pilots), those accepted for training already had some experience as pilots and were soon flying solo. Women of the Army Nurse Corps were deployed in every theater of the war and often served in field hospitals just behind the front. More than 200 were killed in action during the conflict. Women of the Navy Nurse Corps were not sent to combat zones until the close of the war, but many served on hospital ships. Like WACs, those who enlisted in the Navy as WAVES (Women Accepted for Volunteer Emergency Service) were first confined to clerical work but later took on technical tasks.

World War II hit Americans where they lived, making and breaking marriages and separating loved ones. The draft encouraged some couples to marry and have children, because most fathers were deferred by draft boards until military manpower demands increased in 1943. Another incentive for marrying was the emotional pressure couples felt when men were about to leave for a war from which they might not return. That sometimes led people to make commitments they found hard to keep. "I've told him I don't love him," a young woman confided to an interviewer after a serviceman proposed to her. "But he's an aviator and he says I should marry him anyhow and give him a little happiness. He says he knows he'll be dead in a year." When separated by war, couples who wed or became engaged for such reasons often had trouble sustaining their relationships, some of which ended with "Dear John" letters to servicemen abroad.

*A soldier shares a parting embrace with his girlfriend as he departs
New York City's Pennsylvania Station in 1943.*

Most marriages survived the long wartime separations, but life
was not easy for the wives of men in uniform. Military families
often tried to stay together while the husband remained stateside.
Wives and children followed servicemen from base to base, riding
overcrowded trains and living in rented rooms or cramped military housing. When husbands went overseas, their wives received
small monthly allotments from the government to pay for basic
necessities, but many took jobs or went to live with their parents to make ends meet. Parting was doubly painful for servicemen who left both a wife and child behind, often for a year

JOHN MAROTE
A CHILD'S-EYE VIEW

Marote was nine years old when the United States entered the war and as a resident of Hilo, Hawaii, he was closer to the action than most other Americans. But children see the world through their own peculiar lens. Here's how John remembers wartime.

We heard about the attack on Pearl Harbor over the radio. All the relatives got together at our house. What stands out in my mind is that the adults acted scared. This had never happened before. The fear was that the islands would be invaded and occupied by Japan. My concern? The Palace Theater cancelled the Mickey Mouse Club. (What else would a child be upset about?)

Children in wartime are still children. This photo shows John Marote and his dog playing near a river in Hilo.

I believe that Marshall [*sic*] Law was enforced at once. A curfew and blackout were immediately put into effect. Most of Hilo's population was Japanese. Only a few who were close supporters of their homeland or were suspected spies were sent to internment camps. At my age, I had no trepidation about being surrounded by those "people" who attacked Pearl Harbor. I cannot, however, speak for anyone else. We painted all windows a dark green color in order to comply with the blackout. Barbed wire was placed on the beaches and a machine gun emplacement built alongside our road. Gas masks were issued and we were required to carry them at all times. Students were subjected to tear gas and air raid drills. Air raid shelters were built at schools as well as at individual homes. The shelters consisted of an earthen roofed ditch, which would at best have provided protection only from shrapnel. A cement bunker was built at the mouth of the river. Currency in use was replaced with currency that had the word "Hawaii" written on both sides. This was done to allow bills to be put out of circulation if the island were taken over by the Japanese.

Military personnel were housed in town in ever increasing numbers. Rationing and metal collection were everyone's contribution to the war effort. When my father was drafted, we were given PX privileges. That was a plus. An event partly steeped in myth is the eruption of a Mauna Loa crater shortly after the attack. Not only was the glow bright enough to read a newspaper in Hilo, the light could be seen on the island of Oahu. A cloud that formed over the eruption took the shape of [a] woman's head that faced toward Japan. Supposedly, Japan shortly thereafter had a violent earthquake. PELE'S REVENGE!!!

"What stands out in my mind is that the adults acted scared. This had never happened before."

My personal contribution towards the war effort consisted of making solid miniature wooden airplanes to be used by spotters. I palled around with my cousin who was somewhat of an instigator. I did not always follow his ideas, but at times I did. On occasion we wrestled for servicemen in order to make a quarter. Once we dived for quarters off of LSTs [tank landing ships], which were beached for repairs. The loose change we made was paid for dearly when we both broke out with blisters all over our bodies caused by the oil, which leaked, from the LSTs. Our most daring antic was when we climbed a mango tree at night to watch a couple making out on the lawn below. Although branches rubbing together almost gave us away, we were not caught.

When an invasion was no longer imminent, life returned to normal and what still remained of the military became normal. When the war in the Pacific was over, all I could think of was that my father would be coming home. ∎

or two—and sometimes forever. But lengthy separations did not stop couples from starting families. Birth rates rose, anticipating the baby boom of the postwar era.

Families were creative about staying in touch when a loved one was deployed. In order to be able to slip personal information past military censors, some soldiers developed sophisticated methods of exchanging coded messages through the Red Cross mail system. Other soldiers used codes for more war-focused purposes. In one case, Lt. Frank G. Jonelis, held in a prison camp in Japan, managed to send a postcard addressed to "Mr. F. B. Iers" in Los Angeles. Japanese censors did not understand the reference in the address and permitted the note to pass. The postcard reached an alert FBI agent, who recognized that the contents contained a null code—in which certain words are given as "nulls" to be eliminated—and deciphered the message.

THE HOME FRONT

The huge military call-up transformed American society by expanding opportunities for women and minorities, not just in the various armed forces but in war industries as well. America had not yet overcome the Great Depression when it entered World War II, so good work had been hard to find, particularly for minorities and women. In the six months following the attack on Pearl Harbor, roughly 750,000 women sought well-paid jobs in defense plants. Only about one in ten was accepted. There were still lots of men seeking work, and they had priority.

Soon, however, Americans were fighting on two fronts, and there were not enough able-bodied men to meet the needs of both the armed forces and booming war industries. Employers who once thought women too delicate for tasks like welding and riveting found them well suited for such work and faced a new challenge—attracting women to jobs considered unfeminine. Artists and photographers helped out by altering the image of the American woman. The character "Rosie the Riveter," popularized in a 1942 hit song by bandleader Kay Kyser, became an icon and inspired depictions of strong working women. By 1945, as many as three million women worked in defense plants. When asked why even more women did not join the workforce, one who knew what it took to raise a family responded: "Because they don't have wives."

The wartime industrial boom also allowed African Americans to find skilled jobs from which they had long been barred. Aided by the Fair Employment Practices Commission, blacks made up 7.5 percent of the workers in war industries by 1944. Among them were women who had been relegated to domestic work

Workers at a Boeing plant in Seattle stand proudly beside B-17 Flying Fortress number 5,000, covered with placards bearing their signatures.

before the war. As one woman put it: "Hitler was the one that got us out of the white folks' kitchen." By mobilizing all its human and technological resources, the United States overwhelmed its enemies materially and won the production war, turning

out some 1,500 naval vessels, 5,600 merchant ships, 80,000 landing craft, 100,000 tanks and armored vehicles, 300,000 aircraft, 20 million small arms, and 41 billion rounds of ammunition, more than Japan, Italy, and Germany combined.

The huge expansion in the war industry workforce opened the United States to the possibility that workers and others might accidentally pass valuable information to the enemy. To keep Americans from disclosing secrets to spies, the U.S. Office of War Information distributed posters warning of the consequences of careless talk. Produced by leading graphic artists, they were designed to catch viewers' eyes and seal their lips. Some were considered too artistic by critics, who cited a survey in which factory workers thought the poster entitled "He's Watching You," showing a helmeted Nazi, referred to their boss. But most people got the message and heeded these warnings.

Americans on the home front felt the pinch as the nation shifted from producing consumer goods to arming and equipping millions of U.S. and Allied troops—including Soviet forces, who received more than 400,000 American-made trucks and jeeps. To further that massive war effort, officials in Washington urged citizens to sacrifice for the common good. One poster exhorted the public to "Produce and Conserve, Share and Play Square." Beginning in May 1942, the government froze prices on nearly all consumer goods and rationed items considered essential, including sugar, coffee, butter, meat, shoes, and gasoline. Nylon, needed to make parachutes, was denied to the public, forcing women to do without fashionable stockings. One-third of all cigarettes made in the United States were allocated to the armed forces, and new car production was halted so that auto plants could manufacture military vehicles. Not all Americans were content to share and play square. Black markets emerged, with restricted items sold at steep prices, and ration coupons for gasoline were counterfeited and used to purchase as much as 5 percent of the domestic fuel supply by 1944.

Most people responded generously, however, when asked to aid the war effort. Tens of millions of Americans who were not directly involved in the war contributed by planting "victory gardens" to expand food stocks, purchasing war bonds, and conducting scrap drives to collect metals, rubber, and other strategic materials.

After Japan seized most of the world's rubber supply, President Roosevelt called for a scrap drive, which brought in nearly 500,000 tons of used rubber within a month. Much of it proved ill suited for recycling, but the government successfully conserved rubber by limiting the use of gas, autos, and tires. Other public scrap drives brought in an array of materials to be used for munitions, from iron and steel to the glycerin in kitchen fats. One man donated his beat-up old car to a scrap drive—no small sacrifice when new cars were unavailable—and placed a sign on the window playing on a favorite World War II song: "Praise the Lord, I'll Soon Be Ammunition."

Americans made a big financial investment in the war effort as well, opening their pocketbooks and buying government savings bonds. Knowing war was coming, President Roosevelt himself purchased the first of a new series of bonds in May 1941, encouraging other Americans to do the same. Originally known as defense bonds, their name was changed to war bonds after the attack on Pearl Harbor. Authorized by the U.S. Treasury to finance the war effort and curb inflation by reducing the amount of currency in circulation, the bonds were issued in denominations ranging from $25 to $10,000 and offered a modest annual return of 2.9 percent. Typically they were purchased at a discount of 25 percent and redeemed at full face value 10 years later, leaving the cash in the Treasury's coffers for the duration of the war and then some. Patriotic youngsters purchased war savings stamps worth as little as 10 cents, which they pasted in a book until they had enough to buy a bond. In 1944 alone, the stamps and bonds that American schoolchildren purchased more than covered the cost of building nearly 3,000 aircraft and 44,000 jeeps.

War bond poster campaigns, featuring artwork by such renowned artists as Norman Rockwell and Lawrence Beall Smith, encouraged people to purchase a "share in America." Composer Irving Berlin contributed a theme song, "Any Bonds Today?" for the National Defense Savings Program. High-profile bond drives featuring celebrities such as Bette Davis and Rita Hayworth toured 300 cities and towns. One nationwide series of "Stars Over America" rallies sold a prodigious $838,540,000 worth of bonds. Screen stars Hedy Lamarr and Lana Turner raised millions by promising kisses to those who bought high-priced bonds. Singer Kate Smith, renowned for her rendition of "God Bless America," hosted a marathon radio broadcast that rang up $40 million in bond sales in 16 hours. By the time the fighting ended, more than 85 million Americans had bought bonds worth a total of $135 billion—more than a third of the cost of financing the war, estimated at $340 billion.

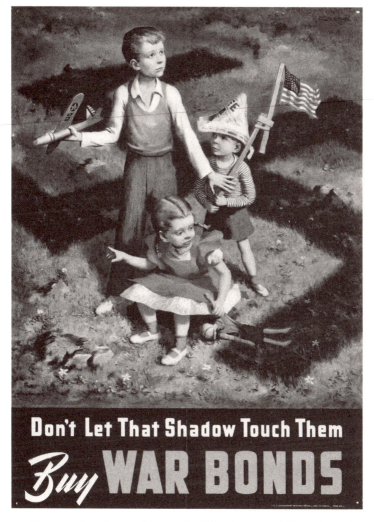

The poster above, by artist Lawrence Beall Smith, promoted the purchase of war bonds as a way to protect children from America's enemies.

When the United States went to war, existing volunteer organizations like the American Red Cross aided service members at home and abroad. During the conflict, the Red Cross collected 13.4 million pints of blood—shipping the life-saving plasma abroad—and sent more than 27 million food and medical parcels to Allied prisoners of war held overseas. National Geographic stepped up too, supplying commanders with accurate maps of remote areas where fighting was taking place, supplementing the work of U.S. agencies such as the Army Map Service and the Navy's Bureau of Navigation. Soon after the attack on Pearl Harbor, President Roosevelt read a military dispatch referring to Simatang, a tiny Indonesian island in the Celebes Sea. Unable to find Simatang on any map at hand, Roosevelt turned to National Geographic, which fulfilled his request and later presented him with a cabinet containing exhaustive, large-scale maps of the world's regions on retractable panels. National Geographic provided a similar cabinet to Winston Churchill.

Men of all ranks sent to the Pacific used National Geographic maps to orient themselves. The U.S. government distributed more than 20,000 copies of a 38-by-31-inch map of the Pacific, with 73 insets detailing Pacific islands, atolls, harbors, and reefs. Early in the war, ships of the U.S. Asiatic Fleet relied on that map when navigating Australian waters, for which they lacked charts. In 1942, Adm. Chester Nimitz was on his way to Guadalcanal when the navigator of the B-17 in which he was flying lost his bearings in a storm. The man grabbed his National Geographic map from under his seat and used it to get back on course.

In 1941, a new volunteer group, the United Service Organizations (USO), arose to meet the emotional needs of lonely recruits. At that time, nightspots near military bases consisted largely of raucous bars and dismal, disease-ridden brothels. What the USO offered instead at canteens set up near many camps was wholesome entertainment, provided mostly by young women who volunteered to talk and dance with servicemen but knew where to draw the line. A volunteer at the USO near Camp Kilmer,

New Jersey, recalled that she and others were escorted there by bus. "At the end of the night," she added, "you got right back on the bus." There was no rule against hostesses corresponding with guests when they went overseas. "We would write to the boys," another volunteer remarked, "especially boys who had no one to write to them."

Celebrities helped entertain servicemen at USO events around the world and at nightclubs founded by other organizations like the Stage Door Canteen in New York's theater district, which

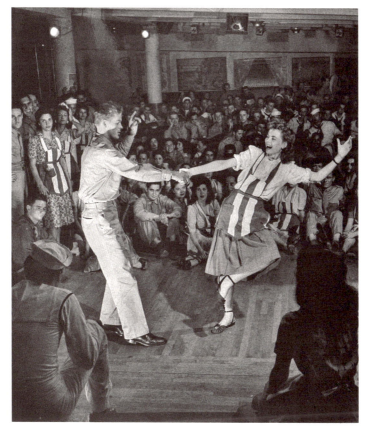

Actress Dorothy McGuire jitterbugs with a soldier at Manhattan's Stage Door Canteen, which was so successful that others like it opened in several cities.

offered guests food, nonalcoholic drinks, and a rare chance to meet and dance with celebrities. But the real stars were the everyday volunteers who kept servicemen entertained and were treated by them in return as someone special. As one USO hostess said, "You felt like the belle of the ball, one soldier after another would cut in to dance with you!"

Other sorts of entertainment were welcome as well. Sgt. Bill Mauldin drew on his own experiences as an infantryman in Sicily and Italy to produce cartoons that captured the essence of the private soldier's war. Mauldin's uncompromising look at the harsh and sometimes humorous existence of the ordinary GI—a term that originally meant "government issue" but came to signify any enlisted man—endeared him to millions of soldiers, who relished his sardonic sketches in the Army newspaper *Stars and Stripes*.

Born in New Mexico in 1921, Mauldin had studied at the Academy of Fine Arts in Chicago. After joining the National Guard, he became part of the 45th Infantry Division and drew cartoons for its newspaper. He served with the 45th in the Mediterranean until 1944, when he went to work full time for *Stars and Stripes*. His most memorable cartoon characters were two bedraggled soldiers named Willie and Joe. "I drew pictures for and about the soldiers because I knew what their life was like and understood their gripes," Mauldin recalled. "I wanted to make something out of the humorous situations which come up even when you don't think life could be any more miserable."

AMERICA'S LOYAL "ENEMY ALIENS"

This newfound American dedication to defeating enemies abroad also had a dark side: racial hatred turned against neighbors at home. In the bitter aftermath of the attacks on Pearl Harbor and the Philippines, Americans were inclined to distrust and disdain all Japanese, including so-called enemy aliens on American soil, many of whom were in fact proud U.S. citizens.

Few people realized that Japanese Americans were among the nation's first war victims on December 7, 1941, when flak from antiaircraft guns went astray in Honolulu and crashed into their homes, killing some and maiming others. Sifting through the rubble in search of survivors that morning was 17-year-old Daniel Inouye, a Japanese-American Red Cross volunteer who would later represent Hawaii in the U.S. Senate. An American citizen by birth, he had no sympathy for imperial Japan. Although only a "generation removed from the land that had spawned those bombers," Inouye wrote later in his memoir, *Journey to Washington,* he looked up at the warplanes and cursed those Japanese. Even as he did so, however, he knew that similar curses would be aimed at him and other loyal Japanese Americans by people who saw them as enemies. No matter how much they did to support and defend their country, he realized, "There would always be those who would look at us and think—and some would say it aloud—'Dirty Jap!'"

Japanese Americans had long faced bias and resentment in the United States, which prohibited further immigration from Japan and other Asian nations in 1924. After war erupted in the Pacific in 1941, Earl Warren—the attorney general of California and future chief justice of the U.S. Supreme Court—called for interning those of Japanese ancestry living on the West Coast, a drastic step that President Roosevelt authorized in February 1942. Warren argued for keeping those detainees in camps even after fears of a Japanese attack subsided. "If the Japs are released," he said in 1943, "no one will be able to tell a saboteur from any other Jap . . . We don't want a second Pearl Harbor in California." Late in life, Warren admitted that Japanese Americans had been wrongly confined without evidence that they were disloyal. He wrote that he "deeply regretted the removal order and my own testimony advocating it, because it was not in keeping with our American concept of freedom and the rights of citizens."

Most Japanese Americans in Hawaii, unlike those on the West Coast, were spared internment. They made up nearly 40 percent of Hawaii's 400,000 inhabitants and were too important to its economy to be removed or isolated. Some influential Anglo Americans vouched for them, including John Burns, a police

Windblown dust envelops the Manzanar camp below the Sierra Nevada, one of many relocation centers situated in remote areas in the West.

captain in Honolulu and future governor who expressed "complete confidence in Hawaii's Japanese Americans." Eighteen-year-old Yoshiaki Fujitani was among those Nisei (first-generation Japanese Americans) who enrolled in the Reserve Officer Training Corps (ROTC) at the University of Hawaii. After the attack on Pearl Harbor, they were inducted into the newly formed Hawaiian Territorial Guard and issued rifles. When they went out on patrols, Fujitani recalled, some people "looked at us very suspiciously . . . to them, we sure looked like the enemy." He and other Nisei were sent to patrol the docks. They joked about what a Marine might say if he arrived there by ship with his buddies to defend Pearl Harbor and saw Japanese guards waiting on shore with guns in hand: "Hey, Mac, we're too late."

Their service in the Hawaiian Territorial Guard lasted only about a month. In late December 1941, Japanese submarines surfaced off Hawaii and shelled port facilities and oil storage tanks. Little damage was done, but the attacks increased concerns in Washington about security in Hawaii and heightened hostility toward Japanese Americans there. In January, Fujitani and his fellow guards "were told that we were going to be inactivated." Rumor had it that they were being cast aside because they "looked like the enemy." Their suspicions were confirmed when the Hawaiian Territorial Guard was reactivated a short time later without them. Although most Japanese Americans in Hawaii remained free, more than a thousand people were arrested as suspected enemy sympathizers. Many of them were Isei (U.S. residents born in Japan) who clung to the traditions of their ancestral land by teaching Japanese or preaching Buddhism. Others of Japanese birth or heritage in Hawaii had their homes searched and their shortwave radios removed or disabled to prevent them from receiving broadcasts

SATO HASHIZUME
JAPANESE-AMERICAN INTERNMENT CAMPS

Hashizume was born in Japan in 1931 and immigrated with her family to Portland, Oregon, as an infant. In 1942, she and her family were sent to the Minidoka internment camp in Idaho.

The people in our apartment house were extremely loyal. After awhile, there used to be an FBI agent who stood across the street from our apartment house. As people left our apartment house, he would question them and say, "Do they have short-wave radio or Japanese flags?" or, "Do they have anything that would suggest loyalty to Japan?" They would say, "No! No! They are Americans! They are born here in the United States! What are you saying?" . . .

We were concerned that they would take away my father or they would think that we were doing something subversive. And so we . . . were going through everything, magazines, our albums, and found the Japanese flag, we went and took them downstairs and burned them in the furnace, to try to get rid of anything that suggested that we may have some loyalties to Japan . . . My father had some books and things that he rather cherished, and he thought, "Well, maybe those should go be burned as well." So, we have gaps in our album where we threw some pictures away that we thought might be incriminating . . . We didn't receive a notice until shortly before we had to leave. At that point, my father had to sell the business . . . so a woman came and gave him an offer that he took and it was way below market value, but we had no choice.

So then we got a notice that said, "This is what you can take, and this is what you must leave behind." . . . They told us that we needed to take our bedding;

> "We were concerned that they would take away my father or they would think that we were doing something subversive."

we needed to take our sheets—not the mattresses or anything like that—but our sheets, and pillows. Then, the other thing that we were supposed to take was one plate, one cup, a knife, fork, and spoon, and our toiletries and then only what we could carry in terms of our clothes . . . We couldn't take any cameras; certainly we couldn't take any pets. I had a cat that I had to get rid of. My sister found a home for it and that was heartbreaking to me . . . Well, we each had a suitcase, and so we filled it—and we didn't know whether we were going to be there for years or days . . . We knew we were going to the assembly center, but from there, we didn't know where we were going to go. ■

Top: *In a desperate appeal for tolerance, a Japanese-American store owner placed this sign in the window of his Oakland, California, grocery on December 8, 1941.* Bottom: *These boys, confined at the Manzanar Relocation Center in California, were among thousands of young Japanese Americans sent with their parents to internment camps.*

from Tokyo. Collectively, they faced hostility and humiliation that few German Americans or Italian Americans with ancestral ties to Axis countries experienced.

Desperate to prove their loyalty, Fujitani and other Nisei at the University of Hawaii formed a group called the Varsity Victory Volunteers and appealed to Lt. Gen. Delos Emmons, the new Army commander at Pearl Harbor and military governor of Hawaii, which was now under martial law. "Hawaii is our home, the United States is our country," they wrote Emmons. "We know but one loyalty and that is to the Stars and Stripes. We wish to do our part as loyal Americans in every way possible and we hereby offer ourselves for whatever service you may see fit to use us." In February 1942, they were assigned to the Army Corps of Engineers as a volunteer labor battalion. They carried no weapons and wielded only hammers, picks, and shovels as they quarried rocks, dug ditches, and built roads and barracks. It was dirty, thankless work, but most of them stuck with it. One exception

"I've been a pretty good American, why should they take my dad? . . . I decided, well, I am not going to cooperate anymore . . . I sort of lost my feeling for America."

Yoshiaki Fujitani, a Nisei member of an Army Corp of Engineers Hawaiian volunteer labor battalion, when he resigned after his father was arrested

was Fujitani, who resigned in April after learning that his father, a Buddhist minister, had been arrested. "I've been a pretty good American," he thought. "Why should they take my dad? . . . I decided, well, I am not going to cooperate anymore . . . I sort of lost my feeling for America." He went to work to support his mother and siblings but later served in the U.S. Military Intelligence Service as a translator in occupied Japanese territory.

The Varsity Victory Volunteers were ultimately rewarded for their efforts. They and other Nisei in Hawaii formed the nucleus of the 442nd Regimental Combat Team, organized in early 1943 when the U.S. Army began inducting Japanese Americans as soldiers. Some of the regiment went directly from internment camps to Army training camps. Others like Daniel Inouye who were not interned jumped at the chance to fight for their country. He had recently enrolled as a premedical student at the University of Hawaii when the ROTC commander addressed Nisei in the auditorium there and informed them that they were eligible to enlist. The officer later told Inouye "that he had a little pep talk all prepared for us, how we now had a chance to do our duty as patriotic Americans, but it was about as necessary as telling those Navy gunners on December 7 to open fire." They burst from the hall and ran to the draft board three miles away. Some who volunteered that day later died in action. Others, like Inouye, were severely wounded and carried the scars of battle with them ever after as living proof that they were neither enemies nor aliens but true Americans, more faithful to their country than their country had been to them.

America's determination to avenge December 7—signaled by this 1942 poster—was especially strong among men of the Pacific Fleet.

CHRONOLOGY

DECEMBER 23, 1941 Gen. Douglas MacArthur abandons the Philippine capital of Manila to the Japanese and withdraws American and Filipino troops to the Bataan Peninsula and Corregidor.

MARCH 11, 1942 MacArthur escapes from besieged Corregidor to command Allied forces in Australia.

STRIKING BACK AT JAPAN

FROM THE BATTLE OF BATAAN TO MIDWAY

O n December 23, 1941, Gen. Douglas MacArthur took a step he had been dreading ever since the Philippines had come under attack two weeks earlier. Japanese troops on the main island of Luzon were now approaching the capital of Manila from north and south. MacArthur's forces, consisting of 22,000 Americans and a larger number of Filipinos, many of them poorly trained, had no chance of holding the city. U.S. warplanes at Clark Field and other bases had been all but wiped out, and the Japanese had command of the air and the sea. In order to spare civilians, MacArthur announced, he would have to declare Manila "an open city, as was done in the case of Paris," which fell without a fight when the French abandoned it to German invaders in June 1940. A proud and aggressive commander who had earlier scrubbed a defensive plan calling for his troops to withdraw to the remote Bataan Peninsula as soon

APRIL 9, 1942 U.S. forces trapped on Bataan surrender and begin a forced march to Japanese prison camps.

MAY 4–8, 1942 Battle of the Coral Sea

JUNE 4–6, 1942 Battle of Midway

APRIL 18, 1942 Lt. Col. James Doolittle leads a raid on Tokyo by bombers launched from the aircraft carrier U.S.S. *Hornet.*

JUNE 3, 1942 Imperial Japanese Navy launches diversionary attacks on U.S. bases on the Aleutian Islands before assaulting Midway Island.

as the Japanese attacked, MacArthur would now have to conduct that retreat with the enemy in hot pursuit.

MacArthur would be remembered as a great American general. But for him as for other accomplished Allied commanders, World War II began disastrously. Like many other top Army officers when the conflict began, the 61-year-old MacArthur was molded by his experiences in World War I, a struggle that unfolded in slow motion compared with the lightning-quick offensives launched by Germany and Japan in this conflict. The startling speed and destructive impact of modern combat, fueled by dramatic advances in aviation and weaponry since 1918, stunned MacArthur and other American officers in December 1941—as it had Polish, French, British, and Soviet commanders who had been overwhelmed by German blitzkriegs in the two years preceding the Japanese onslaught.

In MacArthur's case, the crisis was aggravated by his deep personal attachment to Manila, where his father, Gen. Arthur MacArthur, had served as military governor following the U.S. occupation of the Philippines during the Spanish-American War. Arthur MacArthur's stellar military record, which included a Medal of Honor for his daring charge up Missionary Ridge as a 19-year-old Union lieutenant during the Civil War, had inspired his son to similar acts of heroism as a colonel with the American Expeditionary Forces in France in 1918. Douglas MacArthur's reluctance to retreat from Manila in 1941 stemmed in part from devotion to his father's memory. "You know, I feel Dad's presence here," he remarked. Among the traits he shared with his father was a self-assurance bordering on arrogance. An officer who knew both generals remarked that "Arthur MacArthur was the most flamboyantly egotistical man I had ever seen, until I met his son." Douglas MacArthur's combative pride caused him to spurn the idea of withdrawing to Bataan until that retreat could no longer be avoided—a fallback for which he failed to make adequate preparations. One Army depot near Manila contained enough rice to nourish his men for years, but none of it was shipped to the Bataan Peninsula before they withdrew there and went hungry.

MacArthur's faults were inseparable from his strengths as a commander. His giant ego, which could make him overbearing and overconfident, also made him an inspirational leader in dire circumstances. No one was more aware of MacArthur's flaws than Lt. Col. Dwight D. Eisenhower, who had served under him for several years. "He'd like to occupy a throne room surrounded by experts in flattery," Eisenhower wrote in his diary before leaving MacArthur's staff in 1939. "Will I be glad when I get out of this!" Yet when Ike later achieved prominence as a general, he paid his exasperating old boss a rare tribute. "If that door opened at this moment," he told reporters, "and General MacArthur was standing there, and he said, 'Ike, follow me,' I'd get up and follow him."

After grudgingly abandoning Manila, MacArthur and his officers executed a skillful, fighting retreat to Bataan. Bridges were held just long enough for the troops to cross over, then destroyed to slow the oncoming enemy. MacArthur described the withdrawal succinctly: "Stand and fight, slip back and dynamite. It was savage and bloody, but it won time." His second in command, Maj. Gen. Jonathan Wainwright, fought a valiant delaying action at a vital bridge over the Pampanga River, northwest of Manila, before crossing with his rear guard on New Year's Day 1942, and

> "Stand and fight, slip back and dynamite. It was savage and bloody, but it won time."
>
> Gen. Douglas MacArthur, describing his withdrawal from Manila

demolishing the span behind him. By mid-January, some 80,000 Filipino and American troops and 25,000 civilians were holed up behind fortified lines on Bataan, situated across Manila Bay from the capital. MacArthur made his headquarters on Corregidor, a small island off the southern tip of the peninsula. Sheltered there, in a tunnel blasted out of volcanic rock, with his staff, his wife and young son, and Filipino president Manuel Quezon, he appealed by radio to Washington for aid and reinforcements. Army Chief of Staff Gen. George Marshall hailed him for his "splendid resistance" and promised support. But it soon became clear that neither the Army nor the Navy, still reeling from its losses at Pearl Harbor, could break the Japanese stranglehold on the Philippines.

MacArthur's stranded forces did not yield easily to their Japanese foes. Lt. Col. Philip Fry, the American commander of an elite regiment of Filipino Scouts, recalled how his troops repulsed the initial attack by Lt. Gen. Masahura Homma's overeager troops, who advanced across a minefield into murderous machine-gun fire: "A great shout of 'Banzai!' came from the front and the Japs started an old Civil War charge . . . It was slaughter. All of our guns had been carefully sighted for mutual support and the Japs were caught by terrific fire both frontal and flanking." Homma's next assault was more careful and effective. "This time the enemy brought up his tanks and hit us hard," Fry related. The big guns that MacArthur's men used to combat those tanks fired sporadically, Fry added, because "we had World War I ammunition and averaged about six duds out of every ten rounds fired." Antiquated or deficient weapons, including faulty hand grenades and torpedoes, greatly hampered U.S. forces in the Pacific at the start of this conflict, exposing gaps in the nation's defenses caused by two decades of peacetime complacency and neglect.

Both sides in the grueling battle for Bataan suffered from tropical diseases, festering wounds, and paltry rations. But Homma received thousands of reinforcements in early 1942 and MacArthur received none. "It was Japan's ability to bring in fresh forces and America's inability to do so that finally settled the issue," he wrote. After visiting his troops on the peninsula in January and assuring them that help was on the way—a pledge he made in good faith but could not fulfill—MacArthur returned to Corregidor and remained there. Soldiers mocked their distant commander, calling him "Dugout Doug." He fared better at headquarters than his famished troops did in the field, but life was no picnic on Corregidor, which was constantly under bombardment. The sickening realization that

> "We're the battling bastards of Bataan. No mama, no papa, no Uncle Sam . . . And nobody gives a damn."
>
> Soldiers' song on Bataan

his men on Bataan were trapped gnawed at MacArthur and left him unable to face them again. As their strength ebbed away and their hopes dwindled, they found solace in gallows humor. "We're the battling bastards of Bataan," they chanted, "No mama, no papa, no Uncle Sam . . . And nobody gives a damn."

In truth, their stubborn resistance heartened Americans on the home front and surprised the Japanese, who expected to secure the Philippines by February 1 and were still counting their losses and pouring in reinforcements a month later. By then, Bataan's "battling bastards" were among the last Allied forces in the region holding out against Japanese invaders. In the western Pacific, lightly defended American bases on Guam and Wake Island had been overwhelmed not long after the attack on Pearl Harbor.

HENRY CLAY HENDERSON
DEFENSE OF THE PHILIPPINES

Henderson was serving as a fireman—responsible for operating and maintaining a ship's boilers—on the submarine tender U.S.S. Otus when the Japanese bombed Cavite Navy Yard near Manila on December 10, 1941. Left behind when most U.S. naval forces departed for Australia, Henderson was captured on Corregidor.

Dec. 12, 1941 Fri. morning. I went to the Cavite Navy Yard to try to salvage any submarine spare parts or torpedoes. GOD what a sight. Dead bodies everywhere. Dog, cats, chicken, and pigs were eating the flesh of these bodies. It was a scramble to find a place to put my foot down without stepping on someone or some dismembered part of a body . . .

Jan 2, 1942. All flag personnel were assembled on the USS *Canopus* for assignment to submarines that would ultimately take them to Australia. This included everyone except submarine spare parts personnel. When the Submarine Officers left the area, us so called stragglers were fair prey for any and all dirty details the ARMY could come up with . . .

Mar 1, 1942. . . . The USS *Canopus* was eventually bombed

Captured Japanese infantrymen of the 14th Imperial Army accept the surrender of U.S. troops at the north entrance of the Malinta Tunnel on Corregidor on May 9, 1942.

and had to be scuttled. This crew, as well as all of us stragglers were put in the Beach Defense Sectors, serving under the US ARMY. The US MARINES also suffered this same fate. They were put in charge of training us in the use of the rifle, bayonet, pistol, hand grenades, knife, garrote, and hand to hand combat. BOY!!! They made MARINES out of us in short order. I got so adept with the Enfield rifle that during the invasion of Corregidor, when I got one of the enemy in my sights, he was a downed man . . .

March 15, 1942. I was transferred to the Beach Defense Sector on Monkey Point on Corregidor with the Marines and other stragglers like myself. Being the Junior Chief, I was put in charge of this group. This was a sorry lot, each of us knew just exactly what we were, Cannon Fodder . . .

May 5, 1942 Wed. 2230 hrs. The alert was sounded to repel boarders. The Japanese had landed and where? Right on top of us stragglers. Now I know this was not planned, but none the less, it happened that way. The battle raged until we were told the next morning to resist until NOON, strip our guns and dispose of them and surrender. However, by 1000 hrs. this morning, we knew the end had come, after all my Enfield was no match for the TANKS that had followed the Infantry

"GOD what a sight. Dead bodies everywhere. Dog, cats, chicken, and pigs were eating the flesh of these bodies."

ashore and stomped us into the ground. As all of this was happening, a big shell dropped in on top of us. A small piece of shrapnel hit my left ankle and the concussion stunned me . . . I don't know how long I was in this stupor, some time later, I came to. My rifle had been fired for so long and so many times, that the protective wood around the barrel showed signs of being charred by the heat of this rapid ring. A Japanese soldier was nudging me with his bayonet and pointing in the direction of the 92nd Field Artillery garage. I didn't think I could, but he convinced me otherwise. We were all moved to this location to await further developments . . . The shrapnel in my ankle was killing me by this time. A Corpsman from the USS *Luzon,* a river boat from China, removed this sliver from my ankle with a pair of needle nose pliers. He sewed up the wound, using needle and thread from a sewing kit one of my friends had on him. ■

113

The British lost Hong Kong in late December and suffered a staggering defeat in February when Singapore fell to Japanese troops heavily outnumbered by the hapless defenders of that strategic city at the southern tip of the Malay Peninsula. Winston Churchill, who had sent the battleship H.M.S. *Prince of Wales* and the battle cruiser H.M.S. *Repulse* to defend Singapore and lost both to Japanese bombers, called the surrender of that stronghold the "worst disaster and greatest capitulation of British history."

In Malaya, as in Burma, where the capital, Rangoon, fell to Japanese troops in early March, the invaders moved furtively through the jungle and outflanked British forces defending roads and junctions. The British were further hampered by resistance to imperial rule in their Asian colonies. By posing as liberators and promising to forge a Greater East Asia Co-Prosperity Sphere, the Japanese attracted sympathizers not just in British colonies like Burma—where many nationalists sided with the Japanese against Britain—but also in the oil-rich Dutch East Indies, which were occupied with ease after the Japanese shattered a motley Allied fleet in the Java Sea in late February.

Southeast Asians who endured Japanese occupation soon discovered that their new rulers were more ruthless imperialists than their old European masters. Before World War II erupted, Japan had colonized Korea and Manchuria (reorganized as the puppet state of Manchukuo) and occupied much of China, often subjecting their fellow Asians in those lands to harsh treatment. Ba Maw, a collaborator who served as prime minister of Burma under the Japanese, later denounced what he called the "Korea clique"— Japanese officers who had learned in Korea, Manchuria, and China to behave like "the master race in Asia and to deal with the other Asian races on that footing." They saw "only one destiny for the East Asian countries," he added—"to become so many Manchukuos or Koreas tied to Japan forever." As the new imperial masters of the region, the Japanese siphoned off the natural resources of countries they occupied and forced men to labor for them and women to serve as prostitutes for their soldiers.

Japanese authorities did little to restrain brutal acts by soldiers against civilians or Allied prisoners of war. To the contrary, army officers hardened troops to brutality by beating subordinates and allowing them to do the same to men under their command. Many Japanese soldiers were also steeped in a crude version of the ancient samurai code of *bushido* (way of the warrior), which encouraged them not just to be brave and loyal and to die rather than surrender but also to regard those who surrendered to them as cowardly and contemptible. During the fighting on Bataan, Japanese planes dropped leaflets aimed at Filipino troops, blaming their plight on the United States and urging them to abandon their American allies: "Give up all your weapons at once and surrender to the Japanese force before it is too late, then we shall fully protect you." Few Filipinos were taken in by such appeals. They knew what Japanese occupation meant for Korea and China and recognized that those promises of protection were not worth the paper they were printed on.

THE BATAAN DEATH MARCH

On March 11, 1942, MacArthur left Corregidor with his family and staff aboard a swift PT boat, which evaded Japanese patrols and reached the distant Philippine island of Mindanao, where they boarded a B-17 for Australia. In making this escape, MacArthur was following orders from General Marshall and President

Roosevelt, who did not want him killed or captured by the Japanese and sent him to command Allied forces in Australia. "The President of the United States ordered me to break through the Japanese lines," he declared when he arrived there, "for the purpose, as I understand it, of organizing the American offensive against Japan, a primary object of which is the relief of the Philippines." Then

"I shall return."

Gen. Douglas MacArthur's personal promise on leaving the Philippines in March 1942

he offered a memorable pledge to the Filipino people and the troops stranded on Luzon. "I came through, and I shall return," he vowed. The War Information Office in Washington asked MacArthur's permission to change the "I" to "we" before releasing the story to the press. "We shall return" would signal that Americans as a whole were determined to defeat the Japanese and liberate the Philippines. But MacArthur would not allow his statement to be altered. Reclaiming the Philippines was his personal crusade, and he believed that Filipinos had more trust in him than in the U.S. government, which had seemingly abandoned them to the enemy.

Many American soldiers left behind on Luzon felt abandoned by their commander as well as their government. Some men like pilot Sam Grashio thought that it made sense for MacArthur to carry on the fight elsewhere rather than "fall into the hands of the enemy," but Grashio noticed that others were scornful: "His departure occasioned some bitter remarks about 'Dugout Doug' from men who had long envied the Corregidor garrison for what they presumed was the easier life of the latter or who blamed MacArthur for the inadequate defenses of the Philippines." Morale dropped when he departed, recalled Col. Clifford Bluemel, who assured his troops that MacArthur would indeed return: "Help is going to come. He's going to bring it back." But Bluemel privately doubted that help would arrive in time to save them. "I had to lie a little bit," he admitted. "I didn't believe it." Hunger and disease had weakened the troops, and they could not keep up the fight much longer. In late March, Homma's reinforced army launched fresh attacks and broke through their last lines of defense. A few thousand Americans and Filipinos escaped to Corregidor, where General Wainwright had taken command, but the rest were rounded up when Gen. Edward King surrendered Luzon on April 9. Wainwright would hold out until early May before surrendering the Philippines as a whole.

The Japanese were not prepared to handle the more than 70,000 prisoners of war they seized at the southern tip of the Bataan Peninsula in April. Hasty plans were made to march them nearly 70 miles north to the nearest railroad station, where they would be crowded into boxcars and shipped to Camp O'Donnell, a captured Allied base converted into a prison camp. The prisoners were wary of the Japanese, but few anticipated the terrible ordeal that lay ahead. When Maj. Alva Fitch and his men reached the town of Mariveles at the end of their first day's march, they "expected to find food and transportation to wherever we were going," he said. Instead, "we found nothing except several hundred Americans, as bewildered, hungry, and poverty stricken as ourselves. We were herded into what had been the public square and thoroughly searched." An hour or so later, Fitch added, "a Jap climbed up on a truck and made a speech: 'You take a little walk to Balanga. Maybe you get food there.' Balanga was about 40 kilometers [25 miles] away. I didn't think we could make it, but I was no longer in a position to dispute with the Imperial Japanese Armed Forces."

Many of the prisoners were in poor shape when the march began. Those who lagged behind or fell out were beaten by guards or prodded back into line with bayonets. Those who collapsed were often shot or stabbed and left to die. As Fitch and his fellow prisoners approached Balanga, they noticed "an increase in the number of corpses along the road"—victims who had preceded them on the march and failed to reach that town, where there were in fact no provisions. Nor were there any sanitary facilities at Balanga, Fitch recalled: "This did not concern most of us much, as we had been three days without food and could never get enough water to spare for urine. There were two small spigots at Balanga and it was necessary to stand in line for several hours to get your canteen filled." Fitch managed to dig a few turnips out of the ground with a stick. That helped sustain him, but others in his company were unable to keep up when the march resumed: "I helped Chaplain Duffy along until he quit trying. I then commended him to his maker and left him to the gentle mercies of the Japanese." Fitch later tried to help a fellow officer named Vaughn back on his feet when he fell: "I couldn't get him up and a Jap came along and told me to move on. I tried to explain to him but he jabbed me in the butt with his bayonet. Then he shot Vaughn in the chest."

More than 7,000 Filipino and American prisoners perished on that murderous death march, which concluded with a suffocating train ride from San Fernando to Capas, a few miles from Camp O'Donnell. Up to a hundred men were jammed into each boxcar. "Too crowded to sit, much less lie, they watched the doors slam shut," related one survivor, Capt. John Olson. "Then began three to four hours of excruciating sweltering in this fetid sweat box. Some collapsed, the weakest died. Even the Japanese guards suffered."

The prisoners' ordeal continued when they reached Camp O'Donnell, which Olson likened to Andersonville, the filthy Confederate compound where thousands of Union prisoners died of disease and malnutrition during the Civil War. In fact, the plight of many prisoners of war during World War II was even worse than that of inmates at 19th-century hellholes like Andersonville and Fort Delaware, where Confederate captives died in droves. In this conflict as in the Civil War, many prisoners perished because their captors lacked enough food, medicine, and other supplies to sustain them or were unwilling to expend those vital resources on captured enemies. But the toll during World War II was magnified by fierce national rivalries and racism, which led some guards and officers who oversaw camps not just to neglect prisoners but to despise them and hasten their death. Captured Allied troops suffered worse treatment from imperial Japan—whose soldiers were taught to disdain those of all opposing nations or races who yielded to them—than from Nazi Germany, where Anglo-Saxons like the British and Americans were considered worthy foes while Russians and other non-Aryan adversaries were classified as subhuman and treated terribly. When scarce resources combined with the hostility and fanaticism of prison guards and commandants, as happened all too often during World War II, those who survived confinement sometimes envied the dead.

Major Fitch thought he had endured the worst his captors had to offer when he reached Camp O'Donnell, but he soon learned otherwise: "I was damn glad to arrive, little knowing that the name O'Donnell would make the Black Hole of Calcutta seem a Sunday school picnic." Another prisoner recalled the chilling words of the commandant who greeted them. They were enemies,

*American prisoners of war at Camp O'Donnell on Luzon
carry remains of the dead for burial there.*

he told them, and always would be. His only concern as their enemy was "how many of you are dead every morning." Those who had perished on the Death March, he added, were "the lucky ones." The camp was so crowded and chaotic that no precise casualty count was kept during the war, but roughly half of those held there died there.

REVIVING THE FLEET

"Tell Nimitz to get the hell out to Pearl and stay there until the war is won." With those words, Franklin Roosevelt entrusted the battered Pacific Fleet to Adm. Chester Nimitz. Nimitz had never commanded a ship in battle, but there was no one better suited to restore confidence to officers haunted by the disastrous events of December 7. A mortifying mishap early in his career—when as a 23-year-old ensign in 1908 he took command of a destroyer and ran it aground—taught Nimitz to cope with failure and use it as an incentive to improve and excel. When he arrived at Pearl Harbor a few weeks after the attack there, he commiserated with the commander he was sent to replace, Adm. Husband Kimmel, and assured him: "The same thing could have happened to anybody." Kimmel would soon be dismissed from the Navy for dereliction of duty, but Nimitz did not blame him or his aides for America's collective failure to prepare for war in the Pacific. Staff officers who expected to be sacked by the new fleet commander were stunned when he told them that they had been assigned to Pearl Harbor because they were first rate and he still considered them so. He would try to accommodate those who wished to leave, but he hoped to preserve continuity and there were some officers he would insist on keeping.

No one was more surprised or heartened by Nimitz's words than Lt. Cmdr. Edwin Layton, Kimmel's chief intelligence officer. Layton felt that he had let Kimmel down and assumed that he would be let go by his successor. But failure to foresee the enemy's first strike made Layton all the more determined to anticipate his next move, and Nimitz kept him on. He proved so valuable that Nimitz later denied his request for duty at sea. "You can kill more enemy working at your desk," Nimitz told him, "than if you commanded a division of cruisers."

"You can kill more enemy working at your desk than if you commanded a division of cruisers."

Adm. Chester Nimitz to intelligence officer Lt. Cmdr. Edwin Layton

Indeed, intelligence was the secret weapon that allowed Nimitz to risk battle against a Japanese fleet far larger than his own. He was less concerned by the severe damage done on December 7 to the Pacific Fleet's battleships, which were old and slow, than by the fact that he had just three aircraft carriers to contend with seven big Japanese carriers and four smaller ones. Only by knowing where those carriers were and where they were headed could he gain the advantage of surprise and lessen the odds against his fleet. Using aerial reconnaissance alone to search for enemy warships across the vast Pacific was like seeking needles in a haystack. More effective were the techniques employed by Layton, who had studied in Japan and understood the language, methods, and mentality of Japanese officers. The task he performed for Nimitz was to read the enemy's mind.

Layton did not practice telepathy. His conclusions were based largely on briefings he received from Lt. Cmdr. Joseph Rochefort, a seasoned cryptanalyst who had studied with him in Japan and was fluent in the language. Rochefort ran Pearl Harbor's secret combat intelligence unit, locked behind steel doors in a windowless basement. Listeners there at Station HYPO and elsewhere transcribed Japanese naval radio messages that were enciphered by the Japanese and broadcast as groups of numbers in Morse code. Station HYPO's combat intelligence unit analyzed them with the help of IBM tabulators that were forerunners of the first electronic computers, designed for military use later in the war. Unlike Japanese diplomatic communications—enciphered using a machine that the U.S. Army's Signal Intelligence Service had succeeded in duplicating—Japanese naval communications were enciphered the old-fashioned way, using codebooks and cipher tables that were changed periodically to frustrate enemy cryptanalysts. One such change had occurred shortly before the December 7 attack, and the Japanese strike force had taken extra precautions by observing radio silence.

Like Nimitz, Rochefort did not blame his staff for failing to detect that assault. Forget about it, he told them, "and get on with the job!" Bolstered by fresh recruits—including band members from the sunken battleship *California* whose musical training gave them a strong grasp of abstract symbolic language that suited them well for code breaking—they worked 12-hour shifts seven days a week. A sign above

> "For weeks the only sleep he got was on a field cot pushed into a crowded corner. Always nearly fully dressed, he was ready at a moment's notice to roll out and jump into carpet slippers and an old, red smoking jacket."
>
> One of Lt. Cmdr. Joseph Rochefort's aides on his boss's 24-7 devotion to breaking enemy codes

the desk of one staff member summed up the nerve-racking nature of their efforts: "You don't have to be crazy to work here, but it helps." Rochefort himself lived like a troll, seldom emerging from the unit's cramped, subterranean office. "For weeks the only sleep he got was on a field cot pushed into a crowded corner," wrote one aide. "Always nearly fully dressed, he was ready at a moment's notice to roll out and jump into carpet slippers and an old, red smoking jacket."

Rochefort and his team of code breakers, mathematicians, linguists, and traffic analysts (specialists who used various techniques to determine the origin and destination of a message) were helped by the fact that the Japanese grew more confident and less careful in early 1942 as their stunning early triumphs instilled in them what they later called "victory disease." Changing codebooks was not easily done once their navy was widely dispersed in wartime, and so they relied on the same codes for months on end. That allowed Rochefort's team to detect patterns and begin unlocking the hidden content of those messages. It was a slow process of trial and error.

The Imperial Japanese Navy's JN-25 codebook consisted of more than 30,000 five-digit numbers, each representing a word, phrase, letter, or numeral. To disguise the codes for frequently repeated words such as *battleship* or *attack,* each five-digit code number in a message was altered by adding on a different five-digit number from the cipher table, which had 100,000 possible combinations. The sender then transmitted the message along with a numerical key, indicating the location of the cipher numbers in the table. To decipher the message, the officer receiving it used an identical cipher table and code-book to reverse the process. This system should have been unbreakable, but it had flaws. In the months between the distribution of new codebooks to the far-flung Japanese fleet, there was time for telltale repetitions to become obvious to U.S. cryptanalysts. In addition, some careless operators used the same sequence of numbers from the cipher table time and again. Rochefort's team employed mathematical analysis, assisted by punch-card tabulating machines, to look for such repetitions, strip away the cipher numbers, and reveal the underlying five-digit codes.

Clues to the meaning of frequently repeated code numbers were provided by traffic analysis. Using radio direction finders in two locations, traffic analysts could triangulate readings and determine the location of a ship, which might then be identified by recon-naissance aircraft. Japanese ships could also be distinguished by the idiosyncrasies of their telegraphers. One telegrapher aboard the aircraft carrier *Akagi,* for example, pressed the key so hard it sounded as if he were hitting it with his foot. Knowing which

JAPANESE CODE JN-25

The Japanese Imperial Navy used codebooks filled with five-digit numbers representing words such as those below. The code numbers shown here were then altered using a cipher table, so that when a word appeared a second time in the message, it was represented by a different five-digit number.

attack (ing, ed)	73428
battleship (s)	29781
cruiser (s)	58797
destroyer (s)	36549
enemy	38754

ship was sending a message and its coordinates helped Rochefort's team decode other details of vital significance, such as the ship's destination and when it would arrive there. By April 1942, the combat intelligence unit was able to read about a third of the JN-25 code words and make educated guesses about Japanese naval plans.

The big breakthrough came in May 1942 when the team decoded references to a major operation whose objective was designated "AF." Rochefort and Layton concluded that "AF" stood for Midway Island. To make sure, Layton instructed the base commander at Midway to send an uncoded message stating that the island's water-distillation plant had failed and fresh water was needed. A short time later, Rochefort's team decoded a Japanese message stating that "AF is short of water." Nimitz could then send the bulk of his fleet to Midway to intercept Japanese carriers bearing down on that island.

But when Admiral Nimitz first visited Rochefort and his team in January 1942, they could read only about 10 or 15 percent of any given message—not enough to reveal enemy plans. Until his cryptanalysts achieved their goal, any offensive operations Nimitz conducted with his few aircraft carriers risked exposing them to a superior fleet whose movements he could not yet anticipate. At first, all he dared attempt was hit-and-run raids on enemy bases on the Marshall Islands and other targets at the outskirts of the Japanese-occupied zone, which embraced roughly the western half of the Pacific Ocean. American newspapers touted those attacks as revenge for Pearl Harbor, but Nimitz and his staff knew better. As one officer who took part in the raids remarked, "The Japs don't mind them any more than a dog minds a flea."

One thing they *would* mind and find shocking was a carrier-launched air strike on Tokyo. When that option was first proposed, Nimitz rejected it as too risky because his bombers had a range of only about 300 miles, and any carrier that got close enough to Japan to launch and retrieve those aircraft would likely be spotted and sunk. Lt. Col. James Doolittle of the U.S. Army Air Forces overcame that objection, however, by training pilots to take off from an aircraft carrier in B-25 bombers, which had a range of nearly 1,200 miles. They were too heavy to land on a carrier, but Doolittle, who himself would lead the raid, hoped to reach China after the attack and find refuge among friendly forces fighting the Japanese invaders there.

Assigned to haul the 16 B-25s and their crews to within range of Tokyo was the U.S.S. *Hornet,* a new flattop due to join the

Pacific Fleet along with the U.S.S. *Yorktown,* transferred from the Atlantic Fleet. With five carriers, Nimitz would have been greatly strengthened, but he had lost the recently overhauled *Saratoga* when it was torpedoed by a Japanese submarine and returned to the West Coast for repairs. And he would have to commit a second carrier to the risky Doolittle raid because the heavily loaded *Hornet* had no room for the fighters or reconnaissance aircraft needed to guard against an attack. To escort the *Hornet,* Nimitz chose the *Enterprise* and its pugnacious captain, Vice Adm. William "Bull" Halsey, who made no secret of his hatred for the enemy. "Before we're through with them," he remarked, "the Japanese language will be spoken only in hell."

> "Before we're through with them, the Japanese language will be spoken only in hell."
>
> Vice Adm. William "Bull" Halsey

On April 18, Doolittle and his airmen took off from the deck of the *Hornet* in rough seas 670 miles from Tokyo and embarked on what Halsey called one of the "most courageous deeds in military history." The odds against them appeared steep, but they achieved complete surprise and dropped their payloads on military targets in and around Tokyo before continuing on. One crew landed in Vladivostok, where Soviet authorities who were now officially their allies detained them for more than a year before they escaped. The rest reached China as planned, where they crash-landed or bailed out. Doolittle and 70 others found shelter among friendly Chinese and survived. Nine airmen were captured by the Japanese, who executed three of them in flagrant violation of the Geneva Convention, which war leaders in Tokyo refused to recognize even though it protected their own prisoners taken by the Allies.

Japanese authorities dismissed the attack on Tokyo as trivial and issued statements in English mocking it as the "do-little" or "do-nothing" raid. In truth, they were stung by the assault. "Even though there wasn't much damage," declared fleet commander Adm. Isoroku Yamamoto, "it is a disgrace that the skies of the imperial capital should have been defiled without a single enemy plane being shot down." The Doolittle Raid lent impetus to a sprawling new offensive proposed by Yamamoto, which called for attacks on American bases on the Aleutian Islands and on Midway Island, situated some 1,300 miles northwest of Honolulu and that much closer to Tokyo. Yamamoto's objective was to extend Japan's defensive perimeter in the Pacific—and perhaps lure the American carriers into a decisive battle against his larger force.

By late April, Nimitz had a rough idea of Japanese intentions, thanks to advances by Rochefort's team, aided by another combat intelligence unit in Australia. He knew that Yamamoto was preparing for a big push in the mid-Pacific, although just where he would attack was not yet clear. Nimitz also learned that three of Yamamoto's flattops—the light carrier *Shoho* and the big carriers *Shokaku* and *Zuikaku*—had recently been detached from the fleet to conduct a separate offensive against Port Moresby, New Guinea, situated dangerously close to Australia. If the Japanese seized that port, they could sever the maritime supply line between the United States and Australia and bottle up MacArthur's forces there. Nimitz dispatched a task force led by the carriers *Lexington* and *Yorktown* to meet that threat in the Coral Sea, knowing as he did so that if they were lost in action, he would have little chance of repelling Yamamoto's main thrust.

The Battle of the Coral Sea was unprecedented. For the first time, a naval contest was decided by aircraft launched from opposing warships that never came within sight of each other. On May 7, dive-bombers and torpedo planes launched from the *Yorktown* and *Lexington* scored the first coup in this new form of combat by sinking the *Shoho.* "Scratch one flattop!" radioed a jubilant American squadron leader, Lt. Cmdr. Robert Dixon, as the ship foundered. In carrier warfare, hunters who make a kill announce their presence to the enemy and often become the hunted. Such was the case in this battle, which intensified on May 8 when warplanes from the *Shokaku* and *Zuikaku* swooped down on their prey, damaging the *Yorktown* and rupturing the fuel lines of the *Lexington,* which exploded and sank that evening after its crew was rescued by other ships in the task force. As the battle drew to a close, the *Shokaku* was hit as well, and the *Zuikaku* lost so many pilots that both Japanese carriers were put out

Crewmen abandon the burning U.S.S. Lexington *by scrambling down ropes on the afternoon of May 8.*

of action for months, easing the threat to Port Moresby and depriving Yamamoto of two large carriers he was counting on for his main offensive.

In late May, the battered *Yorktown* entered Pearl Harbor, trailing a long slick of oil caused by a bomb that detonated deep in its hull. The crew had been at sea for three months and was looking forward to extended shore leave while the carrier underwent repairs, which would surely take weeks. But when Nimitz inspected the damage, he told the officers in charge of the task: "We must have this ship back in three days." The tone of his voice made it clear to them that something big was up—and that there could be only one response to his seemingly impossible demand: "Yes, sir."

DESTINATION MIDWAY

Confidence ran high as Admiral Yamamoto's fleet set out on May 28, 1942, to complete the task left unfinished on December 7, 1941. Yamamoto fully expected that the U.S. Pacific Fleet would come out to defend Midway with its aircraft carriers, whose absence at Pearl Harbor on the first day of the Pacific war had enabled his foes to keep up the fight. His plan designated June 7, 1942—precisely six months after that opening attack—as N-Day, the date on which Midway would be invaded and his fleet would be poised to achieve a decisive victory. Yamamoto did not take the Americans lightly. The closely fought Battle of the Coral Sea demonstrated that they could hold their own in a contest where the two sides were of roughly equal strength. But even after the losses his fleet suffered there, Yamamoto had eight operational aircraft carriers to contend with just three opposing flattops, including the damaged *Yorktown*. He had far more cruisers and destroyers than his foe and could deploy more than a dozen battleships, while Nimitz had not one that was fit to fight. As Capt. Yoshikawa Miwa wrote in his diary at sea on May 31: "Everybody in the fleet from its head down to the men entertains not the least doubt about a victory."

> "Everybody in the fleet from its head down to the men entertains not the least doubt about a victory."
>
> Capt. Yoshikawa Miwa, before the Battle of Midway

What Yamamoto and his forces did not anticipate was that the great advantage of surprise, which had been theirs in December, would be seized by their opponents. Nimitz's situation as battle loomed was the opposite of his predecessor's six months earlier. Kimmel had been utterly in the dark as to the movements and intentions of the enemy, but Nimitz had intelligence that cast a floodlight on Yamamoto's plan and exposed it in sharp detail. During the last week of May, he received precise forecasts from Rochefort and Layton, who informed him that the Japanese would commence attacks on the Aleutians on June 3 and begin blasting Midway with carrier-launched bombers on June 4 in preparation for an invasion. On the basis of the latest intercepts, Layton predicted that those carriers would approach from the northwest at a bearing of 315 degrees and would be 175 miles from Midway at 6 a.m. on June 4.

Skeptics considered those startling revelations too good to be true. Officers who knew of Rochefort's code-breaking operation worried that the Japanese were sending out false signals to divert the Pacific Fleet and disguise what could be another attack on Pearl Harbor. Others figured that such secrets could come only from a spy in Japan, peddling material that might be bogus or genuine. "That man of ours in Tokyo is worth every cent we pay him," remarked an officer aboard the *Enterprise,* which returned to Pearl Harbor on May 26, around the same time as the *Yorktown.* Nimitz put great trust in the intelligence he received and saw flaws in Yamamoto's plan that he could exploit. By committing two aircraft carriers and other warships to the Aleutian offensive, which Nimitz recognized as a diversion, Yamamoto was dispersing his forces across a wide area. Furthermore, his plan assumed that Nimitz would not dispatch his carriers from Pearl Harbor until Midway came under assault on June 4. If, however, they were lurking nearby when that attack began, their air squadrons might surprise Japanese carriers while they were engaged in offensive operations against Midway.

By May 28, Nimitz was ready to implement his own plan. He dispatched some cruisers and destroyers to defend the Aleutians, but reserved the rest for two carrier task forces bound for Midway. One, which left Pearl Harbor that day, included the *Hornet* and was led by its escort, the *Enterprise,* whose commander, Admiral Halsey, had been hospitalized and replaced by Rear Adm. Raymond Spruance, an officer as cool and calm as Halsey was fiery. Nimitz likened Spruance to the imperturbable Ulysses S. Grant, noting that he "thought things through very carefully . . . and then when he decided to strike, struck hard."

The other task force was led by Rear Adm. Frank Fletcher, who sailed with Capt. Elliott Buckmaster aboard the *Yorktown,* which departed on May 30 after 72 hours of frantic repair work. Fletcher was assigned overall tactical command at Midway (distant fleet commanders like Nimitz had to delegate that authority to a trusted subordinate destined for battle). Some in Washington thought Fletcher unequal to the task and faulted him for the loss of the *Lexington,* but Nimitz gave him a fair hearing when he returned from the Coral Sea and concluded that he had shown "superior judgment." Nimitz saw the *Yorktown* off and wished Fletcher and crew "good luck and good hunting." By June 2, the two task forces had linked up northeast of Midway, ready to pounce on the approaching Japanese carriers.

Early on June 3, an American base at Dutch Harbor in the Aleutians came under attack. Nimitz was pleased to learn that Yamamoto's offensive was unfolding as anticipated. Although Japanese forces would succeed in occupying a few islands at the far end of the Aleutian chain, they were strategically insignificant compared with Midway, where Nimitz had positioned the bulk of his fleet. Around six the following morning, a Catalina PBY scout plane spotted Japanese carriers and other warships approaching Midway

Smoke rises from a damaged merchant ship in Dutch Harbor, on Unalaska Island in the Aleutians, after an air raid by Japanese carrier-based warplanes on June 3, 1942.

from the northwest at a bearing of 320 degrees and a distance of 180 miles. "Well," Nimitz told Layton, "you were only five miles, five degrees, and five minutes off."

The approaching armada was Yamamoto's First Carrier Striking Force, commanded by Vice Adm. Chuichi Nagumo, who had unleashed the attack on Pearl Harbor. His force was similar to Nagumo's earlier one, with a crucial exception: Rather than six carriers, Nagumo now had just four—his flagship *Akagi,* along with the *Kaga, Hiryu,* and *Soryu.* Awaiting them were the three U.S. carriers as well as several squadrons of fighters and bombers on Midway, which Nimitz had reinforced in recent weeks and planned to use, in effect, as a fourth carrier from which strikes would be launched. With part of Yamamoto's fleet up north attacking the Aleutians and other parts off to the south and west, Nagumo was on his own for now. Armed with accurate intelligence, Nimitz had negated Yamamoto's advantage and achieved virtual parity with the enemy at Midway. His forces were determined to avoid a repetition of the disaster on December 7—and make June 4, 1942, a day that would live in infamy for Japan.

A DECISIVE BATTLE

This time, there would be no American warplanes caught on the ground. Anticipating an attack, the airmen at Midway were up well before dawn and ready for takeoff when radar detected incoming planes from Nagumo's carriers and the siren sounded. By 6:15 a.m., they were all aloft and the airstrip was clear. Advance warning gave them a fighting chance, but they were ill equipped to contend with their Japanese foes. Many of the fighter pilots on Midway were flying stodgy Brewster F2A-3 Buffalos, nicknamed

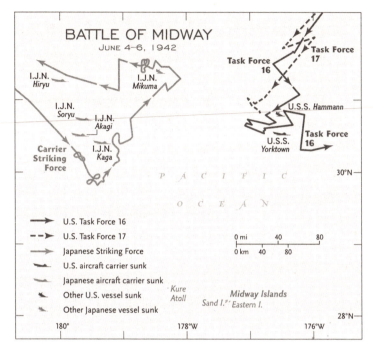

BATTLE OF MIDWAY
JUNE 4–6, 1942

Task Force 17

Task Force 16

I.J.N. Hiryu

I.J.N. Mikuma

I.J.N. Soryu

I.J.N. Akagi

U.S.S. Hammann

Carrier Striking Force

I.J.N. Kaga

U.S.S. Yorktown

Task Force 16

P A C I F I C

O C E A N

30°N

U.S. Task Force 16
U.S. Task Force 17
Japanese Striking Force
U.S. aircraft carrier sunk
Japanese aircraft carrier sunk
Other U.S. vessel sunk
Other Japanese vessel sunk

0 mi   40   80
0 km   40   80

Kure Atoll
Midway Islands
Sand I. Eastern I.

28°N

180°   178°W   176°W

Beginning on June 4, 1942, American and Japanese naval forces clashed in the pivotal Battle of Midway, shown on this map charting the losses suffered by both sides.

"Flying Coffins." Within a matter of minutes, they came up against swift, agile Mitsubishi Zeros and were thoroughly outclassed. More than a dozen Buffalos were gunned down in the ensuing dogfight. Capt. Herbert Merrill, who bailed out and survived, offered a scathing assessment afterward. "The F2A-3 is *not* a combat aeroplane," he wrote. The Zero could run circles around it, and any commander who sent a Buffalo out to fight "should consider the pilot as lost before leaving the ground."

Shielded by the Zeros, most of the Japanese bombers reached Midway unscathed, but the pilots were disappointed to find the airstrip bare. They set oil tanks ablaze and blasted hangars, barracks, and a power station but did little damage to the runway or Midway's big guns. Around 7 a.m., Lt. Joichi Tomonaga ordered the raiders back to their carriers and signaled Nagumo: "There is need of a second attack wave." Nagumo was considering whether to launch that second attack when bombers from Midway appeared on the horizon. He had no radar to warn of such raids, but his carriers were well shielded. Zeros prowled the skies above while battleships, cruisers, and destroyers guarded the perimeter and peppered the incoming torpedo planes with flak. "Black bursts of antiaircraft fire blossomed all around them, but none of the raiders went down," observed Cmdr. Mitsuo Fuchida, who had hoped to lead the first wave that day as he did on December 7 but had fallen ill. "As *Akagi*'s guns commenced firing," he added, "Zeros braved our own antiaircraft fire and dove down on the Americans," destroying three of those planes. Others released their torpedoes before crashing or darting off, but none of the weapons hit home. The greatest threat to Nagumo's flagship, Fuchida recalled, came from a stricken B-26 bomber that flew "straight over the *Akagi*, from starboard to port, nearly grazing the bridge" before bursting into flames. The doomed pilot may have been trying to hit the carrier. His heroism impressed his foes and caused Nagumo's chief of staff to offer a silent prayer for him as he plunged into the sea.

"Zeros braved our own antiaircraft fire and dove down on the Americans."

Cmdr. Mitsuo Fuchida, at the Battle of Midway

The attack convinced Nagumo to launch a second wave of warplanes against Midway. Those aircraft were meant to carry torpedoes against enemy warships but would be rearmed with bombs instead. At 8:30, after repelling further attacks by bombers from Midway, Nagumo learned that at least one enemy carrier had been sighted by aerial reconnaissance. He faced an agonizing decision. His second wave was ready to attack Midway, but the American carrier force was now his primary target. He could send the planes his mechanics had fitted with bombs against those ships, but they would be more effective with torpedoes, for which they were designed. In addition, they would have to proceed without fighter escorts, because Nagumo's Zeros had been aloft for hours and needed to land and refuel—as did the warplanes of the first wave returning from Midway. Nagumo decided to clear the decks for those landings by lowering the planes that were about to take off to the hangar deck below, where they would be rearmed with torpedoes for a concerted assault on the enemy carrier force.

"Nagumo's reasoning was logical enough," Fuchida wrote afterward, but his decision ignored the crucial time factor, which favored commanders who were "quicker to act boldly and decisively to meet unforeseen developments." That advantage went to Admirals Fletcher and Spruance, who acted swiftly and surely while Nagumo proceeded as if his foes would allow him all the time he needed to reconfigure his attack.

At about six that morning, Fletcher had received a message from a scout plane that reported spotting two Japanese carriers northwest of Midway. He promptly signaled Spruance to pursue them with the *Enterprise* and *Hornet:* "Proceed southwesterly and attack enemy carriers when definitely located." Fletcher was waiting for his scout planes to return to the *Yorktown,* and he suspected from intelligence reports that more than two enemy carriers were nearby. By sending Spruance's task force ahead, he prudently held his own force in reserve until he knew better where those other carriers were and also guarded against an enemy attack that would catch all his flattops together and set them ablaze—a risk that Nagumo ran by bunching his carriers and compounded by pausing to rearm his aircraft before launching them.

Spruance, for his part, wasted no time before clearing his decks. He and his chief of staff, Capt. Miles Browning, figured that the first wave of Japanese attackers would return from Midway to Nagumo's carriers by 9 a.m. "We felt that we had to hit him before he could launch his second attack," Browning remarked, "both to prevent further damage to Midway and to ensure our own safety." Spruance was also keenly aware that if his bombers caught Japanese planes as they were refueling and rearming for another attack, the results would be explosive. That meant launching his aircraft promptly, before his carriers were close enough to their targets to ensure that his heavier, short-range bombers would return safely. Furthermore, the bombers would have little protection because many of the fighters would be held back to shield the carriers, as Nimitz had ordered. He and Spruance were no more eager to send pilots to their death than were Yamamoto and Nagumo. But a fierce resolve, fueled by bitter memories of the attack on Pearl Harbor, drove Americans of all ranks to make fearful sacrifices in pursuit of victory at Midway. One squadron leader on the *Hornet,* Lt. Cmdr. John Waldron, summed up that fighting spirit in a message he delivered to his men the night before the battle: "I want each one of us to do his utmost to destroy our enemies. If there is only one plane left to make a final run-in, I want that man to go in and get a hit."

As it happened, Waldron's squadron of 15 Douglas TBD-1 Devastator torpedo planes was the first from Spruance's task force to attack Nagumo's carriers, intercepting them around 9:20. Other squadrons had lost track of the enemy because Nagumo had altered course to get closer to the opposing warships before launching his strike. Waldron had anticipated that move. "He went just as straight to the Jap fleet as if he'd had a string tied to

This group photograph of the pilots of Torpedo Squadron Eight was taken on the deck of the U.S.S. Hornet *a month before Lt. Cmdr. John Waldron led the squadron's 15 TBD-1 Devastators against Japanese carriers at Midway. Only Lt. George Gay, front row center, survived.*

them," recalled Lt. George Gay, who like others in the squadron was entering battle for the first time. Coming in alone, their lumbering, low-flying Devastators made easy targets for Japanese antiaircraft batteries and the recently refueled Zeros. Before long, there was in fact only one plane left, piloted by Gay, who released an errant torpedo at the *Soryu* and then flew right over the carrier. He found himself staring "down the gun barrel of one of those big pom-poms [antiaircraft guns] up forward" but managed to remain aloft until Zeros clipped his wing and sent the plane tumbling. Fished out of the sea by friendly forces after the battle as he clung to an inflatable raft, he was the sole survivor of Waldron's squadron.

Such sacrifices were not in vain. The desperate and seemingly futile assaults by torpedo planes from Spruance's task force, 37 of which went down in about an hour, delayed the rearming and refueling of Nagumo's bombers and brought the Zeros down from

Lt. Cmdr. C. Wade McClusky
Destruction of the *Kaga* and *Akagi*

McClusky led two squadrons of aircraft, Scouting Squadron Six and Bombing Squadron Six, from the U.S.S. Enterprise *in a devastating attack on the Japanese carrier force at Midway on June 4.*

Peering through my binoculars which were practically glued to my eyes, I saw dead ahead about 35 miles distant the welcome sight of the Jap carrier striking force . . . I then broke radio silence and reported the contact to the *Enterprise.* Immediately thereafter I gave attack instructions to my group. Figuring that possibly the *Hornet* group commander would make the same decision that I had, it seemed best to concentrate my two squadrons on two carriers . . . Picking the two nearest carriers in the line of approach, I ordered Scouting Six to follow my section in attacking the carrier on the immediate left and Bombing Six to take the right-hand carrier. These two carriers were the largest in the formation and later were determined to be the *Kaga* and the *Akagi* . . . It was 1222 [10:22 a.m. local time] when I started the attack, rolling in a half-roll and coming to a steep 70 degree dive. About halfway down, anti-aircraft fire began booming around us—our approach being a complete surprise up to that point. As we neared the bomb-dropping point, another stroke of luck met our eyes. Both enemy carriers had their decks full of planes which had just returned from the attack on Midway . . . the planes on deck were being refueled and rearmed for an attack on our carriers . . .

SBD Dauntless dive-bombers close in on a burning Japanese cruiser during the Battle of Midway in June 1942.

In the meantime, our bombs began to hit home. I leveled off at masthead height, picked the widest opening in their screen and dropped to deck level, figuring any anti-aircraft fire aimed at me would also be aimed at their own ships . . . With the throttle practically pushed through the instrument panel, I was fortunate in avoiding a contact with death by slight changes of altitude and varying the getaway course to right and left.

It was quick work to figure the return course, and as I raised my head from the plotting board, a stream of tracer bullets started chopping the water around the plane. Almost immediately my gunner, W. G. Chochalousek, in the rear seat, opened fire. Then a Jap Zero zoomed out of range ahead of me. A hurried glance around found another Zero about 1000 feet above, to the left and astern, about to make another attack. Remaining at 20 feet above the water, I waited until the attacking plane was well in his dive, then wrapped my plane in a steep turn toward him . . . Then ensued about a 5-minute chase, first one Zero attacking from the right, then the second from the left. Each time I would wrap up toward the attacker with Chochalousek keeping up a constant fire. Suddenly a burst from a Jap seemed to envelop the whole plane. The left side of my cockpit was shattered, and I felt my left shoulder had been hit with a sledgehammer.

"As we neared the bomb-dropping point, another stroke of luck met our eyes. Both enemy carriers had their decks full of planes which had just returned from the attack on Midway."

Naturally enough it seemed like the end, we sure were goners. After two or three seconds, I realized there was an unusual quietness except for the purring engine of the old Dauntless. Grasping the inner phone, I yelled to Chochalousek, but no answer. It was difficult to turn with the pain in my left shoulder and arm, but I finally managed and there was the gunner facing aft, guns at the ready and unharmed. He had shot down one of the Zeros . . . and the other decided to call it quits. ∎

LT. JOSEPH POLLARD
ABANDONMENT OF THE U.S.S. *YORKTOWN*

Pollard, a flight surgeon on the U.S.S. Yorktown, *treated the wounded aboard that stricken carrier on June 4 until Capt. Elliott Buckmaster gave the order to abandon ship.*

Battle Dressing Station #1 rapidly overflowed into the passageway, into the parachute loft and into . . . all other available spaces. I called for stretcher bearers to get the more seriously wounded to the sick bay where they could receive plasma, etc., but the passageways had been blocked off due to the bomb hits. So we gave more morphine, covered the patients with blankets, and did the best we could. Many patients went rapidly into shock. All topside lights were out and I never realized that flashlights gave such miserably poor light. . . .

Hit earlier by Japanese dive-bombers, the Yorktown *listed heavily after the torpedoes struck, and sailors struggled for balance on the deck.*

I went up to the flight deck . . . Blood was everywhere. I turned forward and saw great billows of smoke rising from our stack region. We were dead in the water and it suddenly dawned on me how helpless we were lying there . . .

About 1600 [2:00 p.m. local time] our radar picked up enemy planes at 40 to 60 miles coming in fast. We had just begun to gas five F4F-4s that we had succeeded in landing just before the previous attack. Some had only 25 gallons aboard. Nevertheless, they took off post haste. We were just hitting 22 knots but they took a long run and made it off. Just as the last one left the deck I made a dive for Battle Dressing Station #1 and again the AAs [antiaircraft guns] began as before. By the time I could find an unoccupied place on the deck there was a sickening thud and rumble throughout the ship and the deck rose under me, trembled and fell away. One torpedo hit had occurred . . . Then another sickening thud and the good ship shuddered and rapidly listed hard to port. . . . Just then word came over the speaker, "Prepare to abandon ship." . . .

We listed more and more to port until it was almost impossible to stand on the slick deck. We searched frantically for life preservers for the wounded, taking some from the dead. Our stretchers had gone below to the sick bay and we had difficulty finding enough for our wounded. All who could possibly walk did so. I went up on the flight deck and walked along the starboard edge being very careful not to slip and skid the width of the ship and off the port side. The ship rolled slowly with the swells but the water was not rough and after each roll she returned to her former position . . .

Several life rafts were in the water but the lines over the side were not long enough to reach the water. Lieutenant Wilson and I tied some lines together and lowered some wounded. Meanwhile the sick bay wounded were being lowered from the hanger deck. Captain Buckmaster came up and said to abandon ship . . .

I chose a big line and went over the side. I stopped at the armor belt for a rest. It was at least 75 feet from the deck to the water and I still had some 20 feet to go. I worked along the armor belt to a spot which was immediately above a life raft. The line there was a small one and soon after I started down a corner of my life jacket got inside my grip and I began slipping. The fingers of both my hands were rather badly burned before I realized it. Then I released the line and dropped the remainder of the way into the water and swam through the oil to the raft. ∎

> "One torpedo hit had occurred . . . Then another sickening thud and the good ship shuddered and rapidly listed hard to port . . . Just then word came over the speaker, 'Prepare to abandon ship.'"

the lofty heights where they usually patrolled. At 10:20, Nagumo was at last ready to launch his warplanes when a new threat appeared high overhead—squadrons of Douglas SBD Dauntless dive-bombers from the *Enterprise* and *Yorktown,* launched from that carrier by Fletcher, who had decided to join in the attack.

"One remarkable fact stood out as we approached the diving point," recalled Lt. Cmdr. C. Wade McClusky from the *Enterprise:* "Not a Jap fighter plane was there to molest us." Before the low-flying Zeros could rise to this unforeseen challenge, the rugged Dauntlesses bore down like eagles and released bombs that triggered titanic explosions on carrier decks loaded with planes primed to detonate. Fuchida survived the blasts on the *Akagi,* which left "a huge hole in the flight deck," he wrote. "Planes stood tail-up, belching livid flame and jet-black smoke. Reluctant tears streamed down my cheek as I watched the fires spread."

The *Akagi* was doomed, as were the *Soryu* and *Kaga,* whose surviving crewmen were struggling to save the burning ship when the submarine U.S.S. *Nautilus* surfaced and fired three torpedoes, one of which plowed into the carrier but broke apart without detonating. That reprieve allowed the smoldering *Kaga* a few more hours of life before the ship was abandoned and went down. Nagumo's fourth carrier, *Hiryu,* escaped the dive-bombing attack and succeeded in launching its warplanes, which found the *Yorktown* around noon and set it ablaze. Fletcher yielded overall command to Spruance and transferred his flag as task force commander to the cruiser U.S.S. *Astoria.* Captain Buckmaster remained on the *Yorktown,* which was attacked again a few hours later. The carrier eventually sank, but not before its captain and surviving crew had transferred safely to other ships of the task force. A different fate awaited Rear Adm. Tamon Yamaguchi when bombers dispatched by Spruance blasted his surviving carrier, the *Hiryu,* late on June 4 and left it in flames. Yamaguchi chose to go down with his ship. "I have no words to apologize for what has happened," he said in a parting message to Admiral Nagumo, who was dissuaded by staff officers from going down with the *Akagi.* "I only wish for a stronger Japanese Navy—and revenge."

Many Americans felt that they had achieved revenge with their stunning victory at Midway, which forced Yamamoto to withdraw and altered the course of the war in the Pacific. But Nimitz knew how close the battle had been and how much remained to be done. "Pearl Harbor has now been partially avenged," he declared. "Vengeance will not be complete until Japanese sea power is reduced to impotence . . . Perhaps we will be forgiven if we claim that we are about midway to that objective." Midway was in fact roughly halfway between the West Coast and Japan. But U.S. forces would find the second half of that journey far longer, harder, and bloodier than the first.

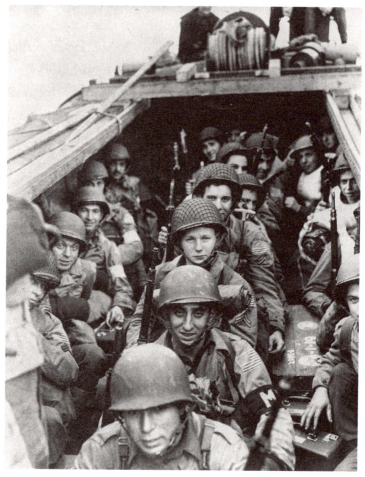

Packed into a landing craft, American soldiers prepare to hit the beach near Oran, Algeria, during Operation Torch in November 1942.

CHRONOLOGY

SEPTEMBER 13, 1940 Italy invades British-occupied Egypt.

NOVEMBER 8, 1942 American troops land in Morocco and Algeria.

FEBRUARY 11, 1941 German Afrikakorps arrive in Libya to support Mussolini's forces.

WAR IN THE MEDITERRANEAN

THE STRUGGLE FOR NORTH AFRICA

When U.S. troops landed in North Africa in November 1942, they were entering an arena that had been hotly contested by Allied and Axis forces for some time. The struggle had begun there in 1940 when troops of the Italian 10th Army led by Marshal Rodolfo Graziani crossed from Libya into Egypt, defended by British forces, including men from various British dominions and colonies. Graziani was acting on orders from Mussolini, who hoped to expand Italy's empire in North Africa— which included Libya and Ethiopia—by seizing Egypt and the Suez Canal, Britain's lifeline to Middle Eastern oil and the Far East. The campaign unfolded in the Western Desert, where

MAY 7, 1943 Axis forces surrender in Tunisia, ending the conflict in North Africa.

JANUARY 14–24, 1943 Roosevelt and Churchill meet at Casablanca and agree to invade Sicily after securing North Africa.

extreme temperatures, sandstorms, and sporadic flash floods tested men and machines to the utmost. The one serviceable road ran along the narrow Mediterranean coastal plain, where forces were vulnerable to attack. Inland, a steep escarpment rose to the Libyan Plateau, which could be reached by tanks and trucks at strategic Halfaya Pass, located in Egypt near the Libyan border. On September 13, 1940, Graziani sent 80,000 of his 200,000 troops into Egypt, where they pushed back a British covering force and seized Halfaya Pass before halting at Sidi Barrani, some 65 miles beyond the border. Graziani's supply lines were overextended, and many of his unreliable Fiat-Ansaldo tanks had broken down. He would soon face a blistering British counterattack that would eventually draw Germany into the campaign, transforming North Africa into a major theater of World War II.

In late 1940, Gen. Archibald Wavell, the British commander in chief in the Middle East, authorized Operation Compass, a raid designed to push Marshal Graziani's troops at Sidi Barrani back toward Libya. Led by Lt. Gen. Richard O'Connor with 30,000 troops of his Western Desert Force, the attack was launched at dawn on December 9 with close support from the Royal Air Force and the Royal Navy, which shelled Italian coastal positions. British tanks of the Seventh Armored Division, backed by two Indian brigades, overran enemy camps and seized Sidi Barrani, capturing nearly 40,000 Italians. One British commander estimated that vast haul at "five acres of officers, 200 acres of other ranks." O'Connor's raid soon turned into an all-out assault on Graziani's army,

"Five acres of officers, 200 acres of other ranks."

A British commander's estimate of what his troops captured at Sidi Barrani, Egypt much of which remained in Libya. After reclaiming Halfaya Pass in mid-December, the British crossed the border and captured the fortified Libyan town of Bardia, where the "Desert Rats" of the Seventh Armored Division and the Australian 16th Infantry Brigade bagged another 40,000 prisoners in early January 1941.

Ahead lay the strategic port city of Tobruk, which Graziani relied on for supplies. Neither O'Connor nor Wavell had had any thought of seizing that prize when the campaign began, but Prime Minister Churchill urged them on now. "Seek, and ye shall find," he wired Wavell in Cairo, quoting Scripture; "knock, and it shall be opened to you."

Supported by massed field guns, Australian infantry broke through at Tobruk and took the city on January 22, corralling an additional 17,000 POWs. O'Connor's troops pursued the remnants of Graziani's army westward across Libya and trapped most of them in early February. In two months, the victors had advanced 500 miles and annihilated the Italian 10th Army, capturing 130,000 prisoners, 380 tanks, and 845 artillery pieces. Their victory so embarrassed Mussolini and the Axis that Hitler felt compelled to intervene.

On February 11, 1941, a small convoy of Italian freighters docked at Tripoli in far western Libya and began offloading men and vehicles. They were the lead elements of the newly created Afrikakorps, two panzer divisions dispatched at Hitler's order to bolster his faltering Italian allies. Commanding the Afrikakorps was Lt. Gen. Erwin Rommel, who had demonstrated his mastery of armored warfare during the blitzkrieg in France. Rommel realized that success in desert combat depended on the daring use of mobile mechanized columns to disrupt and destroy enemy troop concentrations. Despite orders to remain on the defensive, the aggressive general soon attacked. The sudden advance by Rommel's German and Italian forces startled British troops in Libya, who hastily withdrew toward Egypt with their foes in hot pursuit. "The British are falling over each other to get away," wrote Rommel.

On April 7, a German patrol captured General O'Connor and the officer sent to relieve him, Lt. Gen. Philip Neame. General Wavell then decided to hold the port of Tobruk in eastern Libya to deny Rommel a supply base. Wavell entrusted its defense to Australian troops led by Maj. Gen. John Lavarack. Unable to break through there, Rommel laid siege to Tobruk, but the Royal Navy had control of the Mediterranean and shipped supplies and reinforcements to the besieged port.

Meanwhile, much of the Afrikakorps had bypassed Tobruk and crossed into Egypt to occupy Halfaya Pass—known to the British by then as Hell Fire Pass for the hot battles fought there. Wavell's attempts to dislodge those Germans and relieve pressure on Tobruk failed. Churchill replaced him with Gen. Claude Auchinleck. The methodical Auchinleck prepared at length for Operation Crusader, a massive armored offensive by the newly formed British Eighth Army, which broke through to Tobruk in November 1941 at a steep cost in men and tanks. Rommel, short on supplies and unable to replace lost armored vehicles, withdrew westward and dug in around the Libyan port of El Agheila in December.

Bolstered with fresh supplies and reinforcements, Rommel left El Agheila in late January 1942 and resumed the offensive. His forces, redesignated the Panzerarmee Afrika, drove the British Eighth Army back almost 300 miles before Rommel called a halt short of Tobruk to rest and fortify his troops for the next big push. In late May, they forged ahead, breaching Allied lines and capturing Tobruk in June, after which Rommel was promoted to field marshal.

Summer in the desert took its toll as men on both sides struggled to maintain their health and morale. Temperatures ranged as high as 120°F under the summer sun but could plummet overnight, leaving soldiers chilled to the bone. Their food was seldom fresh or appetizing. The rations issued to German troops consisted heavily of beans, zwieback, olive oil, sardines, and the universally detested Italian canned meat. The British made do largely with preserved food, consisting of crackers and canned items such as cheese, fish, and "bully beef," which was "anything but solid," Pvt. Henry Foster of the West Yorkshire Regiment recalled: "with the intense heat, it was quite liquefied." Drinking water was almost always in short supply and often had to be transported over long distances. It was carried by the Germans in sturdy five-gallon containers, dubbed "Jerry cans" by the British, who called the old gasoline cans they used to hold water "flimsies." Bathing and shaving had to wait until sufficient water was available.

More irritating than flies or other pests was the powdery desert sand and dust that reduced visibility, irritated the eyes and sinuses, and fouled weapons, vehicles, and optical equipment. Military operations often came to a standstill when stiff winds stirred up *ghiblis:* blinding sandstorms that engulfed men and vehicles, made breathing difficult, and disrupted radio signals. Helmuth Orschiedt, an artilleryman serving with Rommel's 15th Panzer Division, recalled those maddening desert storms: "Sand and dust everywhere, even inside wristwatches," he wrote. "We wrapped our heads in clothes and laid down. Nothing else could be done to survive."

Of course combat losses did nothing to cheer British troops, and leadership was equally unhappy. Churchill called Tobruk a "shattering and grievous loss" and soured on General Auchinleck, who withdrew to El Alamein in Egypt, only 150 miles west of Cairo. There the British dug in, using the Mediterranean to the north and the impassable Qattara Depression to the south to shield their flanks. In August, Auchinleck was replaced by Lt. Gen. Harold Alexander, who entrusted the Eighth Army to the supremely confident Lt. Gen. Bernard "Monty" Montgomery. "We will finish with Rommel once and for all," Monty vowed.

SOLVING THE ENIGMA

When Montgomery took charge of British forces in North Africa, he told his troops that he knew what Rommel was up to. That was no idle boast, for the British were decoding German wireless communications and reading their plans. German commanders had gone to war in 1939 confident that their communications were absolutely secure. They relied heavily on an intricate electronic coding machine called Enigma, which evolved from a less sophisticated device produced in the 1920s as a way for businesses to hide their secrets from competitors. The Germans vastly improved on that prototype and rendered their coded messages seemingly impenetrable to foes.

When an Enigma operator pressed a letter on the keyboard, an electronic impulse traveled through multiple rotors in turn, each of which had 26 settings for its contact points, and lit up a different letter on a panel atop the machine. The combination for the rotor settings was known only to the sender and the receiver, who typed the encrypted message—a meaningless stream of letters transmitted in Morse code or by teletype—into an Enigma machine set to that combination, reversing the process and unscrambling the text.

The first serious breach in Enigma's security had occurred in the early 1930s when a clerk in the German cipher bureau sold Enigma operating instructions and settings to French agents, who shared the intelligence with their allies in the Polish cipher bureau. That helped Polish mathematician Marian Rejewski and other inspired cryptanalysts solve Enigma's puzzles and reconstruct the machine. They then integrated several Enigma rotors into a device called a "bombe," which raced through countless settings until it found a combination matching that used by German operators on any given day.

In 1938, as war loomed, the Germans had improved Enigma by increasing the number of rotors from three to four or more and adding additional cables, which could be inserted into a plugboard in various ways, further scrambling the message. Frustrated and fearing attack by Germany, Polish code breakers shared what they had accomplished with their Western allies. In August 1939, they had bequeathed their Enigma, bombes, and other breakthroughs to the British Code and Cipher School at Bletchley Park, north of London.

Teams of mathematicians—including the brilliant Alan Turing, a pioneering computer theorist—joined intelligence analysts, linguists, and technicians at the Bletchley campus to crack the improved Enigma codes. Turing and fellow mathematician Gordon Welchman developed a more powerful bombe that could cope with the increasing number of Enigma combinations.

Hands raised in surrender, a crewman of an immobilized German Panzer III tank surrenders to British infantrymen during the early stages of the Battle of El Alamein, which proved to be the one of the worst defeats Germany had yet suffered in the war.

Under the direction of Cmdr. Alastair Denniston, Bletchley Park expanded to include legions of clerks and typists who handled thousands of intercepts. "Secrecy was so great that at the end of a watch we never spoke about what we did," recalled Royal Navy code clerk Betty Warwick Boyd, "nor did we talk to those in other huts or know what they did." Churchill referred to them as "the geese who laid the golden eggs—and never cackled."

Making excellent use of intelligence reports from Bletchley Park, Montgomery launched his October 23, 1942, attack at Alamein with a powerful artillery bombardment that opened gaps in the German defenses for a massed infantry assault. Rommel was away, receiving medical treatment in Germany, and flew back on the 25th to find his forces hard-pressed. The British had taken heavy losses advancing through German minefields, however, and the outcome at El Alamein remained in doubt until November 2 when British armored divisions achieved a decisive breakthrough. Defeated in one of the war's pivotal battles, Rommel fell back slowly across Egypt and Libya to Tunisia, where his diminished army would encounter new foes—Americans who had landed in North Africa just days after Monty's smashing victory.

ENTER THE YANKS

Maj. Gen. George S. Patton could not wait to enter combat. "All my life I have wanted to lead a lot of men in a desperate battle," he wrote before embarking from Norfolk, Virginia, with more than 30,000 troops in late October 1942. They would be among the first American soldiers to cross the Atlantic and wage war. Their objective was not Europe, however, but North Africa, and the opponents awaiting them

> "All my life I have wanted to lead a lot of men in a desperate battle."
>
> Maj. Gen. George S. Patton

were not Germans or Italians but French forces serving the Vichy government, which collaborated with the Axis but remained officially neutral. As much as Patton longed for action, this was not a contest he relished. He and others who had fought as allies of France in World War I found it unsettling to be pitted against their old comrades in arms. "I cannot stomach fighting the French if there is a way to avoid it," he remarked aboard the U.S.S. *Augusta,* the flagship of Rear Adm. Henry Hewitt, as their task force of more than 100 warships and troop transports approached the coast of French Morocco in early November. Whether French forces in North Africa would actively oppose this Allied invasion was uncertain. Some of them felt little loyalty to their Vichy rulers, who had come to terms with Hitler in June 1940 following the German occupation of northern France and retained control of southern France and the French colonies. Adm. Jean-François

Darlan, commander of all Vichy armed forces, met secretly in Algiers on the eve of the invasion with a U.S. official who urged him to yield without a fight. Darlan would bow to the Allies and order a cease-fire—but not soon enough to prevent bloodshed between two countries whose bonds of friendship went back to the American Revolution.

As Patton and Hewitt approached Morocco, two other Allied task forces prepared to land in Algeria. Altogether, nearly 110,000 troops—three-quarters of them Americans and the rest British—took part in this invasion, known as Operation Torch, commanded by Lt. Gen. Dwight D. Eisenhower. His objective was to advance eastward from Algeria into Tunisia and trap Field Marshal Rommel's Panzerarmee Afrika, which was being pursued westward by the British Eighth Army of General Montgomery, which had defeated Rommel at El Alamein, Egypt. Before taking on that larger challenge, however, the troops involved in Operation Torch would have to snuff out any French resistance they encountered.

Patton and Hewitt had to reckon with the French naval base at Casablanca, where forces were on guard against another deadly attack like that launched by the British against the Vichy fleet in July 1940 to prevent French warships from falling into German hands. Wary French gunners manning a big coastal battery at Casablanca opened fire as soon as Hewitt's warships drew within range on November 8.

Patton was standing on the deck of the *Augusta* when an incoming shell splashed into the water nearby and drenched him. He was less concerned for his own safety than for the loss of his landing craft, which was shattered by concussion when the *Augusta* returned fire and spilled his belongings into the sea.

Turning to his aide, he burst out: "Goddamit, I hope you have a spare toothbrush with you I can use to clean out my foul mouth." Any further curses the profane Patton had to offer were soon drowned out by a deafening battle between American naval forces, which included warplanes from the aircraft carrier U.S.S. *Ranger,* and the outmatched Vichy fleet. Several French ships went down at a cost of nearly 500 lives in a clash that the Americans, who suffered few casualties, would rather have avoided. Those defiant Frenchmen in Morocco were not Patton's preferred foes, but the fight was on, and he entered it with gusto. Wading ashore north of Casablanca, he found his forces in chaos after a rough landing and had to whip them into shape before he could whip the enemy. "The beach was a mess and the officers were doing nothing," he noted. One frightened man found cringing in the sand received a swift kick in the rear from his commander. "If I see another soldier lying down on this beach," he vowed, "I'll court-martial him." Heavy surf delayed the landing of tanks and other equipment.

Patton's troops were not in position to assault Casablanca until November 11, his 57th birthday, by which time French resistance in neighboring Algeria had collapsed. "Dear Georgie," Ike wrote him, "Algiers has been ours for two days . . . The only tough nut left is in your hands. Crack it open quickly." That morning Darlan's cease-fire order took effect, sparing Patton the necessity of assaulting Casablanca. As a Christian, he was glad no more blood would be spilled, he said, "but as a soldier I would have given a good deal to have the fight go on." He had not yet had a chance to distinguish himself—nor would he until the raw recruits he and other American officers led became true soldiers. They were lucky to have met with only sporadic opposition from

Pvt. Leo Inglesby
Lost in North Africa

Inglesby's 509th Parachute Regiment took part in the U.S. Army's first ever airborne assault. His C-47 transport plane went off course en route from England, missed its drop zone in Algeria, and landed on November 8, 1942, near a French fort, where he and others were briefly detained.

These French Foreign Legionnaires from Syria served with the British Eighth Army.

It was nearly midnight by the time the plane was aloft . . . The flight plan was to take us across the Bay of Biscay, then south across Spain . . . and over the Mediterranean to our destination beyond Oran, the Tafaroui airfield . . . Even before Gibraltar, a heavy ground fog set in, and a promised and clandestine radio direction beam never was picked up . . . Within the hour, the plane encountered violent turbulence. The pilot told us that during the turbulence his visibility was absolutely zero, and his altimeter was descending at a rate of a thousand feet per minute. Gradually, the plane settled back to normal as it flew through the storm and as the darkness gave way to dawn. By the pilot's reckoning, we could be almost anywhere except where we ought to have been. The storm had blown him in every direction; he had never been more lost . . . After a short while the message came back to us that his gas was getting so low that it would be safer for us to jump rather than risk a crash landing on that rocky surface. Accordingly, we gathered up our gear and hooked up our static lines to the overhead cable. As we started to shuffle toward the mid-cabin exit door, the co-pilot yelled for us to hold up.

From the open door we could see why he shouted. There below us . . . was a square-shaped high-walled fortress-like structure flying at its corner the tri-colored flag of France. The pilot made out the outlines of a landing strip, banked the plane sharply, and glided in for a smooth and bumpless landing.

We didn't have to wait long before the gate of the fort opened. There emerged a heavy-set mustachioed senior non-com who strolled up to the open door. Greeting him was the only member of the plane-load that spoke French, Private Rosario Cyr, our assigned medic. Our pilot, the senior officer aboard, told Cyr to tell him that we were on a training flight and got lost. To which the non-com just grunted. He told us we were to be prisoners, to leave all weapons in the plane and follow him . . . Our captors were a detachment of, as they called themselves, Le Legion Étrangères—or, as known to old Laurel and Hardy fans, the French Foreign Legion. ∎

> "Our captors were a detachment of, as they called themselves, Le Legion Étrangères—or, as known to old Laurel and Hardy fans, the French Foreign Legion."

foes with little incentive to fight. "Had the landings been opposed by Germans," Patton observed, "we never would have gotten ashore."

IKE'S DIFFICULT DEBUT

The man who led Operation Torch was a prodigious military planner, but he had as much to learn about high command as the green American troops who stumbled ashore in North Africa did about fighting. Born in 1890, Eisenhower did not enter West Point until he was nearly 21 and missed out on World War I, which ended before the tank brigade he was training at Gettysburg, Pennsylvania, could enter action. He served for some time as a staff officer under the temperamental Douglas MacArthur before Army Chief of Staff George Marshall called him to Washington and groomed the little-known Eisenhower for greatness. Arriving in North Africa, he found himself overseeing strong-willed generals who far surpassed him in reputation and experience. Even the celebrated Monty, the hero of El

> "Good chap—no soldier! He knows nothing whatever about how to make war or fight battles; he should be kept right away from all that business if we want to win this war."
>
> Gen. Bernard Montgomery on his new boss, Maj. Gen. Dwight Eisenhower

Alamein, would become Ike's subordinate when he reached Tunisia with his army in early 1942. "Good chap—no soldier!" Montgomery said of his new boss. "He knows nothing whatever about how to make war or fight battles; he should be kept right away from all that business if we want to win this war." Gen. Alan Brooke, the British army chief, echoed that scathing assessment: "Eisenhower as a general is hopeless! He submerges himself in politics and neglects his military duties."

Gen. Dwight D. Eisenhower (left), supreme commander of Allied forces in North Africa, stands beside his Western Task Force commander, Lt. Gen. George Patton.

Politics in fact took up more of Eisenhower's time than he wished. One of his first official acts was to cut a deal with Admiral Darlan, which left that Vichy turncoat, who now pledged loyalty to the Allies, in charge of Morocco and Algeria and freed Ike to concentrate on fighting Axis troops in Tunisia. The deal outraged Gen. Charles de Gaulle, who had fled to Britain when Germany invaded his country in June 1940 and proclaimed himself leader of the Free French. Others joined de Gaulle in blasting Eisenhower for embracing an officer who had collaborated with the enemy. "Are we fighting Nazis or sleeping with them?" asked Edward R. Murrow. Ike defended his pact with Darlan as necessary to achieve Allied military objectives, as did President Roosevelt, who cited an old Balkan proverb to justify such unsavory deals: "My children, you are permitted in time of great danger to walk with the Devil until you have crossed the bridge."

The assassination of Darlan in December brought a more acceptable French officer to power and relieved some of the political pressure on Eisenhower. Yet he still had to devote much attention to a task that was more diplomatic than military: strengthening the fragile Anglo-American alliance. More than a few British officers doubted the fighting capacity of the Yanks and the fitness of their commander, and many American officers had misgivings about their British counterparts, whom they suspected of being more concerned with preserving their own empire than shattering Hitler's Reich. General Marshall worried that Americans were being drawn into a long and costly diversion in the Mediterranean that might serve British interests there but would do little to hasten the defeat of Nazi Germany. Ike was a true Anglophile, however, and believed that British and U.S. interests were inseparable. He would not allow American officers to speak ill of their allies and expected his Yanks to serve as faithfully under British superiors as under their own countrymen. "Every subordinate throughout the chain of command," he insisted, "will execute the orders he receives without even pausing to consider whether that order emanated from a British or American source." That was too much to ask of Patton, who felt that American generals should be calling their own shots and complained that Ike was "more British than the British."

The strains in this alliance would ease when Americans proved themselves in battle, but the trials awaiting them in Tunisia were severe. Alarmed by Operation Torch and Darlan's defection, Hitler occupied southern France and heavily reinforced the ports of Tunis and nearby Bizerte, which if captured by the Allies would sever the enemy supply line and doom Axis troops in North

Africa. Ike's headquarters at Algiers was 500 miles from Tunis, and the forces he dispatched to seize that objective moved slowly along muddy roads. American soldiers who had expected to find Africa warm and dry encountered torrential winter rains, fierce winds, and frigid nights. Patton, raised in California, called Tunisia the "coldest damn place I have ever seen" and found it "very hard on the men."

Any hope Ike had of achieving a quick victory ended in December when his ill-equipped troops were stopped short of Tunis by punishing German counterattacks. American light tanks like the M3 Stuart proved no match for the hefty German Mk IV, whose armor-piercing 75-mm gun made the Stuart's 37-mm weapon seem like a pistol by comparison.

Even the more powerful M4 Sherman was at a disadvantage against the heavily armored Mk IV or the huge German Tiger tank. American armored units took savage beatings when they dashed recklessly into battle—a tactic favored by commanders who approached armored assaults like cavalry charges—and fell into traps laid for them by the savvy Germans. During one tank battle in Tunisia, an American lieutenant found his men so shocked by the pounding they were taking that they could barely move. "I walked from tank to tank trying to make them fire and retire," he recalled. "They seemed petrified." The lieutenant "cursed and insulted, climbing on tanks and shouting," but he could not get them to budge and fell wounded. No less petrifying for the Allies were shrieking Stuka dive-bombers that so dominated the skies over one blood-soaked battleground west of Tunis that it became known as Stuka Valley.

In late December, Eisenhower suspended the offensive in Tunisia until his troops there were bolstered and better equipped.

It was a gloomy Christmas for the Allied commander, who was as tough in assessing his own performance as his British critics were. Thus far, he wrote, the campaign in North Africa had "violated every recognized principle of war." When told that he might receive a Medal of Honor for the Torch landings, he objected that he had done nothing to earn the medal. "I don't want it and if it is awarded I won't wear it," he said. "I won't even keep it."

> "I don't want it and if it is awarded I won't wear it. I won't even keep it."
>
> Lt. Gen. Dwight Eisenhower, firmly rejecting the idea that he might be given the Medal of Honor for the Torch landings in Tunisia

In January 1943, Franklin Roosevelt and Winston Churchill met at Casablanca with military chiefs from their two countries. When Eisenhower conferred privately there with the president, he thought he was about to be sacked and said that he was "ready to take the rap for whatever went wrong." Roosevelt was looking beyond the problems of the moment to the Allies' next big step, however, and asked him when he would have Tunisia in hand. "May 15," Ike replied, committing himself to a deadline he was not sure he could meet.

If the Allies secured North Africa by then, they could challenge Axis forces on their own turf that summer by landing in Sicily, which might be used as a stepping-stone to invade mainland Italy. That plan was favored by the British but opposed by Marshall, who considered the Mediterranean "a blind alley to which American forces had only been committed because of the President's insistence that they should fight the Germans somewhere." Taking Italy would be a long and costly struggle, he reckoned, and even a hard-won victory there would pose no direct threat to Germany, which was shielded from Italy by neutral Switzerland and the forbidding Alps. The surest and quickest route to Germany lay through northern France or the Low Countries, Marshall insisted, and the sooner the Allies pursued that course, the better. Marshall's British counterpart, General Brooke, was against risking such an invasion in 1943, citing the disastrous results of an Allied raid across the English Channel against the German-occupied port of Dieppe in August 1942. The Allies could not afford a repetition of that debacle, and they would not be equipped to undertake a massive cross-Channel invasion with any confidence until 1944. In the meantime, Allied forces in North Africa could be used to knock Hitler's partner Mussolini out of the war and keep German troops tied down in Italy while the big push across the Channel unfolded.

The British won that argument by securing approval at Casablanca for an invasion of Sicily and clearing the way at another Allied conference later in the year for an invasion of Italy. Eisenhower accepted the decision. What worried him was the new command structure adopted at Casablanca, which

Wounded Canadians lie near a disabled tank of the 14th Canadian Tank Regiment following a disastrous Allied amphibious raid on the German-occupied port of Dieppe, France, on August 19, 1942.

entrusted ground operations in Tunisia to his British deputy, Gen. Harold Alexander. Eisenhower admired Alexander, but British commanders were also placed in charge of naval and air forces. Ike rightly suspected that his allies doubted his ability and were distancing him from the campaign. As Brooke wrote in his diary: "We were pushing Eisenhower up into the stratosphere and rarified atmosphere of a supreme commander, where he would be free to devote his time to political and inter-allied problems, whilst we inserted under him our own commanders to deal with the military situations and to restore the necessary drive and coordination which had been so seriously lacking of late!"

Eisenhower, who was promoted to full, four-star general to match Alexander's rank, praised the new command structure publicly, but inwardly he was seething. Marshall worried about Ike's health and the pressures that had been on him ever since the Darlan deal. "He may think he has troubles so far," Marshall said, "but he will have so many before this war is over that Darlan will be nothing."

Those words proved grimly prophetic as fighting resumed in Tunisia. Eisenhower remained responsible for appointing American officers in North Africa and replacing those who were not up to task. In February, he drove to the front to confer with Maj. Gen. Lloyd Fredenhall, commander of the U.S. II Corps. Fredenhall's engineers were excavating a deep bunker to shelter the general and his staff. His forces, meanwhile, were widely dispersed on the Allies' southern flank—a dangerous spot as Rommel's Panzerarmee approached from the south to link up with the army of Gen. Hans-Jürgen von Arnim, who had arrived in Tunisia in December. One officer under Fredenhall, Brig. Gen.

Paul Robinett, told Eisenhower that II Corps was in an "impossible" position. Fredenhall had ignored Ike's advice to keep a large mobile force in reserve, and if his front collapsed, he would be hard-pressed to hold the vital Kasserine Pass, which the enemy could use to wreak havoc behind Allied lines.

Fredenhall was clearly a liability. But Eisenhower hesitated to remove an officer recommended by his boss, Marshall, and thought there was no imminent threat to II Corps, having received intelligence that the Germans would attack up north. In fact, Rommel was about to launch an assault in the south—a step he took with some misgivings. If it were up to him, his battle-worn forces would have been withdrawn from Africa to save them for decisive campaigns in Europe. But neither Hitler nor his commander in the Mediterranean, Field Marshal Albert Kesselring, would stand for that. So Rommel decided to attack II Corps before Montgomery's trailing Eighth Army could catch up and trap him. Kesselring added two of Arnim's divisions to the offensive and vowed: "We are going to go all out for the total destruction of the Americans."

> "We are going to go all out for the total destruction of the Americans."
>
> Field Marshal Albert Kesselring, approving an attack on the U.S. II Corps in Tunisia

RETREAT AND REDEMPTION

Perched on a hill with men of his 168th Infantry Regiment, Col. Thomas Drake watched helplessly as Stuka dive-bombers and German armor shattered American defenses around the Tunisian town of Sidi bou Zid on the morning of February 14. Sherman tanks—known to the troops as "Ronsons" after the classic cigarette lighter because they ignited so quickly—lay blasted and burning in the valley below, and artillerymen of the U.S. First Armored Division were abandoning their guns on a distant hill and fleeing. Drake called Brig. Gen. Raymond McQuillin at his command post near the town and told him that his forces were giving way.

"You don't know what you're saying," McQuillin responded. "They're only shifting positions." Drake assured him otherwise. "I know panic when I see it," he insisted. If so, McQuillin shot back, Drake should "take command and stop it." How Drake's lightly armed infantrymen were supposed to stop this rout if American armor and artillery could not was left unexplained. A short time later, Drake learned that McQuillin was pulling out and asked to do the same. McQuillin contacted II Corps headquarters, 80 miles to the rear. Fredenhall, who had positioned his units too far apart to cope with this attack, replied that it was "too early to give Drake permission to withdraw."

Left stranded in what was now enemy territory, the regiment held out under fire for 36 hours before Drake's request was finally granted: "Fight your way out. Time and place yours." Leaving behind their dead and wounded, they escaped in the night with other men of the 34th Infantry Division, only to be overtaken by German troops the next day. "We were young, dumb, outgunned, outmaneuvered, and outsmarted," recalled Capt. Billy Bingham. "By the time the Germans caught up with us we were in poor condition, dead tired," he added. "It was more like a roundup than a battle." Drake told an officer who demanded his surrender to "go to hell," but he and his men had little choice but to yield. More than a thousand Americans were captured. As the prisoners were led away under guard, Bingham stated, "We saw Arabs tearing the uniforms off dead soldiers. Dogs were gnawing on the bodies of those killed on the 14th, the wreckage of a terrible battle."

By February 19, another terrible battle loomed at Kasserine Pass. Rommel's attack there was delayed as he debated whether to push westward through that pass against II Corps and attack the big enemy supply base at Tébessa, Algeria, or to advance northward against other Allied targets in Tunisia. He chose to divide his forces and pursue both options, reckoning that he would not need all his strength to overcome Fredenhall's troops at Kasserine Pass. Stunned by the German onslaught, Fredenhall pleaded for reinforcements. "I haven't got a damn bit of reserve," he said, a situation for which he bore some responsibility. Eisenhower sent troops, but few of them would arrive in time to defend the pass. So Fredenhall called on Col. Alexander Stark, commander of the 26th Infantry Regiment, back near Tébessa. "Alex," he said, "I want you to go to Kasserine right away and pull a Stonewall Jackson. Take over up there."

Like Jackson, Stark was a Virginian, but there the resemblance ended. A former military surgeon who had been decorated for bravery in World War I but seemed out of his depth in this one, he arrived at the pass early on February 19 to find American engineers with minimal combat training occupying the low ground, leaving the heights to be occupied by the oncoming Germans. Stark had little chance of making a heroic stand here but was slow to recognize how perilous the situation was. He had things "well in hand," he told a British officer, who concluded that Stark "had completely lost control of events." On February 20, Stark was overwhelmed as Rommel's tanks challenged the Americans head-on while German infantrymen, who had seized the high ground, poured down flanking fire on the forlorn defenders. Hundreds fell dead or wounded before resistance collapsed that afternoon and the survivors fled.

Eisenhower sent Maj. Gen. Ernest Harmon to prop up the hapless Fredenhall and restore order. On his way to the front, Harmon had to force his way through retreating Yanks. "It was the first—and only—time I had ever seen an American army in rout," he wrote. "Jeeps, trucks, wheeled vehicles of every imaginable sort streamed up the road toward us . . . It was obvious there was one thing only in the minds of the panic-stricken drivers: to get away from the front, to escape to some place where there was no shooting." Had Rommel committed all his forces to a swift thrust through Kasserine Pass, he might have shattered the demoralized II Corps. But as it was, American and British artillery units were able to waylay German tanks as they advanced through rugged terrain on separate paths. On February 22, Rommel and Kesselring conferred and called off the offensive, which achieved no lasting gains but cost the Americans more than 6,000 casualties and destroyed nearly 200 tanks.

The results seemed to confirm the low opinion in which British officers like Alexander held the inexperienced Americans. "They simply do not know their jobs as soldiers," he wrote, "and this is the case from the highest to the lowest." But the fault lay not just with the Yanks but with the entire, ill-coordinated Allied operation in North Africa. "One would have to search all history to find a more jumbled command structure," concluded General Robinett, who felt that II Corps had not been well served by Fredenhall, his British superior Lt. Gen. Kenneth Anderson, or their supreme commander, Eisenhower.

Fortunately, Ike and the Americans under him learned far more from their failures in Tunisia than from their easy success in

Morocco and Algeria. Poorly performing officers were eased out and promising ones promoted. Eisenhower rehabilitated II Corps by placing it first under the stern hand of General Patton—who took on that task temporarily before resuming preparations for the Sicily campaign—and then under the firm grip of Ike's old friend from West Point Maj. Gen. Omar Bradley. He and Eisenhower overcame British qualms and insisted that II Corps be given an important role to play when the Allies launched an all-out attack on their Axis foes in April.

War correspondent Ernie Pyle returned to North Africa shortly before that battle began and noted how Americans there had been hardened by combat. "The most vivid change is the casual and workshop manner in which they now talk about killing," he wrote. Few of them had started out hating Germans, but their losses at Kasserine Pass and else-where left them with the same burning desire to destroy the enemy that Americans serving in the Pacific felt after Pearl Harbor. As Pyle observed, soldiers in North Africa were now eager "to see the Germans overrun, mangled, butchered in the Tunisian trap."

> "The most vivid change is the casual and workshop manner in which they now talk about killing."
>
> War correspondent Ernie Pyle, observing how American soldiers had been hardened by combat in North Africa

By the time the final battle for North Africa began on April 23, Rommel had returned to Germany on sick leave and Montgomery's Eighth Army had rolled in and sealed off the Axis troops. They were trapped with their backs to the sea, prey to relentless Allied air strikes. Bradley's II Corps, assigned to take Bizerte while other Allied forces targeted Tunis, advanced with new-found determination against Germans who were in no mood to surrender. The biggest obstacle in Bradley's path was Hill 609, bristling with mortars and machine-gun nests. "Get me that hill,"

A C-47 of the U.S. Air Transport Command, carrying supplies for Allied forces in North Africa, flies over the famous Egyptian Pyramids at Giza in 1943.

he ordered Maj. Gen. Charles Ryder, whose 34th Infantry Division had been mauled and maligned in recent months. "Take it and no one will ever again doubt the toughness of your division." In contrast to earlier battles, the infantry here was closely supported by armor and artillery. Bradley asked his artillery chief, Brig. Gen. Charles Hart, to throw all he had at the stubborn defenders of Hill 609. "We'll give them a serenade," Hart replied, "and sweeten it with everything we've got."

On April 29, Ryder's infantry advanced up the hill behind a phalanx of Sherman tanks, overwhelming foes who were shaken by Hart's barrage and shocked to see armor ascending the slope. The taking of Hill 609 opened the way to Bizerte for Bradley's men, who seized that port on May 7, the same day Tunis fell.

Nearly 250,000 Axis troops were captured by the Allies in the worst defeat for Hitler since the disaster at Stalingrad earlier that year. Eisenhower, who met his deadline for securing North Africa with a week to spare, displayed the tough new American stance toward the enemy by refusing to speak with the defeated Axis commander, General Arnim. Ike did not "trust his reactions before a representative of the Prussian and Nazi regime," explained his chief of staff. "The only German generals I'm interested in," said Eisenhower, "are the ones we haven't captured yet."

This magazine cover shows a compassionate British medic carrying a Sicilian baby to an aid station to be weighed and fed.

CHRONOLOGY

JULY 10, 1943 Allied troops invade Sicily.

SEPTEMBER 3, 1943 British Eighth Army lands at Reggio di Calabria, launching Allied invasion of Italy.

JULY 25, 1943 Mussolini falls from power.

SEPTEMBER 8, 1943 Italy surrenders; German troops take control.

LONG ROAD TO ROME

THE ALLIED CONQUEST OF ITALY

B ernard Montgomery did not mince words. The Allied plan
for Operation Husky—the code name for the invasion of
Sicily—was, he said, a "hopeless mess." A firm believer in concen-
trating one's forces, he rejected a proposal for far-flung landings
there and wanted them confined to a narrow stretch of Sicily's
south coast and placed under his command. "I should be running
Husky," he wrote. Officially, Eisenhower was running the show,
but operational command of ground forces remained with his
British deputy, Alexander, who trusted in Monty's judgment. Ike
too saw merit in Montgomery's plan, but he placed the American
troops bound for Sicily under Patton. Monty's Eighth Army would
land near Syracuse and advance on Messina, at Sicily's northeastern
tip, where they hoped to cut off Axis forces before they escaped
across the strait to the Italian mainland. Patton's Seventh Army

SEPTEMBER 9, 1943 U.S. Fifth
Army lands at Salerno, Italy.

JUNE 5, 1944 Rome falls
to Allied troops.

NOVEMBER 30, 1943 The Big Three—Roosevelt, Churchill,
and Stalin—meet in Tehran to coordinate their war efforts.

As shown on this map, U.S. troops and the British Eighth Army launch a joint attack on Sicily. The British reach the prize, Messina, shortly after the Americans.

would land farther from Messina and guard the British flank and rear. Patton did not like playing second fiddle, but he fell into line when Ike backed the revised plan. "I've been in this army 30 years," Patton said, "and when my superior gives me an order I say 'Yes, sir!' and then do my god-damnedest to carry it out."

No soldiers involved in Operation Husky had a more perilous task to carry out than the airborne troops assigned to land in Sicily on the night of July 9, 1943, and seize roads, bridges, and other objectives that the enemy could use to assail Allied forces as they came ashore early on July 10. "Many lives will be lost in a few hours," predicted Col. James Gavin of the U.S. 82nd Airborne Division, which was entering combat for the first time. The C-47 aircraft carrying Gavin's men and other regiments were scattered by heavy winds and dropped most of the paratroopers far from their designated landing zones.

"Each aircraft was more or less on its own," recalled Lt. Robert Piper of Gavin's 505th Parachute Infantry Regiment. "We finally picked up the Sicilian coast and were flying up the Strait of Messina over near the British sector when the pilot admitted he wasn't sure where he was. I asked him to turn westerly and give me the green light when we were again over land." Piper and his men were less than 400 feet above ground when they jumped. He landed in an olive tree and managed to free himself. Other paratroopers came down hard that night and broke bones or drifted over enemy positions and were shot before they reached the ground.

The first concern for those who landed unscathed was to find comrades and form companies, using passwords to distinguish friend from foe in the dark. (The call sign for paratroopers in Gavin's regiment was "George," to be answered by "Marshall.") Piper gathered up about a dozen men. Reckoning that they had landed east of their intended drop zone, they "immediately started moving west over rugged, rocky and barren country." Spotting a group of soldiers who were approaching in the gloom, he and his company had only a few seconds to identify and deal with them before becoming targets themselves. "When I said 'Hi,' they responded with 'Heil Hitler,' " Piper recalled, "and there was a brief firefight, which they lost!"

> "When I said 'Hi,' they responded with 'Heil Hitler.'"
>
> Lt. Robert Piper,
> 505th Parachute Infantry Regiment

Most of the paratroopers in the 82nd were far from their objectives that morning, but they fared better than the British airborne forces who landed in gliders, many of which were released too far from shore and plowed into the sea, drowning more than 200 men. Despite such calamities, small, determined groups of Allied airborne troops seized targets such as the Ponte Grande, a vital bridge in the British sector, and caused confusion among opposing forces inland as the greatest amphibious assault yet attempted unfolded on the coast. Seven Allied divisions (two more than would later land at Normandy on D-Day) comprising more than 80,000 men were transported from North Africa, along with 600 tanks and thousands of other vehicles, by an armada of more than 3,000 ships and landing craft, including newly designed DUKWs that operated as boats at sea and trucks on land. That immense amphibious fleet "resembled a distant city" on the horizon, wrote Ernie Pyle. "It covered half the skyline . . . I hope no American ever has to see its counterpart sailing against us."

Heavy surf made the Allied landings on July 10 nauseating and treacherous. Enemy air strikes and land mines took their toll as the troops came ashore, but resistance on the beaches was lighter than Eisenhower had feared. Credit for that went partly to Allied intelligence officers, who could not hide the huge buildup for Operation Husky in North Africa but conducted ingenious deception campaigns that kept their foes guessing as to where the blow would fall. On April 30, 1943, a fisherman trolling in the Atlantic off the Spanish port of Huelva recovered what appeared to be the body of a British officer floating in the sea, seemingly one more victim of a war that had already claimed countless lives. In fact, the body was that of a man who had taken his own life, little knowing that his remains would be used in Operation Mincemeat, one of the most successful deceptions of World War II. The macabre plot was carried out by MI-5, Britain's counterintelligence agency, to conceal the upcoming invasion.

MI-5 entrusted the mission to Flight Lt. Charles Cholmondeley of the Royal Air Force and Lt. Cmdr. Ewen Montagu of

Naval Intelligence. Their goal was to place false documents in the hands of German commanders indicating that Allied forces massing in North Africa across from Sicily were destined for two other targets: German-occupied Greece and Sardinia. The documents would be carried by a corpse disguised as a deceased military courier who had apparently drowned after his aircraft crashed off the Spanish coast. Although Spanish officials were officially neutral, they cooperated with German authorities and could be expected to bring such sensitive documents to their attention.

Cholmondeley obtained a suitable dead body from a London coroner—that of a 34-year-old drifter named Glyndwr Michael who had committed suicide by taking rat poison, leaving no marks on his body inconsistent with drowning. "In life he had done little for his country," Montagu wrote, "but in death he did more than most could achieve by a lifetime of service."

> "In life he had done little for his country, but in death he did more than most could achieve by a lifetime of service."
>
> Lt. Cmdr. Ewen Montagu, British Naval Intelligence, on the corpse used in Operation Mincemeat

The officers established a backstory for their fictitious courier, whom they dubbed Maj. William Martin of the Royal Marines. Secretaries at MI-5 composed romantic letters from Martin's fiancée and provided a charming photograph of her. Cholmondeley carried the letters in his wallet, repeatedly folding and unfolding them to add authenticity before placing them on the dead man once he was suitably clothed. Other convincing items in Martin's pockets included a bank overdraft notice, a military identification card, theater tickets, receipts, matchbooks, and keys. His briefcase included a letter from Lt. Gen. Archibald Nye of the Imperial General Staff to Gen. Harold Alexander in Tunisia that

In reply, quote: S.R. 1924/43.

COMBINED OPERATIONS HEADQUARTERS,

1A, RICHMOND TERRACE,

WHITEHALL. S.W.1.

Telephone:
WHitehall 9777

21st April,
1943.

Dear Admiral of the Fleet,

I promised V.C.I.G.S. that Major Martin would
arrange with you for the onward transmission of a
letter he has with him for General Alexander. It is
very urgent and very "hot" and as there are some
remarks in it that could not be seen by others in the
War Office, it could not go by signal. I feel sure
that you will see that it goes on safely and without
delay.

I think you will find Martin the man you want.
He is quiet and shy at first, but he really knows his
stuff. He was more accurate than some of us about the
probable run of events at Dieppe and he has been well
in on the experiments with the latest barges and
equipment which took place up in Scotland.

Let me have him back, please, as soon as the
assault is over. He might bring some sardines with him -
they are "on points" here!

Yours sincerely

Louis Mountbatten

Admiral of the Fleet Sir A.B. Cunningham, G.C.B.,D.S.O.,
Commander in Chief Mediterranean,
Allied Force H.Q.,
Algiers.

*British MI-5 counterintelligence packed a briefcase for the fake "Major Martin"
with this letter, which was signed by Admiral Lord Louis Mountbatten
himself and refers slyly to "sardines," meant to be interpreted by the Germans
as alluding to Sardinia.*

detailed Allied plans for an invasion of Greece and referred to a second operation, which another letter in the briefcase suggested was Sardinia.

The body was then packed in dry ice to retard decomposition and placed aboard the submarine H.M.S. *Seraph* for the voyage to Spain. Only its commander knew the true nature of the mission. Before dawn on April 30, the *Seraph* surfaced off Huelva, and Major Martin, with briefcase chained securely to him and life vest inflated, was slipped into the sea.

The body was quickly found by the fisherman and turned over to local authorities, who passed the remains along to the British consulate for burial but sent the contents of the briefcase to Spanish Naval Headquarters in Madrid. There, an officer allowed agents from the German embassy to open the letters and take photographs. Code breakers at Bletchley Park monitored communications by the Abwehr (German military intelligence) and confirmed that information from Martin's briefcase had been sent to Berlin. On May 12, the German High Command directed that measures for the defense of Greece and Sardinia "take precedence over everything else." So successful was Operation Mincemeat in diverting enemy attention and troops to those other targets that only two German divisions were in Sicily to support its Italian defenders when the Allies landed there in July.

Other ruses conducted shortly before the invasion began, when the threat to Sicily was obvious, indicated that the invaders would come ashore near the island's western tip, a long way from the actual landing zones. On July 10, one of the two German divisions in Sicily was far off to the west awaiting a possible invasion there. The other was closer to where the Americans came ashore but arrived too late to disrupt the initial landings.

Some Italian troops fought the Allies intently, but many others were ill equipped and demoralized, having lost faith in Mussolini, now widely disdained by his own people as Hitler's lackey. Italians were soon surrendering in droves to the Allies, who could not handle them all at once. Sgt. Bill Mauldin of the 45th Infantry Division wrote of those willing captives: "It's hard to work up a good hate for soldiers who are surrendering so fast you have to take them by appointment."

> "It's hard to work up a good hate for soldiers who are surrendering so fast you have to take them by appointment."
>
> Sgt. Bill Mauldin, 45th Infantry Division, as Italian troops surrendered in droves

American troops and supplies were still coming ashore around the town of Gela on the morning of July 11 when the Hermann Göring Panzer Division—named for the chief of the Luftwaffe, to which their outfit was attached—attacked in force and advanced to within a half mile of the beach. "Situation critical. We are being overrun by tanks," reported an officer in the First Infantry Division, known proudly to its troops as the "Big Red One" for the scarlet number on their shoulder patches. Their commander, Maj. Gen. Terry Allen, appealed for armor to meet the threat, but many of the Seventh Army's tanks were stuck with other vehicles in thick sand on the beach. With only a few Shermans to throw into the battle, Allen relied mightily on his antitank gunners, who had honed their skills against panzers in North Africa. When an aide suggested withdrawing the division's hard-pressed troops, Allen shot back: "Hell, no. We haven't begun to fight. They haven't overrun our artillery yet." By midday, the Germans were being pounded by a lethal combination of artillery fire—including blasts from fearsome 155-mm Long Toms that could fire 95-pound projectiles up to 15 miles or pulverize tanks at short range—and salvos from Admiral Hewitt's warships offshore. The Germans "wisely concluded that the 26-ton Mark IV is no match for a cruiser," wrote Allen's corps commander, Bradley. The attackers soon took to their heels, leaving nearly half of their 60 tanks behind in flames.

The hardest losses for U.S. forces in Operation Husky occurred that night as C-47s flew in over Gela with another wave of paratroopers and were mistaken for enemy aircraft. Nearly two dozen planes were shot down, and several hundred men were killed or wounded. The sad fact was that another airborne assault was not needed to secure the beachhead or allow forces there to advance inland. It soon became clear that the Germans were shifting to a defensive stance that eased pressure on the American sector while making it harder for the British to advance toward Messina. On July 11, Field Marshal Kesselring flew to Sicily from mainland Italy to confer with his generals. An agile and adaptable commander, Kesselring recognized that the Allies were now too well established to be driven back into the sea. But with an additional 20,000 Germans troops who began arriving that evening, his forces could make a stand around towering Mount Etna in northeastern Sicily and shield Messina.

Montgomery found his direct route to Messina—a narrow corridor between Mount Etna and Sicily's east coast—blocked by stout German defenses near Catania. So he sent his XXX Corps on a wide sweep to the west around that volcanic peak, which brought those troops into the path of Patton's forces as they advanced inland along Route 124, the only serviceable road for tanks and trucks in the area. Montgomery prevailed on General Alexander to shunt the Americans aside. "Monty wants the road right away," a deflated Patton told Bradley, whose corps would have to backtrack toward their landing zone to comply with Alexander's directive. "General Bradley executed this preposterous order silently and skillfully," wrote an aide, "but inwardly he was as hot as Mount Etna."

Unwilling to wait idly in the wings while Monty stole the show, Patton persuaded Alexander to "take the wraps off" and let his forces advance on Palermo, a major port in northwestern Sicily. That quick dash to Palermo, seized on July 23, brought Patton's army more Italian prisoners and a major supply base. But otherwise, wrote Bradley, "there was little to be gained in the west. Certainly there was no glory in the capture of hills, docile peasants, and spiritless soldiers."

Greater glory lay in beating Monty to Messina—a contest that unfolded when the British Eighth Army failed to crack the enemy's formidable Etna Line in the east. Belatedly, Alexander committed both armies to that task, with the Americans advancing along Sicily's north coast while the British pressed forward to their south.

> "We must take Messina before the British."
>
> Lt. Gen. George S. Patton

"This is a horse race in which the prestige of the U.S. Army is at stake," Patton declared. "We must take Messina before the British." That so-called race often slowed to a crawl, however, as the Germans fought fiercely and withdrew stubbornly, wrecking bridges and blocking tunnels behind them. It cost the First Infantry Division 500 casualties and the better part of a week to pierce the Etna Line at Troina, Sicily's highest town. There was little left of the place when they got there, a reporter wrote, except weeping civilians, "torn streets, heaps of rubble that had been houses, grief, horror and pain."

On August 17, American troops entered Messina, arriving there a few hours ahead of the British. The Yanks had won the race by

Pvt. Harvey White, a medic with the U.S. Third Infantry Division, administers blood plasma to Pvt. Roy Humphrey, wounded by shrapnel during the fighting on Sicily in August 1943.

a nose. Yet the Allies had gained less through competition than they could have achieved through cooperation and coordination. In recent days, Kesselring had managed to evacuate more than 100,000 Axis troops and 10,000 vehicles across the Strait of Messina to the mainland. As Bradley observed, this promising Allied campaign had come to an "unspectacular end"—one that allowed too many of their enemies to escape and fight again another day.

Patton basked briefly in glory after taking Messina, but was soon mired in scandal. Two soldiers in his army were charged with massacring Axis prisoners of war and court-martialed. Both men admitted to the deeds, but stated in their defense that Patton had urged them in pep talks to be merciless to their foes. As one soldier recalled, Patton told them "to kill the enemy wherever we found

STAFF SGT. CHARLES BEARDSLEY
THE LONG ROAD TO PALERMO

Beardsley served with the 30th Regiment of the Third Infantry Division as Patton's troops crossed the rugged terrain of western Sicily at a grueling pace and captured Palermo.

Displaying white sheets to signal a truce, residents of Palermo greet men of the U.S. Second Armored Division, arriving in M4 Sherman tanks after Axis troops abandoned the city on July 23, 1943.

As the day wore on water became more and more of a problem [and] by 5 p.m. we were starting to drink water from the horse troughs along the side of the road . . . As the night darkened the temperature lowered and it became a little more comfortable, but fatigue was a problem. We were now already down to less than half strength since many soldiers had dropped out from heat exhaustion, blisters and other foot problems.

From 10 p.m. on, every time we took a rest break, I fell asleep as soon as my butt hit the ground . . . At around 11 p.m. the men were dropping out from just pure exhaustion. The next day I saw a couple of men that were leading a mule carrying a heavy machine gun and ammo, which weighed around 250 pounds. They used up three mules this way. I saw the first one go down around noon . . .

About three miles down the road . . . the bridge had been blown. Everyone had to climb down into a deep canyon about 300-feet deep to cross a dry riverbed and then climb up the other side. The enemy must not have realized they could have held us up for hours with just a couple machine guns properly placed. We continued on to our objective which we reached at 2 a.m. after twenty hours. The battalion started out with 800 men and by the time our objective was reached there were only 200 left since so many of the soldiers fell apart physically . . .

Now [a] town had to be taken, but fortunately there were only Italian soldiers there so it was just a matter of walking through, taking cover as you went and firing a few rounds that bounced off the stone walls. In 20 minutes the town was ours. When I reached the other side of town I was so completely exhausted there wasn't an ounce of strength left in me. My bones ached and even my skin was tired. I collapsed between the rows in a vineyard and didn't know a thing until the next morning . . .

The next day when we moved out we hiked through the area and we saw the destruction. There were many dead lying around bloated and smelling like something that would gag a maggot. It was my first real smell of rotting bodies on a battlefield but not to be the last . . . About four days later we reached Palermo meeting little resistance which was agreeable to us. We had covered 150 miles in six days and we needed a rest. ∎

> "As the day wore on water became more and more of a problem [and] by 5 p.m. we were starting to drink water from the horse troughs along the side of the road."

him . . . and not to fool around with prisoners. He said that there was only one good German and that was a dead one." One of the defendants was acquitted, and both cases were hushed up by the Army to shield American POWs from reprisals.

Another scandal involving Patton became public, however, when it was revealed that he had insulted and slapped two hospitalized soldiers in Sicily whom he considered shirkers. Patton called one of those men—suffering from what was then labeled shell shock—a "yellow son-of-a-bitch" and waved a pistol at him. "You ought to be lined up against a wall and shot," he railed. "I ought to shoot you myself right now, goddamn you!" Patton could have been court-martialed for that outburst, but Eisenhower chose instead to reprimand him and require him to make apologies. He later cut Patton down a notch by placing him under his temperamental opposite, Bradley, who remarked that for all Patton's skills as a commander, "he had not yet learned to command himself." To win this brutal war, however, Ike needed men like Patton, who told him on one occasion: "You name them; I'll shoot them."

THE COLLAPSE OF IL DUCE

Had Sicily been defended only by Italian troops, it would have fallen much sooner. The ease with which those disheartened soldiers yielded to the Allies signaled that Mussolini, who had ruled Italy with an iron fist for more than two decades, was losing his grip. From the start, he had been the junior partner in his so-called Pact of Steel with Hitler. When he tried to rival German conquests by invading the Balkans and North Africa, Il Duce had stumbled badly, forcing the führer to bail him out. Heavy losses in those campaigns and in the Soviet Union had embittered

Italians, who felt less affection for Germany—their foe in the last war—than for America, home to many Italian immigrants. "In Italy, we can rely only on the Duce," warned Hitler, who feared that Mussolini would be overthrown and made plans, if that happened, to seize control of Italy, an operation code-named Alaric after the Germanic chieftain who sacked Rome.

On July 25, 1943, six days after the first Allied bombing raid on Rome, Mussolini met with King Victor Emmanuel III, who had been reduced to a ceremonial role when Il Duce seized power but remained popular in Italy. Mussolini expected the king to back him in his feud with the Fascist Grand Council, which had turned against him. But Victor Emmanuel told the faltering dictator that it was time for him to step down. "At this moment, you are the most hated man in Italy," he said. "You have not a single friend left, except me." Mussolini was arrested that evening and replaced by Field Marshal Pietro Badoglio, who pledged that Italy would remain loyal to Germany but entered into secret peace talks with the

> "At this moment, you are the most hated man in Italy."
>
> King Victor Emmanuel III
> to Benito Mussolini

Allies. Hitler was not fooled and set Operation Alaric in motion while those talks were under way in August. Eight divisions led by Erwin Rommel would occupy northern Italy, where Mussolini would later be installed as a Fascist figurehead after German commandos freed him from prison in September. Other German forces led by Kesselring, including troops withdrawn from Sicily, would patrol the country from Rome southward and guard against Allied landings there.

In making plans to invade mainland Italy, Eisenhower had to reckon with strong German resistance. His task was further complicated by preparations in Britain for Operation Overlord—a

A bullet-riddled portrait of Italian dictator Benito Mussolini hangs pinned to a tree by a bayonet soon after the Allied invasion of Sicily, which led to Mussolini's downfall. Many Sicilians chafed under Fascist rule and resented the intruding Germans, who placed their stamp on Italy by installing their own road signs.

cross-Channel invasion of France in 1944—which limited the number of troops, landing craft, and other resources committed to Italy. Ike and his staff considered ways of expediting the Italian campaign, including an airborne assault on Rome that would spare troops from having to fight their way to that city from Italy's toe, 300 miles away. But any quick leap to Rome was rejected as too risky. Instead, Allied troops would land in southern Italy, closer to their staging grounds.

On September 3, Montgomery's Eighth Army came ashore virtually unopposed at Reggio di Calabria, just across the Strait of Messina. The U.S. Fifth Army, which was led by Lt. Gen. Mark Wayne Clark and included some British forces, would land six days later at Salerno, roughly halfway up the coast to Rome. The plan called for Montgomery's and Clark's forces to link up, take Naples, and advance on Rome, but no one knew what the Allies would do next if and when they seized Italy's capital.

"Before we embark on major operations on the mainland of Europe, we must have a master plan," objected Montgomery, who concluded that there was no such plan. Like many other costly campaigns during World War II, this one was launched not because the territory at stake was crucial or the strategic objective was clear but simply because the enemy was there in strength and showed no signs of yielding until he was defeated on all fronts and his strength was gone.

Few of the soldiers who embarked on this long and painful Italian venture knew what they were in for. On the evening of September 8, as Clark's forces prepared to land at Salerno, they learned that Italy had surrendered. Unaware that German troops had stepped into the breach and were ready to fight them tooth and nail, they began celebrating. "The war is over," cheered sailors on the destroyer U.S.S. *Mayo*. Gleeful soldiers of the Second Battalion Scots Guards asked their bagpiper to compose a tune for their victory march through Naples. "I never again expect to witness such scenes of sheer joy," wrote an aide to Clark. "Speculation was rampant, and it was all good . . . We would dock in Naples harbor unopposed, with an olive branch in one hand and an opera ticket in the other." Officers who knew better tried to bring men to their senses. "Stop it, you bloody fools," yelled one British captain, who foresaw bloody days ahead. Maj. Gen. Ernest Dawley, commander of the U.S. VI Corps, told troops that they would have to fight like "Comanches if we mean to get ashore and stay there."

STRUGGLE AT SALERNO

"It was dark as hell, and we were just waiting out there," recalled an American soldier whose landing craft lurked offshore as the first wave of troops hit the beach at Salerno before dawn on September 9. "If we thought we were going to sneak ashore, we were nuts," he told author and war correspondent John Steinbeck. "They had machine guns in the sand dunes and 88's [artillery] on the hills." As he and other troops in the landing craft waited their turn to enter the fight, they saw soldiers stumble onto the beach—illuminated by tracer fire and bursting shells—and collapse. It was like watching a war movie in a dark theater. "Then all of a sudden it came on me that this wasn't a moving picture," he said. "Those were guys getting the

> "It was dark as hell, and we were just waiting out there . . . I was just getting real scared when we got the order to move in, and I swear that is the longest trip I ever took, that mile to the beach."
>
> An American soldier, after landing at Salerno

hell shot out of them . . . I was just getting real scared when we got the order to move in, and I swear that is the longest trip I ever took, that mile to the beach. I thought we'd never get there . . . Then we bumped the beach and the ramps went down and I hit the water up to my waist."

Unlike the landings on Sicily, the Germans anticipated the invasion at Salerno and had one armored division ready to greet the Allies when they arrived that morning and more on the way. Soldiers who made it ashore unscathed like the man Steinbeck interviewed remained at great risk as the day dawned. Enemy gunners perched on slopes above the beach continued to pound the incoming Allies, who were divided by the Sele River as it entered the sea, separating the Americans to the south from British forces to the north. In the morning light, they made conspicuous targets for German warplanes and tanks, which caused havoc before DUKWs delivered artillery to help deal with them. Once again, as in Sicily, Allied warships brought their big guns to bear and blasted enemy positions, clearing paths for troops on the beach, who advanced a few miles inland by nightfall. They made further progress over the next two days, but Germans clung to the high ground overlooking the Salerno plain and prepared to counterattack. Earlier in the month, Patton had reviewed plans for the invasion and predicted where that blow would fall. "Just as sure as God lives," he said, pointing to the Sele on a map, "the Germans will attack down that river."

Patton's recent problems kept him away from the action at Salerno. It was Clark, an officer of lofty ambition but little battle experience, who decided to land troops on both sides of the river. The risks involved in doing so did not fully dawn on him until he came ashore in the American sector on September 12 and

ORESTE MAINA
ITALIAN DEPORTEE

When Italy signed its armistice with the Allies in 1943,
Germany occupied the country and fought the Allies for control.
At the same time, it ramped up its labor deportation program,
abducting Italian men to become "guest workers" in Germany.
Oreste Maina was one of these men.

September 23, 1943
Casale di Carinola

German soldiers with machine guns are positioned on all the streets of Casale. At around 8:00, a loudspeaker announces that all the townsmen must meet in the main square for a German official's speech. Upon arriving in the square, we realize that we are surrounded on all sides. Our ID cards are collected and we are given an hour to go home and pack some things. We are told we'll be taken away to work for two or three days. We are warned that if we don't return, reprisals will be taken against our families. I suspect they'll be taking us to Germany but out of fear of reprisal against my wife, my two children, and my father, I return to the square. After an hour we all re-gather in the square. They load us into trucks and drive up to the mountains near Massico.

We sleep outdoors that night, encircled by German soldiers.

September 24, 1943

They load us into trucks again and we are taken to the Sparanise train station. Here, they load us into cattle cars. There are men from Casale, Carinola, San Donato, San Ruosi, and Ventaroli. They close the doors and there is no way out. We depart that same night. We are covered in sweat and can barely breathe. The night goes by like this. We stop at a station and they let us out to relieve ourselves, but we're only allowed to do so on the tracks surrounded by Germans armed with rifles and machine guns.

September 26, 1943

We're at the Verona train station. I tried to escape. I stepped out on the opposite side of the tracks and tried to climb into a freight train that was at the station. I heard a shout behind me and saw a German with his rifle pointed straight at me. I immediately stepped back into the cattle car.

We've arrived in Dachau, a concentration camp. We slept on wood planks.

September 30, 1943

We've arrived in Munich. It's night, they take us to a grand hotel. Here, we exchanged some of our Italian money for German Marks. We bought some beer. At night we had to sleep on wood planks on the stage of a theater.

We were taken to the employment office. People come to collect us as if we were objects. They call out our names and take the men with them, some take 20 men, some take 30 men, some take 10. They call out the names of Oreste Maina and Donato Russo from San Donato. The man is a wholesale produce merchant. That night we're taken to a dormitory where over 500 men are lodged. While sleeping, the siren goes off. The siren hollers, it frightens us, we are led to the basement. When the siren stops,

we go back up to the quarters. The windows are all broken and glass is scattered on the beds and the floor. The wall plaster has crumbled and there are cracks in the walls. On nearby streets, the firemen are working all night, making deafening noises.

October 1, 1943

Donato Russo and I went to work today. We unload apples, cucumbers, and vegetables from Italian freight cars. At night, we go back to our dormitory. The only thing we eat here is "suppe": warm water with wheat bran and not a bit of seasoning. At 20:00 we must take an obligatory shower, and at 20:30 everyone must go to sleep. Every morning we go to the same place. We walk three kilometers through the city to reach the loading dock. We load trucks with cases of apples and take them to the place where the boss has his office and from where he sells produce to organizations, restaurants, and whatnot with proper ration cards. At midday we have lunch at a restaurant: suppe and kartoffel. At night, they accompany us to the dormitory. ∎

established his headquarters at a villa near the Sele River and its tributary, the Calore. The corridor between those two rivers seemingly offered a path by which his troops could advance and break out; instead, the Germans used it as a path to break in. By evening, elements of several panzer divisions were bearing down on the American sector, forcing Clark to withdraw to a hastily improvised command post near the beach. The counter-attack intensified the next day as armored columns overran exposed units of the 36th Infantry Division, made up largely of inexperienced soldiers from the Texas National Guard. One battalion lost more than 500 men captured or killed in a matter of hours. Those who withstood frontal and flank attacks had to watch their rear as they pulled back. "Tonight, you're not fighting for your country," one officer told his men bluntly as Germans enveloped them, "you're fighting for your ass."

Heavy artillery fire halted the panzers that evening, but Clark feared that they would soon renew their advance along the Sele and reach the sea, driving a wedge through his forces with dire results. He asked Admiral Hewitt to prepare to remove troops from the threatened American sector and ferry them northward to the British sector. But Hewitt—who had a new German threat to contend with in the form of radio-guided glide bombs that badly damaged several warships—worried that using landing craft to extract troops would prove disastrous and was relieved when other measures eased the pressure on Clark. On the night of September 13, Maj. Gen. Matthew Ridgway, commander of the 82nd Airborne, sent in a battalion of 1,300 paratroopers, who landed safely among the American soldiers, offering them hope that more help would soon be on the way. Morale improved further the next day when the Allies renewed

ITALIAN MAINLAND CAMPAIGN
SEPTEMBER 3, 1943–MAY 2, 1945

ALLIED ADVANCES
- - - ▸ British Eighth Army
——▸ U.S. Fifth Army
Sept. 9, 1943 Date Allies controlled city

GERMAN DEFENSIVE LINES
xxxxxxx Gothic Line
▭▭▭ Gustav Line

MILAN
Brescia April 28, 1945
April 29, 1945 Padua
Verona April 26, 1945
VENICE April 28, 1945
Turin
Parma April 24, 1945
Bologna April 21, 1945
Ferrara April 23, 1945
Genoa April 27, 1945
La Spezia April 23, 1945
Pisa July 23, 1944
Florence
Monaco
Ligurian Sea
Sept. 21, 1944 Rimini
San Marino Sept. 19, 1944
Ancona July 18, 1944
Aug. 4, 1944
Arezzo July 16, 1944
June 14, 1944 Orvieto
June 16, 1944 Spoleto
Elba June 18, 1944
CORSICA (France) Late Sept. 1943
ITALY
Ortona Dec. 28, 1943
Civitavecchia June 7, 1944
Termoli Oct. 6, 1943
ROME June 5, 1944
Foggia Sept. 27, 1943
May 23, 1944 Anzio
Cassino May 18, 1944
Campobasso
U.S. Sixth Corps Jan. 22, 1944
Bari
Oct. 1, 1943
Avellino Sept. 28, 1943
NAPLES
Acerno
Sept. 18, 1943 Salerno
Brindisi
Taranto Sept. 9, 1943
SARDINIA (Italy) Late Sept. 1943
Gulf of Salerno
Sapri
Castrovillari Sept. 12, 1943
Gulf of Taranto
Belvedere Marittimo
From Oran
Palermo
Messina
Bagnara
Reggio di Calabria Sept. 3, 1943
SICILY
Strait of Messina
Ionian Sea
Bizerte
Tunis
MEDITERRANEAN SEA
TUNISIA
From Tripoli

0 mi   100   200
0 km 100 200

The land invasion of Italy was long and costly. Montgomery's British forces crossed the Strait of Messina while the U.S. Fifth Army, which included some British forces, landed at Salerno. The two armies proceeded up opposite coasts, confronting Germany's entrenched defensive lines.

the naval bombardment and air strikes that had helped push back the enemy several days earlier and would do so again now. On September 18, the Germans began withdrawing from Salerno before Montgomery's army could arrive from the south and place them in an even worse bind.

No U.S. troops who fought at Salerno fared better against their tough foes than Lt. Col. William Darby's Rangers. Trained rigorously by British commandos, they seized the Chiunzi Pass, on the Allied left flank, on the first day of the battle and held it tenaciously. "We'll stay here until hell freezes over if necessary," Darby vowed. In late September, the Germans abandoned attempts to reclaim that pass, and the Allies proceeded northward to Naples. Entering that city on

"We'll stay here until hell freezes over if necessary."
Lt. Col. William Darby at Chiunzi Pass

October 1, Clark found windows shuttered and the streets empty. Some Neapolitans came out later to cheer the troops, but many were left speechless by the damage done to their city after Italy surrendered and the Germans became their enemies. Some of the actions taken by German occupiers before they abandoned Naples could be justified on military grounds—such as wrecking railroads and port facilities to deny them to Allied forces—but other measures served mainly to punish the populace, including destroying the water and sewage systems in Naples and torching libraries filled with rare books and manuscripts. (Elsewhere, Germans looted public and private art collections and hauled their treasures away.) Hundreds of structures in Naples were demolished to block streets, and bombs were placed in public buildings and timed to detonate after the Germans departed. One blast shattered the city's main post office on October 7, killing or wounding scores of civilians and soldiers. "The first two floors were blown completely away," said one witness. "Chunks of steel and marble were thrown as far as 100 yards."

The devastation in Naples was part of a larger German campaign to make Italy and its people pay dearly for abandoning the Axis. More than a million Italian troops were detained by German authorities. Most refused to fight for the Germans and were classified as military internees rather than prisoners of war, thus denying them any rights under the Geneva Convention. Nearly 700,000 of those internees ended up as slave laborers in German camps, along with millions of other captives, many of them civilians seized in eastern European countries. Other victims of the German occupation included Italian Jews, who had not been rounded up under Mussolini but were now at risk of being seized by Nazi agents and sent to concentration camps. Nearly 10,000 Italian Jews suffered that fate, but many more were harbored by

German soldiers display a painting taken from the Uffizi Gallery in Florence, Italy. The Germans looted more than 800 paintings and sculptures from Italian collections.

sympathetic neighbors, priests, and officials who risked their own lives to save them.

The Allied war effort brought misery and death to many civilians, including hundreds of thousands of people who perished in massive bombing raids on German and Japanese cities. But Allied commanders like Eisenhower firmly believed that they were engaged in a necessary struggle against an evil far greater than any harm done by their own forces. "We are told the American soldier does not know

> "We are told the American soldier does not know what he is fighting for. Now, at least, he will know what he is fighting *against*."
>
> Gen. Dwight Eisenhower, after Nazi war crimes came to light

what he is fighting for," Ike said late in the war when the full magnitude of Nazi war crimes came to light. "Now, at least, he will know what he is fighting *against.*"

TENSIONS AT TEHRAN

As 1943 drew to a close, the Allies had yet to draw up a master plan for winning the war in Europe. American and British forces were now cooperating closely in Italy, but the Soviets were waging their own bitter struggle against German invaders, who were falling back but remained in Soviet territory. President Roosevelt and Prime Minister Churchill were in constant communication, but the two did not confer jointly with Joseph Stalin until the Big Three, as they were known, met on November 30, 1943, in the Iranian capital of Tehran—a site chosen because Iran had sided with the Allies after being occupied by British and Soviet troops.

A vast gulf separated Stalin from the two Western leaders at that conference. He feared that they would postpone Operation

Overlord—allowing Hitler to throw more troops against the Soviets—and might even make a separate peace with Germany despite Roosevelt's declaration that the Allies would accept no terms other than unconditional surrender. Roosevelt and Churchill were concerned that if the Soviets pushed the Germans back to Berlin and occupied Poland and other countries, Stalin would make a mockery of their stated purpose, which was to defeat totalitarianism and defend democracy. As Roosevelt declared before the United States entered the conflict, America's goal was to help build "a world founded upon four essential freedoms": freedom of speech, freedom of worship, freedom from want, and freedom from fear. Nothing in Stalin's past suggested that he would promote or preserve those freedoms in any country under his control.

The simmering tensions boiled over at dinner on the second night of the conference. Stalin taunted Churchill by suggesting that his reluctance to launch Overlord stemmed from his "secret affection" for Germany. Churchill let that pass but was appalled when Stalin declared that when the war ended, "at least 50,000 and perhaps 100,000 German commanders must be physically liquidated."

Churchill knew for a fact that Soviet agents had executed 10,000 Polish officers and buried them in a mass grave after Stalin and Hitler carved up that country as part of their short-lived Nonaggression Pact in 1939. "The British Parliament and public," Churchill told Stalin, "will never tolerate mass executions." Stalin reiterated that 50,000 German officers must be shot, to which Churchill replied: "I would rather be taken out into the garden here and be shot myself than sully my own and my country's honor by such infamy." Unlike the outspoken Churchill, Roosevelt often disguised his true thoughts and feelings behind a mask of geniality. He chose to treat Stalin's threat as a joke and remarked that perhaps they could compromise by shooting only 49,000 officers. But others at the dinner shared Churchill's impression that Stalin was in earnest. Churchill knew of secret American efforts to develop an atomic bomb and came away from his confrontation with Stalin fearing the consequences if this conflict did not end hostilities between the world's great powers. "There might be a more bloody war," he told his physician that night. "I believe man might destroy man and wipe out civilization."

"I believe man might destroy man and wipe out civilization."

Winston Churchill at Tehran

The one bond holding the Big Three together was their mutual determination to defeat Hitler. Before leaving Tehran, they agreed that Operation Overlord would be conducted in spring 1944. "Who will command Overlord?" Stalin asked. "Nothing will come out of the operation unless one man is made responsible." The decision lay with Roosevelt because the United States would commit most of the troops and supplies needed to liberate France and invade Germany. He put Stalin off and left Tehran undecided as to who would be supreme commander of that supreme effort. The leading candidate was U.S. Army Chief of Staff George Marshall. Roosevelt did not want to part with Marshall, a highly respected figure in Washington with great influence in Congress. At the same time, he thought that Marshall deserved the chance to win fame as a commander abroad. As Roosevelt said to Eisenhower when he stopped to visit him on his way to Tehran: "Ike, you and I know who was the chief of staff during the last years of the Civil War, but practically no one else knows." Roosevelt was referring to Henry Halleck, who oversaw the Union Army in

Washington while Ulysses Grant and William Sherman won lasting glory in the field. Roosevelt did not want his Army chief to end up like Halleck: "I hate to think that 50 years from now practically nobody will know who George Marshall was."

The president shared those thoughts with Eisenhower because he would be called on to serve as acting chief in Washington if Marshall became supreme commander in Britain. Marshall, who had raised Ike to prominence and knew that his command experience in the Mediterranean qualified him to take charge of Overlord, scrupulously declined to campaign for that prestigious appointment. He told Roosevelt that "the issue was too great for any personal feelings to be considered" and that he would honor the president's decision. Roosevelt chose Eisenhower to be supreme commander, in part because he was more acceptable and more attuned to the British than Marshall was, but also because he valued his chief so highly. "I feel I could not sleep at night with you out of the country," Roosevelt told him. As it turned out, Marshall would long be remembered, not just for all he did in Washington to win the war but for his inspired Marshall Plan, which helped rebuild postwar Europe.

HARD ROAD TO ROME

Eisenhower's departure from the Mediterranean in December did not bode well for Allied operations there. Joining him soon in Britain to prepare for Overlord would be other accomplished commanders—including Patton, Bradley, and Montgomery—as well as seven Allied divisions, which left Italy at a time when the Germans were being reinforced and strengthening their defenses. Since pulling back from Salerno in September, Field Marshal

Kesselring had formed a forbidding barrier, known as the Winter Line, that snaked across the mountainous Italian peninsula north of Naples and barred the way to Rome. "Don't worry," said General Clark, who remained in Italy as commander of the Fifth Army, "I'll get through the Winter Line all right, and push the Germans out." But smashing that line would make the battle at Salerno seem like a skirmish by comparison.

> "Don't worry, I'll get through the Winter Line all right, and push the Germans out."
>
> Lt. Gen. Mark Clark, commander of the U.S. Fifth Army

Depleted by the demands of Overlord, Clark and his British superiors—General Alexander and Field Marshal Henry Maitland Wilson, Ike's successor in the Mediterranean—needed all the help they could get. Help soon arrived from various forces that joined the Allies in a broad coalition known as the United Nations (today's UN was not founded until war's end). The first non-American unit attached to the Fifth Army was the British X Corps, which landed with Clark's forces at Salerno in September 1943 and fought alongside the Americans that winter at Cassino. In spring 1944, the X Corps was relieved by the French Expeditionary Corps, consisting of Algerians, Moroccans, Tunisians, and French North Africans who cast their lot with the Allies when the Vichy regime collapsed. Led by Gen. Alphonse-Pierre Juin, an Algerian-born French patriot, they were adept at mountain warfare and accompanied by tribesmen called Goumiers who relished close combat with knife in hand. When the French Expeditionary Corps broke through the enemy line in May 1944, General Clark reported that "knife-wielding Goumiers swarmed over the hills . . . and General Juin's entire force showed an aggressiveness hour after hour that the Germans could not withstand." In summer 1944, Clark was reinforced by the Sixth South African Armored

Division. Later that year, his forces were joined by men of the Brazilian Expeditionary Force, including three regimental combat teams and artillery.

The British Eighth Army, now commanded by Gen. Oliver Leese, had long been a multicultural force, whose recruits included Rajputs from India, Gurkhas from Nepal, and Maori from New Zealand, and—in early 1945—the Jewish Brigade, consisting of more than 5,000 Jewish volunteers recruited in Palestine. Joining them for the punishing assault on the Winter Line were Canadians, South Africans, and more than 50,000 Polish troops. The Poles' leader, Lt. Gen. Wladyslaw Anders, had been captured when the Soviet Union invaded eastern Poland in 1939 and detained for more than a year in Moscow's dreaded Lubyanka Prison before being released to fight the Germans, whom Anders hated for devastating his homeland even more than he did the Soviets. "We never take prisoners," said one officer in Anders's Polish Corps of their German foes. "After all, they started it."

U.S. forces fighting in the Mediterranean were ethnically diverse as well, though segregated. They included Hispanics in the 36th Infantry Division, several of whom were cited for bravery at Salerno, and Native Americans from several western tribes in the 45th Infantry Division, known as the Thunderbirds. The 442nd Infantry Regiment, made up of Japanese Americans, would enter combat in Italy in summer 1944, as would the African-American 92nd Infantry Division. African-American troops of the Second Cavalry Division had arrived earlier in North Africa but were relegated to noncombat duty, as were many other black units in an Army that remained riddled with racial prejudice.

*Lt. Gen. Mark Wayne Clark inspects Japanese-American soldiers
of the 442nd Infantry Regiment in northern Italy in 1944. The 442nd was composed of Nisei (Japanese Americans born in the United States), who proved their
loyalty by fighting with distinction in Italy, southern France, and Germany.*

Among the African Americans who defied doubters and proved
themselves in battle were the Tuskegee Airmen of the 99th Fighter
Squadron, who trained at the Tuskegee Institute in Alabama and
flew missions in Sicily and Italy with the 15th Army Air Force.
Their commander, Lt. Col. Benjamin Davis, had endured more
than the usual hazing at West Point. During his four years at the
academy, white classmates refused to speak to him. He and his
fellow airmen were at first given little opportunity to test their
skills against enemy pilots by commanders, one of whom stated
that the "negro type has not the proper reflexes to make a first-
class fighter pilot." When Lt. Gen. Ira Eaker took charge of Allied
air forces in the Mediterranean in late 1943, however, he overruled
such objections. Thrown into the thick of the fighting over central

Italy in January 1944, the 99th Fighter Squadron downed more than a dozen German warplanes in two days.

Airpower was crucial to Allied success in the Mediterranean and in Europe at large. From bases in southern Italy, bombers struck targets vital to the German war effort, including heavily defended oil refineries at Ploesti, Romania, which were blasted repeatedly in raids that cost the lives of thousands of airmen but reduced the flow of oil to German factories and armed forces substantially. When crews learned in the briefing room that Ploesti was their target, one bomber pilot in the 15th Air Force recalled, they reacted with "half-stifled groans" and shifted in their seats "as if to move out of harm's way . . . The man beside me leaned forward and muttered, 'Oh, Christ, here we go.'" Ploesti missions were so perilous that each one counted as two in the number required for airmen to complete their tour of duty until mid-1944. By then, the German fighter squadrons defending the refineries had been degraded, but airmen continued to suffer heavy losses to antiaircraft batteries at Ploesti and challenged the presumption at headquarters that the mission was now less hazardous. After one costly raid, members of the 449th Bomber Group invited their general "to visit Ploesti on our next mission—single sortie! No flak vest will be issued."

Allied fighters and bombers also flew numerous missions against enemy bases and supply lines in Italy. Close air support of ground troops attacking the Winter Line was hampered by bad weather, however, and often failed to dislodge entrenched German defenders. Before leaving Italy to join Eisenhower in Britain, Montgomery expressed skepticism about trying to overcome those stout enemy defenses in a season when frequent storms reduced roads to mud and flooded rivers. "I do not think we can

LT. CLARENCE "LUCKY" LESTER
A TUSKEGEE AIRMAN OVER ITALY

*Clarence Lester was among the Tuskegee Airmen
in the 99th Fighter Squadron, 332nd Fighter Group,
15th Air Force. On July 18, 1944, he downed three German
fighters within six minutes over Italy. He earned the
nickname Lucky, as he put it, "because of all the tight
situations from which I had escaped without a scratch or even
a bullet hole in my aircraft."*

We were flying a loose combat formation, 200 feet apart and zigzagging. The flight leader commanded "hard right turn and punch tanks" [drop the external fuel tanks] . . . I saw a formation of Messerschmitt Bf 109s straight ahead, but slightly lower; I closed to about 200 feet and started to fire. Smoke began to pour out of the 109 and the aircraft exploded. I was going so fast I was sure I would hit some of the debris from the explosion, but luckily I didn't.

As I was dodging pieces of aircraft, I saw another 109 to my right, all alone on a heading 90 degrees to mine, but at the same altitude. I turned onto his tail and closed to about 200 feet while firing. His aircraft started to smoke and almost stopped. My closure was so fast I began to overtake him. When I overran him, I looked down to see the

> "I looked down to see the enemy pilot emerge from his burning aircraft. I remember seeing his blonde hair as he bailed out at approximately 8,000 feet."

Trained at the Tuskegee Institute, Lt. Clarence Lester (far right) and fellow pilots of the 99th Fighter Squadron pose in August 1944 beside one of their P-51 Mustang fighters. African-American pilots were barred from flying in the military before 1940, and underwent continued adversity in the war despite ongoing acts of bravery.

enemy pilot emerge from his burning aircraft. I remember seeing his blonde hair as he bailed out at approximately 8,000 feet.

By this time I was alone and looking for my flight mates when I spotted the third 109 flying very low, about 1,000 feet off the ground. I dove to the right behind him and opened fire. As I scored hits, he apparently thought he had enough altitude to use a "split S" maneuver [a half loop where the aircraft rolls upside down and pulls through until it becomes right side up] to evade me. As I did a diving turn, I saw the 109 go straight into the ground. ∎

conduct a winter campaign in this country," he wrote. "If I remember, Caesar used to go into winter quarters—a very sound thing to do!" But this was a war without letup, and those left in charge of the Italian campaign had little choice but to continue seeking ways of puncturing the Winter Line. It was a grueling process of trial and error, and the errors were costly. By January 1944, Allied planners had concluded that an amphibious landing at Anzio, on Italy's west coast north of the Winter Line, might succeed in unhinging German defenses and lead to the capture of Rome. Churchill strongly favored that option and managed to secure enough landing craft—most of which were being diverted to Britain for Overlord—to bring at least two divisions ashore at Anzio in late January. That would be a smaller force than landed at Salerno, and it would be at considerable risk unless Allied troops put renewed pressure on the Winter Line and kept Germans there from being diverted to Anzio. In mid-January, French, British, and American forces attacked the heart of the Winter Line, around the town of Cassino, where the main highway to Rome crossed the rain-swollen Rapido River. The French advanced north of town near the ancient Benedictine monastery of Monte Cassino but made little progress in that mountainous terrain. The British fared better initially to the south but bogged down at the Garigliano River, into which the Rapido flowed.

That left the Americans, assigned to cross the Rapido River between the British and French, in a bind. Their task would have been difficult even had their allies on either flank succeeded, but it was all but impossible now. Clark nevertheless decided that he "must make this attack, fully expecting heavy losses," and sent the 36th Infantry Division into battle on January 21. "We had the feeling we were being sacrificed," said Sgt. Billy Kirby, "but we'd give it our damnedest." Even hardened veterans of Salerno had never seen anything as desperate as this fight. Germans firing from the rubble of the bombed-out town of Sant'An-gelo on the far bank gunned down many of them as they

"We had the feeling we were being sacrificed, but we'd give it our damnedest."

Sgt. Billy Kirby

struggled across a mine-strewn bog to reach the Rapido. Others perished in the river when the rubber rafts or wooden boats they launched were blown apart. Kirby was among the remnant that made it across the Rapido before he too fell wounded. "Just about everyone was hit," he recalled. "I didn't have a single good friend in the company who wasn't killed or wounded." Some men in the 36th never forgave Clark for ordering the futile attack, but commanders caught up in this grinding war of attrition often felt compelled to demand such sacrifices with little assurance of success.

More trials and errors lay ahead for the Allies, who proceeded with the landing at Anzio despite their setbacks at the Winter Line. The troops who came ashore there on January 22 achieved almost complete surprise and met with little opposition initially. Their commander, Maj. Gen. John Lucas, had orders to advance inland and cut roads linking the Winter Line to Rome, which was only about 30 miles from Anzio. But Lucas hesitated to break out of the beachhead until he had all his men and equipment ashore. Clark had warned him not to stick his neck out, and he heeded that advice by refusing to be rushed by higher-ups like Churchill who hoped for a daring stroke that would end the stalemate in Italy. "I will not be stampeded," Lucas vowed. By the time he was ready to advance at month's end, Kesselring had him hemmed in. Clark sent reinforcements, but the

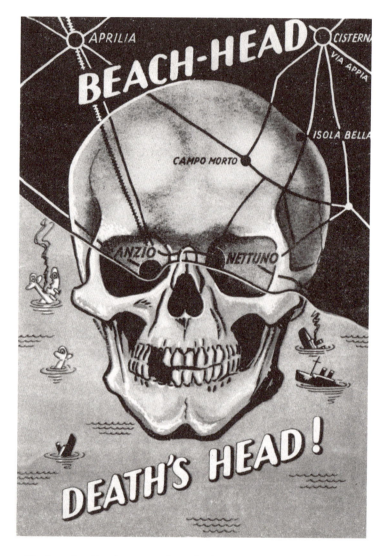

The Anzio beachhead is portrayed as a death trap in this German propaganda leaflet, air-dropped to Allied troops to break their morale.

Germans remained stronger and launched a furious assault in mid-February led by hulking Tigers, the largest tanks in their arsenal. The hard-pressed 45th Infantry Division was nearly driven back into the sea, but Lucas withstood the attack with help from the dynamic Maj. Gen. Lucian Truscott, who then took his place. Lucas had long expected to be treated as a sacrificial lamb. They would put him ashore "with inadequate forces," he predicted before the operation began, then saddle him with the blame. Kesselring agreed that Anzio as conceived was a weak "halfway measure."

Allied commanders miscalculated again in March when they launched another assault at Cassino, preceded by bombing raids that shattered the historic mountaintop monastery, killing scores of monks and civilians sheltered there. Contrary to Allied suspicions, the Germans were not using Monte Cassino as an observation or command post, but they occupied the ruins soon after the bombing ceased and found them better suited for defensive purposes than intact buildings. Troops from New Zealand and India launched determined attacks on the defenders but were unable to oust them from the rubble of the ruined monastery or the battered town of Cassino. "Almost every building or stump of a building contained a sniper's or a machine gunner's post," stated the New Zealanders' battle report. When the fighting ended in late March, the Allies were no closer to their goal, and Cassino had earned the title "Little Stalingrad."

The costly struggles of international forces who battered the Winter Line without breaking it were not entirely in vain. German casualties were steep, and defenders who escaped injury were worn down by persistent air and ground assaults. Allied commanders learned from their mistakes and stopped fixating on Cassino. In May, they attacked on a broad front, seeking out the enemy's weak spots, one of which proved to be well south of Cassino where North African troops threaded steep mountain passes and outflanked the Germans. Other breakthroughs followed as the line buckled. The final blow was delivered by Polish troops who took Cassino at a cost of 4,000 casualties and buried their dead on a hill overlooking the ruined town. In an inscription addressed to the people of Italy, they honored their fallen Polish comrades, who died "for our freedom and yours."

In late May, Truscott's troops broke out of the Anzio beachhead and linked up with others in Clark's Fifth Army who had breached the Winter Line. Truscott had a chance to cut off large numbers of German troops before they escaped northward to take up new defensive positions, but Clark was intent on taking Rome before the British got there and circumvented orders from his British superior, Alexander, by diverting most of Truscott's forces to that city. As Clark put it, he wanted people back home to know that it was his American-led Fifth Army that "did the job," when in

British and South African troops show off a Nazi flag captured at Cassino as bulldozers clear a path through the rubble of the bombed-out town in May 1944, shortly after German troops retreated.

fact the British-led Eighth Army had contributed significantly to this hard-won victory.

Critics charged that Clark neglected his duty to pursue the enemy and instead pursued fame in Rome. If so, his triumph was appropriately short-lived. His entry into the Eternal City on June 5, 1944, was overshadowed in less than 24 hours by a greater sensation: the Allied landings in Normandy on June 6. "How do you like that?" Clark said when he heard the news. "They didn't even let us have the newspaper headlines for the fall of Rome for one day."

Howard Brodie, an enlisted artist for the new Army magazine
Yank, *sketched men of the 25th "Tropic Lightning" Division*
fighting on Guadalcanal.

CHRONOLOGY

AUGUST 7, 1942 U.S. Marines land on Guadalcanal, launching American ground campaign against Japanese forces in the Pacific.

SEPTEMBER 1942 Gen. Douglas MacArthur sends U.S. troops to Papua New Guinea to join Australians fighting the Japanese there.

JANUARY 1943 American forces secure Guadalcanal and Buna in Papua New Guinea.

NOVEMBER 20, 1943 American forces land on Makin and Tarawa Atolls in the Gilbert Islands.

★ ★ ★ ★ ★   CHAPTER 6   ★ ★ ★ ★ ★

ISLAND FIGHTING

GUADALCANAL TO THE INVASION OF SAIPAN

While U.S. troops and their allies were advancing on the historic city of Rome, others were fighting on obscure islands in the Pacific that few Americans had heard of before the conflict began. Officially, President Roosevelt gave the war against Germany priority over that remote struggle against Japan. But unlike Hitler, Roosevelt did not dictate to his commanders. His stated policy of "Europe First" did not prevent the U.S. Navy or Army from launching counteroffensives to halt menacing Japanese advances in the Pacific before Americans entered battle across the Atlantic. Gen. Douglas MacArthur, after escaping from the Philippines in March 1942 and taking charge of Allied forces in Australia, insisted that the best way to shield that country from invasion was to oust Japanese troops from nearby New Guinea, which he hoped to use as a stepping-stone to reclaim the Philippines. "We

JUNE 14, 1944 U.S. Marines land on Saipan in the Mariana Islands.

AUGUST 3, 1944 Allied troops led by Lt. Gen. Joseph Stilwell defeat Japanese forces in Burma at Myitkyina.

JUNE 19-20, 1944 Battle of the Philippine Sea

must attack, attack, attack!" MacArthur declared. In Washington, meanwhile, Adm. Ernest King, chief of the U.S. Navy and Marine Corps, was pressing for swift retaliation against Japan.

The Pacific Fleet's stunning victory at the Battle of Midway in June set the stage for the first American ground assault on Axis troops, launched in August 1942 against the Japanese on Guadalcanal, situated east of New Guinea near the southern tip of the Solomon Islands. Although Guadalcanal lay farther from Australia than New Guinea, it offered the Japanese a platform for air strikes on Australia's maritime supply lines. For troops engaged on Guadalcanal and other Pacific islands in months to come, and for many Americans following their strenuous campaigns back home, beating Japan was the nation's first order of business. In fact, not until mid-1944 would there be more Americans fighting in Europe than in the Pacific.

The American assault on Guadalcanal was launched from New Zealand, situated 2,000 miles from Japanese-occupied territory and at less risk of attack than Australia. The First Marine Division, led by Maj. Gen. Alexander Vandegrift, began arriving there in late June 1942 and was supposed to undergo at least a half year of training before entering combat. That same month, however, Martin Clemens, a British resident on Guadalcanal who served as a coastwatcher—assigned to spy on enemy movements for the Allies—reported by radio that the Japanese were building an airfield there. It was May 18, 1942, when Clemens, who served as district commissioner for the British Solomon Islands Protectorate, left his post at the village of Aola on the north coast of Guadalcanal and traveled to the tree-covered high ground near Lunga Point. He had received radio reports that a Japanese naval task force was on its way to the southern Solomons. From his vantage point, Clemens watched troops of Japan's elite Special Naval Landing Force come ashore on the nearby islands of Tulagi and Gavutu-Tanambogo.

Clemens's interest in the Japanese operation was not simply that of a civilian official. The 27-year-old Scotsman was a volunteer in the British Solomon Islands Protectorate Defense Force and held a reserve commission as a lieutenant in the Royal Australian Navy. His primary wartime duty was to act as part of a far-flung network of coastwatchers, who remained behind Japanese lines to spy for the Allies in the southwest Pacific. If apprehended by the Japanese, he and others conducting such surveillance were subject to execution.

Coastwatcher Martin Clemens (center) stands with scouts of the British Solomon Islands Protectorate Defense Force who helped him spy on the Japanese on Guadalcanal, including Andrew Langabaea and Daniel Pule (standing, left and right), and Olorere, Gumu, Chaparuka, and Chaku (seated, left to right).

Recruited from among colonial officials, planters, and missionaries, the coastwatchers were organized into a network of field stations by Lt. Cmdr. Eric Feldt of the Royal Australian Navy. By mid-1941, Feldt had established 64 coastwatcher stations, equipped with radio sets capable of both Morse code and voice communications. By 1942, Feldt's network numbered around 800 agents across an area of more than 500,000 square miles. Coastwatchers like Clemens on Guadalcanal were supported by scouts native to the area, including men of the police or local defense forces who blended in with the populace and attracted little attention as they monitored Japanese movements.

Clemens promptly reported the arrival of the Japanese expedition on Guadalcanal, relaying his message through a chain of stations in the northern Solomon Islands and Papua New Guinea to Allied intelligence officers in Australia. Clemens and his scouts established an observation post above Lunga Point to observe enemy warships and watch activity at the new Imperial Japanese Navy seaplane base on Tulagi. On July 1, 1942, he sent a report that the Japanese had begun work on an airstrip at Lunga Point. As enemy activity increased, Clemens withdrew deeper into the jungle to avoid detection. The Japanese soon became aware that a clandestine radio was operating on the island, and Clemens had to move frequently, shifting his bulky radio and batteries. No longer able to observe progress on the airstrip, Clemens sent scouts to join the labor force there and report back to him.

The urgent task of seizing the Japanese airstrip before it became operational fell to Vandegrift and his Marines. "I didn't even know the location of Guadalcanal," he recalled. "I knew only that my division was spread over hell's half acre, one-third in Samoa, one-third in New Zealand, and one-third still at sea." Vandegrift had less than five weeks to assemble his division of nearly 20,000 men and prepare for the mission. Their training consisted of brief landing exercises, which he described as "a complete bust."

The Marines who approached the Solomons in early August, like many later assault forces in the Pacific, found such tropical islands seductive from afar and sickening up close. Guadalcanal "was beautiful when seen from the sea," recalled Pvt. Robert Leckie, who landed there with Vandegrift's division and later chronicled the campaign. "She was beautiful, but beneath her loveliness, within the necklace of sand and palm, under the coiffure of her sun-kissed treetops with its tiara of jeweled birds, she was a mass of slops and stinks and pestilence; of scum-crested lagoons and vile swamps inhabited by giant crocodiles; a place of spiders as big as your fist and wasps as long as your finger . . . She was sour with the odor of her own decay, her breath so hot and humid, so sullen and so still, that all those Marines who came to her shores on the morning of August 7 cursed and swore to feel the vitality oozing from them in a steady stream of enervating sweat."

> "[A]ll those Marines who came to her shores on the morning of August 7 cursed and swore to feel the vitality oozing from them in a steady stream of enervating sweat."
>
> Pvt. Robert Leckie, on the landing at Guadalcanal

At first, Vandegrift's men met with little opposition on Guadalcanal. Japanese construction crews abandoned the half-finished airstrip there to the Marines, who dubbed it Henderson Field for a pilot who had died in action at Midway. Most of the fighting occurred initially on Tulagi, a small island north of Guadalcanal where some 2,000 Japanese troops were stationed. "Enemy force overwhelming," their commander reported that morning. "We will defend our posts to the death." They did just that. In three days of savage combat, not one Japanese soldier surrendered willingly, and only two dozen were captured alive. The rest perished, many of them in desperate attacks that left scores of Marines dead.

Taking Tulagi and Henderson Field offered small comfort to Vandegrift, who faced mounting opposition at sea and in the air. Before dawn on August 9, Japanese warships surprised an Allied task force between Guadalcanal and nearby Savo Island and sank four cruisers, killing more than a thousand sailors. That same day, Vice Adm. Frank Fletcher, a veteran of Midway, withdrew the three aircraft carriers shielding the landing forces. Those were the Navy's most precious assets, and Fletcher and his commander in the South Pacific, Vice Adm. Robert Ghormley, were unwilling to risk them at Guadalcanal any longer. Without close support from the carriers and their warplanes, vulnerable transports also had to be withdrawn, taking with them nearly 1,400 Marines, heavy artillery and equipment, and other essential supplies on ships that had not yet been unloaded. "God only knew when we could expect aircraft protection," remarked Vandegrift, who told his officers to break the bad news to their men but assure them that there would be no repetition on Guadalcanal of the recent disaster at Bataan. Since the birth of their corps in 1775, "Marines had found themselves in tough spots," Vandegrift said. "They had survived and we would survive—but only if every officer and man gave his all to the cause."

The Navy did not abandon the Marines on Guadalcanal. Cruisers, destroyers, and PT boats continued to patrol the waters offshore—known as Iron Bottom Sound for the many vessels sunk there as the campaign intensified—and the carriers remained out at sea, where they were less exposed to attack but close enough to launch air raids on enemy warships around the Solomons. Japanese skippers were adept at evading detection at night, however, and brought troops in under cover of darkness so swiftly and successfully that their sorties became known as the Tokyo Express.

Fortunately for Vandegrift and his men, their foes underestimated their strength and determination. Many Japanese officers, in the wake of their dramatic advances in the Pacific, suffered from "victory disease" and assumed that pampered American soldiers were no match for their own dedicated warriors. According to a Japanese army training manual, "Westerners—being very haughty, effeminate and cowardly—intensely dislike fighting in the rain or mist or in the dark. They cannot conceive night to be a proper time for battle—though it is excellent for dancing. In these weaknesses lie our great opportunity."

> "Westerners—being very haughty, effeminate and cowardly—intensely dislike fighting in the rain or mist or in the dark."
>
> Japanese army training manual

When Col. Kiyano Ichiki landed on Guadalcanal with 900 troops in mid-August, he was overconfident and did not wait for reinforcements. On August 21, he launched a reckless nighttime assault near the Tenaru River and his troops were scythed down by artillery and machine-gun fire from Marines warned of their approach by coastwatchers. Ichiki committed suicide, and Vandegrift wiped out lingering resistance by sending in tanks, which crushed men under their tracks. "The rear of the tanks looked like meat grinders," he reported. The attack cost the Japanese "some 800 dead with only a handful escaping to the jungle," Vandegrift added. "Our own casualties came to 100 with 43 dead."

*Corpses of Japanese soldiers lie half-buried in the sand near the mouth of the
Tenaru River after the disastrous assault by Col. Kiyano Ichiki's forces.*

By late August, Henderson Field had been completed by a naval
construction battalion—designated CB and staffed by hardwork-
ing men known as Seabees. That allowed fighters and bombers
to land on Guadalcanal and strengthened Vandegrift's position.
But there was no respite for the Seabees who maintained the
runway or the Marines who defended the field, which was subject
to repeated air and ground attacks as the Tokyo Express funneled
more Japanese troops and artillery to Guadalcanal. On the night
of September 12, a fierce battle erupted on Bloody Ridge, overlooking Henderson Field. Several thousand Japanese soldiers
attacked there, shouting in broken English: "U.S. Marines be
dead tomorrow!"

Lt. Col. Merritt Edson urged the commandos of his First
Marine Raider Battalion to stand fast. "There is only us between
the airfield and the Japs," he told them. "If we don't hold, we will

lose Guadalcanal." After being forced back to within a half mile of the airstrip, they repulsed the enemy at dawn with support from Col. William McKennan's battalion, whose machine gunners shredded the attackers. "When one wave was mowed down—and I mean mowed down—another followed it into death," McKennan recalled. Once again, the Japanese lost more than 10 men for every Marine they killed and gained no ground.

Unwilling to concede defeat, Japanese commanders committed still more naval power and some 20,000 additional troops to the long-running battle for Guadalcanal. Vandegrift received reinforcements as well, but Japanese warships menaced his supply lines and pounded Henderson Field mercilessly, rendering it almost useless for the few warplanes that survived the bombardment. "I can hold," Vandegrift told his superiors, "but I've got to have more active support than I've been getting."

At Pearl Harbor, Adm. Chester Nimitz concluded that his Pacific Fleet was losing the campaign and replaced the cautious Ghormley with the aggressive Vice Adm. Bull Halsey. "Jesus Christ and General Jackson!" Halsey exclaimed when he received his orders. "This is the hottest potato they ever handed me." Soon after he took command in the South Pacific in mid-October, the aircraft carrier U.S.S. *Hornet* went down off Santa Cruz Island, east of Guadalcanal, in a bruising battle that damaged another carrier, U.S.S. *Enterprise,* and knocked two Japanese flattops out of action. Undeterred, Halsey had the *Enterprise* hastily repaired and committed his only available carrier to what Admiral King later called "one of the most furious sea battles ever fought."

Casualties were steep on both sides in that pivotal Naval Battle of Guadalcanal. By the time the smoke cleared on November 15, the U.S. Navy had lost nine warships and more

Pfc. James A. Donahue
To Hell and Back: A Guadalcanal Journal

*In his journal, 21-year-old Private Donahue of the Second
Battalion, First Marine Regiment, described the Japanese frontal assault
on his entrenched position near the Tenaru River on August 21.*

*James Donahue—shown here in a 1945 photo, sitting at left with his wife Cass
and war buddy Art Dignan—kept the Pacific diary.*

It all started about 3 a.m. in the morning. However, we were warned about 11 o'clock to "Stand by your guns."... Was this going to be the real test? All of a sudden our listening posts reported troops moving toward us... The point was heavily fortified. I don't mean with big guns, but we had a platoon of machine gunners there and a 37mm gun crew... The Japs still came across and we kept knocking them off. Their machine guns would throw up a barrage for them but their field of fire was limited. They finally succeeded in getting a machine gun across, which was set up right below. Len Beer threw a hand grenade, which silenced it... The 37mm gun did plenty of damage with its canister shot. The Japs brought up their field pieces and started laying them into the line... soon our 105's silenced them. Japs were using rifle grenades and mortars. After about two hours, reinforcements came up. They sent two light machine guns, which were mounted between Bottles' and my position and Beer's and Dignan's. Within ten minutes the whole two crews were shot up, this due to the fact that they were not below the deck.

At this point, Sgt. Muth picked up a gun and started running down the line. He would stop, fire a few good bursts and then take off to a new position. J. moved up behind Murray, and I and he had a BAR [Browning automatic rifle]. He shouted if there was room for him in the foxhole. There wasn't, so we had to make room. He would be killed if he stayed on the deck. A machine gun had been mounted in an abandoned alligator [amphibious warfare vehicle] and they were throwing plenty of lead our way. J. crept as close as possible and made a dive for our hole. He landed okay and Murray and I continued our fire. About five minutes later, I said to Bottles, "Why the hell don't he fire?" Murray said

> "About five minutes later, I said to Bottles, 'Why the hell don't he fire?' Murray said slowly, 'He's dead.' I said, 'Are you sure?' And he said, 'Here is his blood; feel his pulse.'"

slowly, "He's dead." I said, "Are you sure?" And he said, "Here is his blood; feel his pulse." But we couldn't determine whether he was alive. We couldn't move an inch either, for the Japs were really spraying our lines. So I reached over and felt his pulse. His face was sunken and there was no pulse. The blood began to fill the hole, so we fixed a poncho so that the blood would stay on the other side. The next morning I saw that he had been hit in the head and chest.

While our artillery was finding the Japs' range, they landed three in our lines so close to us that we were covered with dirt … We thought that the next one would land square on top of us. Another Jap machine gun was set up on our side of the river. Bottles said, "Let's go down and get them." I said he was crazy. It was suicide to go down that bank. We had no grenades, so we called to Dignan to heave a pineapple [grenade]. He did and another crew was wiped out. ∎

than a thousand lives, but the Japanese toll was even steeper, including two battleships, a heavy cruiser, three destroyers, and no fewer than 10 troop transports, which went down with thousands of soldiers aboard. "We've got the bastards licked!" exulted Halsey. In the words of his opponent, Rear Adm. Raizo Tanaka, Japan's "last large-scale effort to reinforce Guadalcanal" had ended in failure.

The Navy had ended the struggle, but no one forgot who had done the early work that made the victory possible. Shortly after U.S. Marines landed on Guadalcanal, the gaunt, bearded coast-watcher Martin Clemens and his ragged band of scouts had entered the American camp carrying a British flag, and throughout the campaign, the team had continued to provide vital intelligence to General Vandegrift at First Marine Division headquarters. "We relied heavily on information brought to us by Martin and his charges," wrote Vandegrift, who credited them with providing the "margin of victory" in some instances. Admiral Halsey offered even higher praise. "The coastwatchers saved Guadalcanal," he stated, "and Guadalcanal saved the Pacific."

Halsey received a hero's welcome when he visited the Marines on Guadalcanal in the wake of the victory. The fighting was not over, but the flow of Japanese troops and supplies to the embattled island had been reduced to a trickle. The Marines loved their new leader's combative posture and his well-publicized contempt for the enemy, signaled by a sign Halsey erected at the naval base on Tulagi that proclaimed in large letters: "KILL JAPS. KILL JAPS. KILL MORE JAPS." He sometimes referred to Japanese soldiers as "monkeys," one of many disparaging terms that American fighting men in the Pacific applied to enemies they loathed as much as they did the dense jungle. Some soldiers claimed the body parts of dead Japanese soldiers as trophies. One of the men who fought at Guadalcanal recalled that when they overran a Japanese encampment there, they found "pictures of Marines that had been cut up and mutilated on Wake Island. The next thing you know there are Marines walking around with Jap ears stuck on their belts with safety pins . . . We began to get down to their level."

> "The next thing you know there are Marines walking around with Jap ears stuck on their belts with safety pins . . . We began to get down to their level."
>
> A Marine on Guadalcanal

The same war that dehumanized men and brought out the worst in them also inspired remarkable acts of courage and devotion. Battle-hardened officers like Lt. Col. Evans Carlson, commander of the Second Marine Raider Battalion, combined utter ruthlessness toward the enemy with selfless dedication to their fellow fighting men. "We never take a prisoner," Carlson said of the commandos he drilled in guerrilla warfare and led in perilous missions against the Japanese on Guadalcanal and elsewhere. "That's not our job. I tell my men to kill every Jap they meet—lame, halt, and well . . . They're too treacherous, for one thing. They killed most of our medical corpsmen who tried to help them, so we take no chances." At the same time, Carlson practiced and preached the heroic team spirit called "gung ho": a Chinese concept meaning "work in harmony" that he had witnessed in action while observing Mao Zedong's Communists in China in the 1930s. What he admired was not their ideology but their tireless dedication to their cause and their comrades. "He tried to make Chinese out of us," recalled one of Carlson's men. "He'd say that the Chinese could march 50 miles in a day on nothing but a handful of rice, so that's what we had at Guadalcanal." Traveling light and moving furtively through the jungle, Carlson's Raiders wiped out stubborn pockets of Japanese resistance on Guadalcanal in late 1942 and dispelled any lingering notion among their foes that Americans were too soft to succeed at the nasty business of jungle warfare.

Stereotypes of the Japanese held by American troops could be just as misleading. Not all Japanese soldiers felt compelled to die rather than surrender. One reason that so few yielded to the Americans is that neither side expected mercy if they surrendered. Some Japanese, including fleet commander Adm. Isoroku Yamamoto, saw nothing dishonorable in retreating to fight again another day and considered officers who sacrificed themselves and their men when faced with defeat foolhardy. By early 1943, the surviving Japanese troops on Guadalcanal were starving, and many were suffering from tropical diseases. Instead of abandoning them to their fate, Japanese sailors risked their own lives and rescued 13,000 emaciated soldiers from the island. As shown by such devotion to duty, the gung ho spirit was confined to no one nation or corps engaged in a struggle as heroic as it was horrific.

MACARTHUR STRIKES BACK

"We'll defend Australia in New Guinea," General MacArthur declared in August 1942 as the American campaign on Guadalcanal unfolded. At the time, Japanese troops in New Guinea were

"We'll defend Australia in New Guinea."
Gen. Douglas MacArthur

advancing on Port Moresby in the Australian-administered territory of Papua (now Papua New Guinea). It was one of the worst places on earth to wage war. Swollen rivers descended from the towering peaks of the Owen Stanley Range through dense jungle infested with pythons, crocodiles, leeches, and a maddening host of disease-bearing insects. Allied forces in Australia needed strengthening, and committing them to a counteroffensive in forbidding New Guinea was risky. "MacArthur without fear of criticism might have remained on the defensive until sufficient forces could be made available," remarked his air commander, Maj. Gen. George Kenney. "A lesser general might even have considered the abandonment of Port Moresby, his only base in New Guinea." Instead, MacArthur set out to drive enemy troops from New Guinea as the first step toward his goal of liberating the Philippines and defeating Japan.

Interservice rivalry lent some urgency to MacArthur's campaign. After much wrangling, the Joint Chiefs of Staff in Washington had narrowed his theater of operations in the southwest Pacific slightly and expanded that of the Navy and Marines to allow them to launch their offensive in the Solomons. MacArthur was eager to match them stride for stride to justify his repeated appeals for more troops and supplies. Adept at public relations, he used reporters to press his case that resources should be diverted from Admiral Nimitz's theater to bolster his own efforts and hasten victory over Japan. Such infighting could be counterproductive, but MacArthur's boss, Gen. George Marshall, and Navy chief Ernest King managed to reach an accommodation that kept competition between their services from undermining the war effort. Army troops relieved battle-weary Marines on Guadalcanal and joined in many later Pacific campaigns under Nimitz's jurisdiction. In return, Nimitz provided a fleet to support MacArthur, who required warships and transports for amphibious landings.

Although MacArthur seldom got along with anyone whose ego and reputation rivaled his own, he took a liking to the prominent

CAPTURED JAPANESE DIARY
THE FATE OF IMPERIAL SOLDIERS ON GUADALCANAL

This diary, found on the body of an unidentified noncommissioned officer of the 38th "Nagoya" Division on Guadalcanal, records the suffering of Japanese troops as the battle drew to a close.

25 December 1942 Today is Christmas, a very important day for the enemy. Artillery bombardment is a terrible thing. Again I became sick with malaria and my temperature began to rise, so I fell asleep in the trench. I prayed for a complete recovery, because this is the third time that I had this fever.

26 December 1942 Corporal Abe found some sweets on a dead enemy and divided them . . .

27 December 1942 I went with Corporal Abe to get some more meat, because it was so good yesterday. It was to be eaten by the company. It was buried in the company cemetery to keep it secret. However, maggots had started to develop in it.

1 January 1943 Gave 3 banzai for the Emperor and sang

Too weak to resist, a starving Japanese soldier is captured by American troops at a strongpoint on Mount Austen.

the national anthem. We toasted with whiskey. We are fortunate to drink whiskey on this island. A number of shells burst around the position at about 1400. It is surprising how many shells the enemy has.

5 January 1943 Sergeant Takeya is missing. It is not possible for an active NCO to desert.

12 January 1943 I ran out of ink, so I have to write in pencil from now on. I reconnoitered the enemy situation in front of the 3rd Battalion.

14 January 1943 Men are dying one after another, and now the company roster has 20 men, besides the company commander. The enemy keeps firing from distance, so we shall have to be careful of stray bullets. The enemy does not come close enough that we can kill them and get their rations. I am very hungry. I wonder if this is how it is when a man is starving. Rice cakes and candies appear in my dreams. I must train myself to suppress these desires.

16 January 1943 I heard one of the enemy talking busily in Japanese over a loud speaker. He was probably telling us to come out. What fools the enemy are! The Japanese Army will stick it out to the end. This position must be defended with our lives. There was no artillery shelling because of the broadcast . . . It will probably have no effect at all.

19 January 1943 Ant nests are good to eat when one is starving. I received some meat from battalion headquarters. My orderly is sick, so I had to cook it myself. Enemy artillery began to fire about 1100, and there was an enemy attack in front of the 8th Company about 1300. We fired on them with light machine gun, and I believe they got a surprise . . . I felt very dazed and only semi-conscious because of my empty stomach. At 1330, I prepared my equipment to put it in my haversack so that it can be packed on a moment's notice. It will be so heavy that I don't know whether I'll be able to carry it or not, because of my run-down condition . . . Only my spirit keeps me going. ∎

> "The enemy does not come close enough that we can kill them and get their rations. I am very hungry. I wonder if this is how it is when a man is starving."

Admiral Halsey and invited him to command his fleet. "If you come with me, I'll make you a greater man than Nelson ever dreamed of being," promised MacArthur, referring to Horatio Nelson. Halsey chose to remain as naval commander in the South Pacific under Nimitz, but he and MacArthur made a powerful tandem as their respective forces closed in on the big Japanese base at Rabaul, situated on the island of New Britain, between New Guinea and the Solomons.

MacArthur's offensive began inauspiciously in September 1942 when he sent raw American troops to reinforce the Australians who were defending Port Moresby. Many of those Aussies were battle tested and had succeeded in driving Japanese troops—who had landed at Buna on the east coast of Papua and crossed the rugged Owen Stanley Range—back toward Buna and nearby Gona, where the Japanese dug in and held fast. The Australians were assigned to take Gona, while soldiers of the U.S. 32nd Infantry Division stormed Buna—a daunting task for which they were ill prepared. Their corps commander, Lt. Gen. Robert Eichelberger, a former superintendent at West Point, wrote that they were "in no sense ready for jungle warfare" and were "not sufficiently trained to meet Japanese veterans on equal terms." Like other American soldiers rushed into combat in 1942, they would have to learn to fight in the line of fire.

Eichelberger remained with MacArthur in Australia to train the rest of the corps while Maj. Gen. Edwin Harding led the division into battle in New Guinea. One regiment flew to Port Moresby and trekked over the mountains toward Buna on a trail so narrow and tangled that men had to hack their way through the brush with machetes. Others had an easier trip, landing at an airfield closer to Buna, but the rainy season had begun and few soldiers were in that sweltering jungle for long before contracting dysentery, malaria, or other maladies. Attacking in mid-November, they made little progress amid hostile terrain and fierce Japanese resistance. "Everywhere men cursed, shouted, and screamed," reported one American lieutenant whose platoon reached the outskirts of Buna and tried to break through there. "Brave men led and others followed. Cowards crouched in the grass, frightened out of their skins." When the offensive stalled, MacArthur sent in Eichelberger with instructions that left no room for retreat: "Bob, I want you to take Buna, or not come back alive."

Eichelberger found the troops in disarray. "Their clothing was in rags," his inspectors reported. "They were receiving far less than adequate rations and there was little discipline or military courtesy." Units were badly jumbled, and some officers had lost touch with their men. Eichelberger called a halt to the fighting while he restored order and replenished the division's supplies. Morale improved when the men were well fed and well led. Honoring the age-old maxim that "a commander must be seen by his troops in combat," Eichelberger visited the front soon after the offensive resumed in December and urged on companies that were bogged down near Buna. Although officers there had taken to removing their insignia because it exposed them to sniper fire, he wrote, "I was glad on that particular day that there were three stars on my collar which glittered in the sun. How else would those sick and cast-down soldiers have known their commander was in there with them?"

Generals could inspire men by appearing up front, but the task of leading soldiers in battle fell largely to lowly sergeants and lieutenants, who often took even greater risks in combat than the

NEAL HOOK, U.S.
31ST INFANTRY DIVISION, U.S. ARMY
FRIENDLY FIRE . . . AND THE OTHER KIND

At the urging of his family, 90-year-old Neal Hook wrote a memoir of his military service, an account striking for its vivid details and frank honesty. What follows begins with his company's first deployment, just a few days after landing at Port Moresby in New Guinea.

Company B and our company were advancing in line and started firing at each other. One of our own guys was shot in the head and killed by a 30 caliber; the Japanese used 25 caliber, so it was one of our own. It was estimated 50% of our casualties in WW2 were caused by friendly fire. That included artillery, bombs, small arms fire, etc. This was just about correct according to our experiences. Our company formed a perimeter and dug in for the night. I was in the center area with two sergeants. The outer parameter [*sic*] started firing and kept it up most of the night. I wasn't scared, I was terrified. Tracers were going overhead often enough for us to know rising up or getting out of our foxhole would have gotten us killed. The two other

Neal Hook (right) poses with a buddy during basic training.

guys were as scared as I was. It is a helpless feeling, and from all the firing, we expected the Japanese to come leaping into our foxholes at any minute. A long night; next morning, not a sign of any Japanese. Heard a few other green troops firing their first nights like that. No substitute for experience, and after that night, firing usually meant something was going on . . .

Moved on to the Driniumor

River where we established a line on the riverbed for well over a month. Dug our regular foxholes for two or three guys; that night I woke up hearing terrible screaming. Thought my hair was standing up. A medic had dug a hole for himself, and a Jap had jumped in with a knife and killed him, slitting his throat. That helped us stay awake at night . . .

Sometimes it would rain so intensely we thought we were coming to a rushing river, but it was just rain moving towards us, splashing against the jungle vegetation. Our artillery shells began falling on the other side of the river. Thought that could be helpful if the Japanese attacked until it started towards us and behind us. A couple of our men were killed by the friendly artillery fire.

Our line along the river was going to be held for some time, so we built pillboxes. We dug a hole 2 or 3 feet deep and cut big logs with axes and machetes. It was a foot or so wide and solid on top and three sides, so we could sit up inside. The side facing the river was partially open for the field of fire. Lots of work building but well worth it for security. Even though we had this place, we regularly sent out troops for reconnaissance patrol. Our reconnaissance patrol heard the Japs chopping, and a few minutes later one of our BAR [Browning automatic rifle] men was shot and killed. Morton, our jeep driver when jeeps were useful, was also a machine gunner. He fired and made a huge cloud of smoke. Later the captain said "Morton, that gun should be fired in bursts." Morton answered, "I did, Captain, in bursts of a belt." 30 caliber air cooled guns would jam if fired continuously and not rested occasionally to cool. The battalion was camped in a large area and supplied with ammunition, food, etc. by C-47 planes. Occasionally, they missed our area, and the Japs got the supplies. They would fly in low, and the men would push out the items through the cargo door. Notice was given prior to the dropping—"take cover!!!" One guy left for cover too late, and a case of rations hit him in the back and killed him. ∎

troops they watched over. The first significant American break-through at Buna was achieved by Staff Sgt. Herman Bottcher, an exile from Germany who had fought against fascists during the Spanish Civil War before enlisting in the U.S. Army. On December 5, Bottcher led his platoon of fewer than 20 men through a gap in the enemy line above Buna and reached the beach, where they dug in and used their rifles and a single machine gun to repulse swarming attackers, inflicting on them more than 120 casualties. "With his hand on the hot machine gun, Bottcher was able to mow them down like wheat in a field," Eichelberger related. "For days after, the evidence of Sergeant Bottcher's victory rolled in and out with the tide . . . drifting bodies of Japanese soldiers." Wounded, Bottcher earned his first Distinguished Service Cross (DSC) in that battle. He won his second DSC two weeks later when he offered himself as a target to draw enemy fire away from his men and again fell wounded. The award that meant most to him, however, was U.S. citizen-ship, which he had been denied for fighting in Spain but was granted by an act of Congress several months before he died in action in the Philippines in late 1944.

By January 1943, American and Australian troops had crushed enemy resistance at Buna and Gona, where the victors found corpses piled high in Japanese bunkers. "Rotting bodies, some-times weeks old, formed part of the fortifications," a British correspondent reported. "The living fired over the bodies of the dead, slept side by side with them." Eichelberger's men uncovered the diaries of Japanese soldiers, which recorded their thoughts as their plight worsened and no help arrived. "Now we are waiting only for death," wrote one man. "The news that reinforcements had come turned out to be a rumor . . . Even the invincible

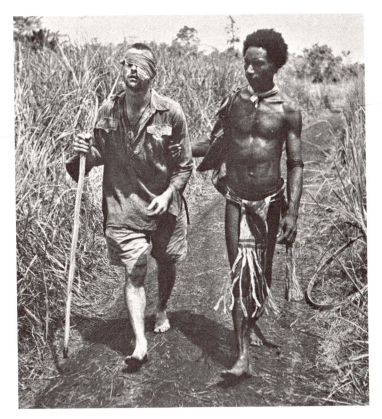

Australian soldiers were often aided and sheltered by compassionate islanders like the Papuan shown helping a blinded Australian infantryman along a road near the Buna-Gona battlefront.

Imperial Army is at a loss. Can't anything be done? Please, God." Spectacular early triumphs in the Pacific had tempted the Japanese to expand their conquests and threaten Australia. Now they were overextended and lacked the resources to cope with simultaneous Allied assaults on their bases in New Guinea and the Solomons.

Eichelberger knew better than to risk MacArthur's wrath by seeking renown for the victory at Buna. He turned down a request to be interviewed for a cover story in *Time,* but stories about him appeared in other magazines and earned him a scolding from his boss, who did not want anyone overshadowing him. "Do you realize I could reduce you to the grade of colonel tomorrow and send you home?" MacArthur asked Eichelberger, who heeded those words and told a public relations officer: "I would rather have you put a rattlesnake in my pocket than to have you give me any publicity."

MacArthur was hard on his subordinates, but he was even harder on the Japanese. Throughout 1943, he and Halsey confounded opposing commanders by circumventing enemy bases where attacks were anticipated and defenses were well prepared and striking more vulnerable targets instead. By "island hopping," leapfrogging over one Japanese position to strike another, they covered more ground at less cost. Some battles were unavoidable, however, and left thousands dead, maimed, or broken in spirit. From Guadalcanal, Halsey's forces leapfrogged to New Georgia, midway up the Solomons chain, where another Japanese airfield was under construction. Soldiers of the 43rd Infantry Division, most of them former National Guardsmen from New England with little combat training, found the dense jungle there appalling. Many were wounded by friendly fire from troops unnerved by strange noises in the night. "Some men knifed each other," one report stated. "Men threw grenades blindly in the dark." Hundreds of soldiers cracked under the strain each week on that embattled island and were hospitalized with combat neuroses. Ultimately, more than 50,000 U.S. Army troops and Marines were needed to subdue fewer than 10,000 Japanese defenders on New Georgia.

HELP FROM ABOVE

Crucial to Allied success in pushing back the determined Japanese was General Kenney's Fifth Army Air Force, which supported MacArthur's offensive and supplemented naval airpower as Halsey's Solomons campaign intensified. A resourceful and inventive commander, Kenney found a way of making air raids on enemy warships and transports more accurate and less dangerous. Hitting moving ships with bombs released at high altitude was a long shot that seldom paid off. Dive-bombers like the SBD Dauntless were far more accurate in that role, but they were vulnerable to attack because of their slow cruising speed and proximity to enemy antiaircraft guns as they swooped down and pulled up. Naval aviators joked that SBD stood for "slow but deadly" and achieved success with the Dauntless by "hell-diving"—dropping down abruptly from high altitude and catching Japanese defenders off guard, a tactic used with devastating impact at Midway.

The Dauntless lacked sufficient range and speed for Kenney's purposes, however. Using longer-range B-25s, he perfected a tactic called skip-bombing, developed in 1941 by Italian pilot Giuseppe Cenni. The B-25s came in low and released their bombs a few hundred feet above the water and a few hundred yards away from their target. The bombs skipped like stones toward their mark while the pilot pulled up and over the enemy ship. "Upon passing over the target, the element of surprise is lost," one pilot warned, "so it is best to pull all power you can and make a hurried departure." Flying mostly at night, Kenney's 43rd Bombardment Group, known proudly as "Ken's Men," achieved a "high percentage of hits" through skip-bombing in 1943 and reported "no losses to date."

> "Upon passing over the target, the element of surprise is lost, so it is best to pull all power you can and make a hurried departure."
>
> Pilot of the Fifth Army Air Force, describing skip-bombing tactics

Another asset for Kenney's fliers was the Lockheed P-38 Lightning fighter, which entered service in the Pacific in late 1942. With a top speed surpassing 400 miles an hour and plenty of firepower, it could outduel the Mitsubishi Zero and helped make legends of skilled pilots like Maj. Richard Bong of the 49th Fighter Group, who became America's top ace with 40 kills and received the Medal of Honor personally from General MacArthur before plummeting to his death while testing a jet fighter a few days before the war ended. Capt. Thomas Lynch scored 20 kills and won a DSC for leading a dozen P-38s against 40 Japanese fighters and bombers over Buna in December 1942 and shooting down two enemy aircraft while others in his squadron destroyed 10 more. "All you gotta do is see them first," he said of his Japanese opponents. "If you see them first, you can get in position. If you see them coming up on your tail, it's too bad—you've seen them last." Promoted to lieutenant colonel, Lynch saw his last battle in March 1944 over Aitape Harbor in northern New Guinea, where he died in action.

By then, MacArthur's American and Australian troops were wrapping up their arduous conquest of New Guinea and preparing to retake the Philippines. Halsey's forces had advanced in late 1943 from New Georgia to Bougainville, near the northern end of the Solomons. That move forced Japanese warships to abandon Rabaul and neutralized the armed forces remaining at that once formidable base. Taking Rabaul—which at its peak harbored dozens of warships, scores of warplanes, and more than 100,000 troops—could have cost the Allies far more casualties than they suffered at Buna and Guadalcanal combined. Instead, they pinched it off and blasted it from the air, reducing that dwindling garrison to impotence.

Japan was no longer capable of offensive action in the Pacific and faced the grim task of defending its home islands with a weakened navy, which had lost its top strategist in April 1943 when a plane carrying Admiral Yamamoto from Rabaul to Bougainville was shot down by a P-38 pilot flying from Henderson Field with guidance from naval code breakers. Even more devastating for Japan was the death in battle of hundreds of expert naval airmen who had trained for years and had to be replaced by less capable fliers. The Imperial Japanese Army remained formidable, but many of its troops were mired in China. Army commanders were reluctant to transfer them to the Pacific theater, and the Imperial Japanese Navy was losing the capacity to safeguard shipments of troops and supplies. Halsey was delighted to hear of enemy transports going down with Japanese soldiers aboard and referred to one such sinking as a "rich, rewarding, beautiful slaughter." Lest any of his subordinates ease up on their faltering foes, he often closed dispatches with the words, "Keep 'em dying."

THE STRUGGLE FOR CHINA

When Japanese troops invaded China in 1937, Emperor Hirohito was told that his Imperial Japanese Army had the situation in hand and the war "could be finished up within two or three months." Four years later, nearly one million Japanese troops were engaged in China, and no end to the conflict was in sight. Gen. Hideki Tojo rejected the option of withdrawing those troops and coming to terms with the United States—which was aiding opposing Chinese Nationalists led by Chiang Kai-shek—and embarked on a sweeping offensive against America and its allies that was supposed to secure Japan's grip on China but failed to do so. Soon after the attack on Pearl Harbor, Japan invaded Burma to stop the Allies from funneling troops or supplies from that British colony to bolster the Nationalists in China. When the Burma Road between those two countries was sealed off, supplies were airlifted to Chiang's forces and Allied commanders made plans to retake Burma and reopen the road. Their main objective was to keep the Nationalists fighting and tie down Japanese troops who might otherwise be sent to oppose American advances in the Pacific. But some strategists had a more ambitious goal: to use Nationalist air bases in China to bomb Japan into submission.

The fate of China was so closely linked to that of Burma and India during World War II that the U.S. Army lumped them together under the acronym CBI (China-Burma-India). Commanding in that theater was Lt. Gen. Joseph Stilwell, known as Vinegar Joe for his quick temper and sharp tongue. Stilwell escaped from Japanese-occupied Burma in 1942 by

> "I claim we got a hell of a beating. We got run out of Burma, and it is humiliating as hell."
>
> Lt. Gen. Joseph Stilwell

leading soldiers and civilians on a long, harrowing trek to India, where reporters touted him as a hero and expected him to celebrate his feat. "I claim we got a hell of a beating," he said bluntly. "We got run out of Burma, and it is humiliating as hell." He vowed to go back and retake that country.

Stilwell never had many Americans serving under him. To retake Burma, he would need help from British and Indian forces and from the Chinese troops he trained in his dual role as Chiang's chief of staff. That assignment caused him much aggravation, because Chiang was reluctant to commit his forces to battle in

Burma. As China's generalissimo, he claimed to have nearly four million soldiers under his command, but many of them were not combat-worthy. Others who were fit to fight were led by officers he distrusted. Chiang preferred to remain on the defensive against the Japanese and preserve his strength for a postwar showdown with his Communist rival, Mao Zedong, who had reached a fragile truce with the Nationalists to keep both sides from being drained by a bloody civil war and crushed by the invaders.

Stilwell thought that Chiang was holding out on the Allies who aided him and referred to him in writing as a "stubborn, ignorant, prejudiced, conceited despot who never hears the truth except from me and finds it hard to believe." As Stilwell's relationship with him deteriorated, Chiang and his influential wife grew closer to Maj. Gen. Claire Chennault, who was Stilwell's subordinate

A Chinese soldier at an airfield in Kunming guards Curtiss P-40K fighters of the U.S. 23rd Fighter Group, painted with the Flying Tiger emblem of Claire Chennault's prewar American Volunteer Group.

but challenged his plan for a renewed ground war in Burma by proposing to use airpower to supply the Nationalists and defeat the Japanese. A veteran of the prewar Army Air Corps, Chennault had recruited American volunteers in 1937 to form the Flying Tigers, and fly combat missions for the Nationalists against the Japanese. When the United States entered the war, he rejoined the U.S. Army and organized the airlift from India to China, carried out by daring pilots who went "over the Hump," flying in turbulent skies above the towering Himalaya to land their overloaded cargo planes on primitive runways. More than a thousand airmen died in crashes on that perilous route during the war.

In March 1943, Chennault was named commander of the 14th Army Air Force, which targeted Japanese forces and their supply lines with fighters and medium-range bombers. His ultimate objective was to blast Japan itself with long-range B-29 bombers, launched from new airstrips he was building for that purpose. Stilwell warned that Japanese troops would respond to that threat by overrunning those bases, but Chennault forged ahead, dismissing the CBI commander as a hidebound old soldier who disdained airpower and distrusted "any weapon more complicated than a rifle and bayonet."

Stilwell hoped to reclaim all of Burma but had to settle for a pared-down offensive whose purpose was to secure the northern part of that country and funnel troops and supplies to China along a new road from Ledo in India that would connect with the old Burma Road and supplement the airlift. He used his authority over the shipment of goods to the Nationalists as leverage to persuade Chiang to commit two Chinese divisions to the offensive. Trained by Stilwell and his officers, those soldiers were

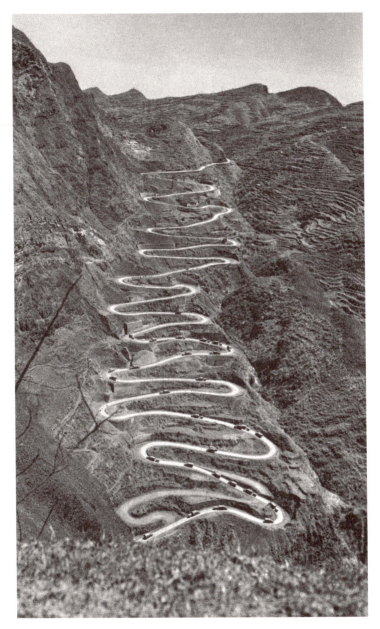

To haul more supplies to Nationalist forces opposing the Japanese in China, engineers improved the Burma Road, including a spectacular stretch near Annan, China, known as "21 curves," shown above with an Allied truck convoy wending its way upward.

LT. JOHN RUSSELL
FLYING OVER THE HUMP

In 1944, 19-year-old Lieutenant Russell, with the First Combat Cargo Group, flew American-trained Chinese troops over the "Hump" of the Himalaya to fight in Burma against the Japanese. Here's his account of a tricky landing in the mountains.

They overloaded us with fifty Chinese soldiers, who, fortunately, were not very well equipped with guns and other supplies so didn't weigh much. I was really shocked by the poor condition of these Chinese soldiers. They were not at all what we expected of American trained troops. We had to climb rather high and the coldness filled the plane. We had some heat up front, but they had none in the back. Consequently, the body lice left them and crawled all over our controls . . . we found a solid layer of clouds in all directions . . . there were no radio devices to bring us in to landing fields, most of which were located in small valleys surrounded by mountains, so when clouds settle down over a field, that field is closed.

This day our delivery of the soldiers to the fighting front came to a stop, as we heard the voice from the field tower tell the plane ahead of us that the field was socked in and landing was not possible. We were then told to divert to another field not too far away, but as we approached them, I radioed that tower for landing instructions, and received that same reply, "socked in." Remember, the Chunking deal was no gas from them for our return trip, so that didn't allow

Lt. John Russell (right) embraces a buddy at their training camp in India's eastern province of Assam.

much time to circle around and wait for the clouds to blow away. We were now down to 50 gallons and choked back as much as safely possible, and even that allowed for only 25 minutes of flying time.

At this time we were on top of the overcast at thirteen thousand feet and could see the peaks of many mountains sticking up through . . . After much conversation, we knew that running out of gas sitting up here would eliminate all choices to land thereafter, so in a desperate move, we chose an area where we thought maybe the clouds didn't have hard centers. Henry, flying on instruments through the clouds, would put the plane in a very tight spiral while descending at a very slow rate, and I would put my face against the glass trying to see anything at all. And indeed I did, as I saw the upraised wing brush against tree tops on the side of the hill which caused me to pull back instantly on the stick to get us back on top again . . .

> "I saw the upraised wing brush against tree tops on the side of the hill which caused me to pull back instantly on the stick to get us back on top again."

The contact with the tower was good, but there was such a disturbance that the compass stuttered and spun, giving us little direction at all. We had been warned of misdirections brought on by the placement by the Japanese of radio devices on the hillsides. A quick-thinking control operator told me to change frequency, and he would talk to us from a radio in a plane on the ground. He would home on our signal, and we would home on his. They worked together perfectly and brought us right over the field, which lay under a blanket of clouds. Then a most amazing thing happened: we saw a circular hole in the overcast exactly over the landing strip. Henry cut the engines back to idle and dove through the hole and onto the ground. We knew every second was critical and once parked, I had the crew chief drain the tanks. All that was left was two gallons: one minute of flying time. ∎

better fed and better equipped than most other Nationalist troops, many of whom were shortchanged by corrupt commanders who profited at their expense.

Supporting Stilwell's Chinese recruits were the 77th Indian Infantry Brigade, dubbed Chindits by their leader, Maj. Gen. Orde Charles Wingate. An unconventional British officer born in India, General Wingate drilled his men relentlessly in harsh conditions to prepare them to operate behind enemy lines in the dense Burmese jungle. Wingate's tough Chindits (a mix of British, Indian, and Burmese troops) were models for a special unit of 3,000 American commandos recruited to fight in Burma by Brig. Gen. Frank Merrill, a staff officer under Stilwell. Known as Merrill's Marauders, many were veterans of jungle warfare in the Pacific and all were volunteers—although some chose to join Merrill rather than serve time for offenses they committed in uniform.

Among those with good records who volunteered freely for what the War Department called this "particularly hazardous, self-sacrificing mission" were more than a dozen Nisei who had enlisted as translators and interrogators in the Military Intelligence Service. After joining Merrill's Marauders, they did more than translate. Unlike most Nisei in uniform, who served in Europe, they went into combat against Japanese troops, often creeping up on enemy units at great risk to assess their strength, listen for commands and other clues as to their plans, and report back. Some of those volunteers had relatives in Japan. Sgt. Roy Matsumoto, for instance, was born in California and remained there as a young man after his parents and siblings returned to Japan and settled in Hiroshima, where they later survived the atomic blast that obliterated much of that city on August 6, 1945. Fighting against men from their ancestral homeland was a sacrifice that Matsumoto and other Nisei Marauders who had been sent to internment camps in the United States made to show that they were true Americans. As one of them said, "Each of us in our own way looked beyond the 'barbed wires' [of the war relocation camps] to a better America."

> "Each of us in our own way looked beyond the 'barbed wires' [of the war relocation camps] to a better America."
>
> A Nisei commando who volunteered to fight the Japanese as part of the special unit Merrill's Marauders

Stilwell's offensive, launched in late 1943, inaugurated six months of furious action in the CBI theater, during which the momentum swung back and forth. In early 1944, the Japanese counterattacked, crossing into India in a drive that threatened to cut off Allied forces operating in Burma and stem the flow of supplies to Nationalist China. Many Indian troops remained loyal to Britain and opposed that invasion, but some sided with Japan against their British rulers, who had jailed Mohandas Gandhi and other advocates of Indian independence when they refused to support the war effort. Allied pilots who had been flying over the Hump to China shifted their efforts to keep their stranded forces fighting while hard-pressed Japanese troops ran out of food and ammunition and withdrew from India in the spring.

Meanwhile, Stilwell's multinational forces were closing in on their objective in northern Burma: Myitkyina, a vital town near the Chinese border where the Japanese maintained an air base and were reinforced by rail. Merrill's Marauders led the advance and took the runway there in May, but they were stalled by Japanese troops holding the railhead and settled in for a siege.

Many of the Marauders were sick and had to be evacuated. Meanwhile, monsoon downpours mired Stilwell's Chinese troops and held them back. "Rain, rain, rain," he wrote glumly as his campaign bogged down. "Mud, mud, mud, typhus, malaria, dysentery, exhaustion, rotting feet, body sores." One thought consoled him: "If we are so badly off, what about the Japs?" In fact, they were in even worse shape. Chindits cut the railroad below Myitkyina and denied aid to the Japanese defenders there, who lost more than half their men to disease and battle wounds within a few months before the survivors escaped and their commander committed suicide. "Myitkyina over at last," Stilwell wrote in August. "Thank God."

> "Mud, mud, mud, typhus, malaria, dysentery, exhaustion, rotting feet, body sores."
>
> Lt. Gen. Joseph Stilwell, on conditions in Burma

Allied gains in Burma were offset by simultaneous losses in China, where the enemy offensive Stilwell had predicted unfolded, driving Nationalist troops back hundreds of miles and reducing the threat posed to Japan by Chennault's air campaign. By mid-1944, the Joint Chiefs in Washington had concluded that islands in the Pacific would serve better than China as platforms from which to bomb and, if necessary, invade Japan. Future operations in CBI would focus on securing Burma and providing enough aid to the Nationalists to keep the Japanese from conquering all of China and redeploying their troops elsewhere. That strategy proved successful. Before surrendering, Japan had nearly two million soldiers on the Asian mainland, most of them in China and countries bordering it. Having gone to war with the Allies rather than withdraw from China, Japan ended up squandering much of its strength there without achieving victory in Asia or averting disaster in the Pacific.

UNDERWATER WARFARE

The war in the Pacific placed a heavy burden on Japan—defending its maritime supply lines, on which it depended for oil, rubber, iron, and other essential commodities that were scarce or nonexistent on its home islands. That burden grew even heavier as the U.S. Navy achieved supremacy both above and below the waves. During the war, American shipyards with secure and abundant sources of raw materials outproduced Japan by a ratio of nearly 10 to 1 in aircraft carriers, cruisers, destroyers, and other surface ships. The American edge in submarine production was smaller, and it took nearly two years for the Navy to refine its tactics and technology and achieve mastery underwater. Once it did so, however, Japan was in a terrible bind, for subs rivaled and often

This sequence of photographs, taken through the periscope of the Seawolf *by its captain, Lt. Cmdr. Royce Gross, shows Japanese Patrol Boat No. 39 sinking after being torpedoed near Japan's Bonin Islands on April 23, 1943.*

surpassed bombers as strategic weapons, inflicting severe economic damage and stifling the enemy's capacity to wage war.

"Tankers—those were the ships we wanted most to sink."

Vice Adm. Charles Lockwood

American subs sank more than 1,000 merchant ships and reduced the flow of oil to Japan by 80 percent, throttling its war effort. "Tankers—those were the ships we wanted most to sink," wrote Vice Adm. Charles Lockwood, who took charge of all submarine forces in the Pacific in 1943.

Lockwood had done much to increase the effectiveness of those forces and raise their morale, which had been near rock bottom when he received his first combat assignment in 1942. After serving as a staff officer in Washington and London, he reported to Fremantle, Australia, that April to command submarines in the southwest Pacific, where captains and crews had been prowling intently for Japanese ships since the war began but had little to show for their efforts. Even when firing at slow-moving freighters or warships that had been crippled in combat and were sitting ducks, they often missed their marks. One captain launched 15 torpedoes at various targets and scored just one hit, and others fared little better

Submariners blamed the newly introduced Mark 14 torpedo, which one skipper insisted was simply "no damned good," but their complaints fell on deaf ears until Lockwood arrived. Heeding their objections, he conducted target practice using Mark 14s armed with live ammunition—something the cost-conscious Navy Bureau of Ordnance had chosen not to do because such tests ruined those expensive torpedoes. He found that they were running at least 10 feet deeper than their settings indicated, which meant that many torpedoes fired in combat were passing harmlessly under their targets. Further examination revealed that the

Mark 14's detonating device, designed to trigger an explosion when it entered the magnetic field of a ship's iron hull, was also defective and that the torpedo worked properly only when rigged to explode on contact.

The weapon's glaring defects were not fully remedied until Lockwood was called to Pearl Harbor to command the entire Pacific submarine fleet. One of his first moves in that capacity was to fly to Washington to demand that the Bureau of Ordnance "provide us with torpedoes that will hit and explode." His blunt words offended the bureau's chief, but Lockwood did not back down. "If anything I have said will get the bureau off its duff and get some action," he declared, "I will feel that my trip has not been wasted."

Lockwood won that bureaucratic battle and returned to the Pacific to combat the enemy with effective torpedoes, innovative tactics, and a strategic emphasis on targeting Japan's maritime supply lines. Earlier in the war, American submarine commanders had given enemy warships priority as targets over merchant ships, but Lockwood recognized that subs were most effective when used to destroy the vulnerable freighters and oil tankers that kept Japan's armed forces and war industries running. Those vessels were slower than submarines and more susceptible to attack than aircraft carriers, battleships, or cruisers, which were faster and often shielded by destroyers equipped with sonar to detect subs and depth charges to sink them. Like Allied merchant ships in the Atlantic, Japanese freighters sometimes traveled in convoys with destroyers as escorts to defend against submarines. Lockwood responded by adopting the tactics of German U-boats, which hunted together in so-called wolf packs to increase their chances of success against convoys and their escorts. The chief drawback of those large German wolf packs was that commanding and coordinating them generated considerable radio traffic, which could betray their location. So Lockwood sent out small packs of three subs and minimized radio contact between them.

Hunting in packs improved the odds that one or more subs would penetrate the convoy's defenses and make kills. But doing so was still risky, as Capt. Samuel Dealey discovered in November 1943 when his sub, the U.S.S. *Harder,* became separated from the two others in its pack and encountered a Japanese convoy in the mid-Pacific. Dealey attacked on his own and sank two freighters before submerging to avoid their armed escort, which dropped more than 60 depth charges. Shaken but unscathed, Dealey and crew resurfaced several hours later and dispatched a third freighter. Under Dealey's command, the *Harder* became one of the fleet's deadliest sea wolves, sinking more than a dozen other ships, including three destroyers sent down within the span of a few days in June 1944 before he returned to base at Darwin, Australia.

Dealey's boss there thought that the five grueling war patrols Dealey had completed were enough for any captain and urged him to relinquish command of the *Harder.* But much of its crew was being replaced, and Dealey felt obliged to make one more outing and bring the newcomers up to speed before entrusting his sub to another captain. "I've got to lead this patrol," he insisted. Two months later, off the coast of the Philippines, the *Harder* submerged under attack and never resurfaced. Dealey and his crew were lost at sea, but they were not forgotten. He was one of eight U.S. submarine captains to receive the Medal of Honor, awarded to him posthumously, and he and his men were later memorialized in a book by Admiral Lockwood, *Through Hell and Deep Water.*

Submariners formed an elite corps within the U.S. Navy, all of them volunteers and rigorously trained for their hazardous duty. Roughly one man in every five died in action—a higher percentage than in any other American branch of service during the war—but losses were even steeper among their foreign counterparts. Japanese submariners spent much of the conflict stalking Allied warships at great risk or conducting covert missions, including a daring but futile foray in February 1942 when a Japanese sub surfaced off Santa Barbara, California, and shelled an oil refinery there, inflicting little damage. Later that year, after Japanese warships lost the Naval Battle of Guadalcanal, more than a dozen submarines were diverted from offensive operations to carry food and other supplies furtively to soldiers holding out against U.S. Marines on that island. "We must help them," Vice Adm. Teruhisa Komatsu said of those troops, "no matter what sacrifices must be made."

Two subs were lost in that desperate relief effort; another was damaged and ran aground, killing many of the crewmen. Overall, Japanese submariners suffered a much higher casualty rate than Americans did in that same capacity while inflicting far less damage on opposing warships or merchant ships. As casualties mounted, one Japanese commander responded to an officer's complaint that lives were being sacrificed in vain by declaring fatalistically: "No matter what the difference may be between our capability and that of the enemy, we must still carry out our orders, mustn't we? That

> "No matter what the difference may be between our capability and that of the enemy, we must still carry out our orders, mustn't we?"
>
> A Japanese commander on the sacrifice of so many lives

JULIA CONNER
PRAYING FOR A SON'S SAFETY

Julia Conner, a deeply religious woman, had watched her son Durrell almost be snatched from her in his infancy by spinal meningitis. He then survived the attack on Pearl Harbor only to set off to war as a yeoman second class aboard the battleship California. *She wrote this poem sometime between September 1942 and September 1943, when Durrell was fighting in the Pacific and she couldn't know that he would survive the war and go on to lead the rich, full life she wanted for him.*

A Mother's Poem

Baby mine, so pink and sweet,
Tiny body all complete.
Sent to me from God above,
What a wonderful thing of
   love.

A boy! A boy had someone
   said?
Had something gone wrong
   in my head?
Everything was in a whirl,
For twice before they said
   – a girl!

My girls are lovely, to be sure,
But I had two of them before.
This time a boy we wanted
   most,
Now his dad can truly boast.

Twenty-four years have come
   and flown,
And to manhood he has
   grown.
Now he sails the deep blue sea,
Writing letters home to me.

He sends me coral and trea-
   sures rare,
Which he gathers everywhere.
Oh, they miss a world of joy,
Those who never had a boy.

Father, the boy Thou gavest
   me,
To manhood now has grown.
He's a sailor on the sea,
Sailing far away from me.
Going far from home.

I pray Thy will, not mine, be
   done,
But if it pleaseth Thee,
And if I ask it not amiss,
Please send him back to me.

And while he's far away from
   me,
And I'm not there to bless,
Wilt Thou look down upon
   him, Lord;
Look down in tenderness.

Now I ask Thee not to grant
   that he be President,

But if he humbly follows
   Thee,
Then a leader he shall be
On land or sea.

Keep him safe from harm,
   dear Lord,
And fill his heart with joy.
Yes, I know he's now a man,
But he's still my little boy. ∎

In a pause in her reading, Julia Conner's eyes rest on her son Durrell. When he later fought in the Pacific, she prayed every day that God would keep him safe through all dangers.

has always been the battle spirit of Japanese submarine men, has it not?"

ADVANCING ON SAIPAN

In June 1943, Admiral Nimitz received permission from the Joint Chiefs in Washington to proceed with an ambitious offensive that he believed offered the quickest route to victory in the Pacific. Since defeating the Japanese fleet at Midway a year earlier, he had awaited the opportunity to advance westward toward Japan across tiny islands in the Central Pacific—a term used operationally during World War II to refer to the tropical zone above the Equator. Those islands lay closer to Tokyo than large islands in the South Pacific such as New Guinea and the Solomons. Nimitz had given priority to the Solomons campaign in 1942 because the Japanese threat to Australia and its supply lines was too great to be ignored and because the U.S. Navy needed more ships, landing craft, and troops before it could operate effectively across the vast distances separating the island chains of the Central Pacific.

First to be targeted would be Japanese bases on the Gilbert and Marshall Islands, located near the Equator some 2,000 miles southwest of Pearl Harbor. Another thousand miles beyond that lay the Japanese-occupied Caroline and Mariana Islands. Invading those Central Pacific islands, many of which were part of atolls, involved navigating treacherous coral reefs and landing on desolate shores offering little or no cover for troops exposed to furious fire from entrenched defenders. Once captured, however, coral islands could readily be converted into U.S. naval and air bases to support the next leap forward across the Pacific.

Seizing Saipan in the Marianas would bring B-29 bombers within range of Tokyo and U.S. troops within striking distance of Iwo Jima and Okinawa, the last bastions shielding Japan's home islands.

Nimitz entrusted this offensive to Vice Adm. Raymond Spruance, of Midway fame. Thanks to the prodigious output of American shipyards, Spruance's Fifth Fleet alone was larger than the entire U.S. Pacific Fleet had been before the attack on Pearl Harbor. At his command were 10 big aircraft carriers and seven smaller ones designed to escort and protect amphibious forces as they landed, 12 battleships, a similar number of cruisers, and more than 60 destroyers. Yet despite that formidable display of sea power and airpower, the 35,000 Marines and soldiers who came ashore on the Gilbert Islands in November 1943 struggled

Lt. Walter Chewning, catapult officer aboard the U.S.S. Enterprise, *climbs to the cockpit of a burning Grumman F6F-3 Hellcat to aid the pilot, Ensign Byron Johnson, who escaped after his plane crashed on landing.*

desperately to overcome foes who were vastly outnumbered but deeply entrenched and fiercely determined. On Makin Atoll, it took four days for 6,500 attackers to root out several hundred Japanese troops while the escort carrier *Liscome Bay* and its crew stood by offshore, exposed to attack. On November 24, a Japanese submarine torpedoed the ship, which sank at a cost of more than 600 lives.

Victory came at an even steeper price on Tarawa Atoll, where 4,000 defenders were holed up in pillboxes dug out of coral and reinforced with steel, concrete, and logs from coconut trees felled to provide Japanese gunners with clear lines of fire as Marines came ashore. Rear Adm. Howard Kingman planned to pulverize those fortifications with a devastating naval and aerial bombardment that would end the battle before Marines hit the beach. "Gentlemen," he vowed, "we will not neutralize; we will not destroy; we will obliterate the defenses." But nothing went as planned when the attack unfolded at dawn on November 20. Ineffective air strikes were followed by thunderous naval barrages that cheered the Marines but failed to dislodge their foes. "There aren't 50 Japs left alive on that island," one officer reckoned, shortly before the resilient defenders unleashed concentrated artillery and machine-gun fire on Marines as they approached the beach. Many were stranded in water several feet deep when their landing craft ran aground on a coral reef. Other troop carriers called amtracs (amphibious tractors) kept churning forward when they reached the reef but exploded when shots punctured their fuel tanks. One Marine saw an amtrac ahead of his "burst into flames, with men jumping out like torches." His own vehicle stalled, and he was one of the few men aboard who leaped out and waded ashore without being hit by the Japanese, who were "laying lead to us from a pillbox like holy hell."

Of the 700 Marines in one battalion, only a hundred reached the beach intact, where they remained pinned down through the night with other survivors. Not until the tide rose the following day and allowed landing craft to cross the reef with reinforcements and heavy weaponry were the Marines able to advance in force and blast the enemy with tanks, grenades, and flamethrowers. More than a thousand Americans died and nearly 3,000 were wounded before resistance was wiped out. Only a dozen or so Japanese troops survived the battle as prisoners. An official account called it "the bitterest fighting in the history of the Marine Corps," but horrific contests loomed that would challenge Tarawa for that dubious distinction.

Hard lessons learned in combat on the Gilbert Islands made later assaults more effective. Amtracs were sheathed in heavier armor, and naval aviators were trained in precision bombing using bunker-busting rockets. Like MacArthur and Halsey, Nimitz and Spruance bypassed some Japanese outposts, which were left to "wither on the vine," and targeted others that had greater strategic value as naval or air bases. But nothing commanders did to strengthen or speed the offensive did much to lessen the terrors of island fighting in the Central Pacific, where the great fear was not being enclosed in jungle, as troops were on the Solomons and New Guinea, but being exposed to attack on open water or bare sand.

When Spruance advanced on the Marshall Islands in early 1944, warships and bombers did a better job of softening up Japanese defenses there, and landing craft brought heavy artillery ashore to support the Marines. They remained woefully vulnerable, however, to opposing gunners who survived the bombardment and to the volcanic impact of their own big guns on enemy blockhouses, packed with explosives. One such eruption on Namur, a tiny island within Kwajalein Atoll, cost a Marine battalion as many casualties as were felled there by Japanese bullets or shells. "An ink-black darkness spread over a large part of Namur such that the hand could not be seen in front of the face," one officer reported after the blockhouse exploded. "Debris continued to fall for a considerable length of time which seemed unending to those in the area who were all unprotected from the huge chunks of concrete and steel thudding on the ground about them . . . Men were killed and wounded in small boats a considerable distance from the beach by the flying debris."

The Japanese navy was spread thin across the Pacific and hard-pressed to contest the advance of Spruance's mighty Fifth Fleet. After securing the Marshall Islands, Spruance sent a fast carrier task force led by Rear Adm. Marc Mitscher to attack Truk in the Caroline Islands, which served as the main base for the Japanese fleet. Yamamoto's successor, Adm. Mineichi Koga, withdrew aircraft carriers and other big warships from Truk rather than risk losing them to the oncoming Americans, who blasted the base in mid-February, destroying many vessels left behind there and more than 200 aircraft.

After falling back before the American onslaught, Koga resolved to wage a decisive naval battle against his foes—code-named Operation Z—but died in March in a plane crash off the coast of the Philippines before he could put his plans into action. Lost in the crash was a briefcase containing documents detailing Operation Z, which fell into the hands of Filipino guerrillas, who turned them over to an American agent. What those documents revealed was not one plan of attack but various proposals for securing Japan's "last line of defense"—which encompassed the Marianas and the Philippines—and achieving the great naval victory that both Koga and his successor, Adm. Soemu Toyoda, hoped for. One proposal involved luring U.S. carriers assigned to protect amphibious landings into a reckless pursuit of Japanese carriers, whose aircraft would then join with other warplanes launched from Japanese bases on land to shatter the American fleet and halt any further advances toward the home islands by U.S. Marines or soldiers.

Spruance learned of Operation Z as he was preparing to oust Japanese forces from Saipan and other Mariana Islands in June 1944. Furnished with that intelligence, he reacted cautiously

On June 19, the Japanese launched disastrous attacks, losing some 300 aircraft in clashes with American fighters like the F6F-3 Hellcat, one shown here landing on the U.S.S. Lexington.

Pfc. Henry Kagan
Letters Home From Saipan

Kagan, a heavy equipment operator with the 805th Engineer Aviation Battalion, landed on Saipan in June 1944, soon after the invasion began there, to help build an airfield for B-29 bombers. On August 24, he wrote home describing a Japanese air raid on his first night in Saipan.

Dear Honey,

Just got some interesting news over the radio, that we are now in Paris and going strong. It looks very close for the end of the European war. Then we can all look for big things to happen. The end of this whole war will come soon after that. I think there will be peace on Earth and I will be coming home to you and our son . . .

I grew my mustache back and it is shaping up pretty well. Last night was the first beautiful night I can remember in a long time. When I say night, I mean the sky was beautiful, the stars were shining in the heavens as I lay in my cot looking upward, and that is the only way I want to go through life, with my head up.

Right now I am sort of between Heaven and Earth and when I say the Heavens were beautiful I also wish I could say the Earth was also beautiful, the grass and the mountains etc. But I'm afraid that beautiful day won't come until I set foot on good old U.S. soil.

A faithful correspondent who wrote letters home almost every day, Kagan asked Bella to save them as a record of his service.

"I lay in my cot looking upward, and that is the only way I want to go through life, with my head up. Right now I am sort of between Heaven and Earth and when I say the Heavens were beautiful I also wish I could say the Earth was . . . But I'm afraid that beautiful day won't come until I set foot on good old U.S. soil."

I think I have changed a great deal. I believe in the right things and I fight for what is right, and I will admit I'm wrong. Also you might be interested in knowing I have sworn, that night, that horrible night when we first set foot on Saipan and I was awakened by a roar of a Jap motor and a tremendous burst of bombs all around me, I crawled out of my pup tent like a scared rabbit, my teeth were chattering and my knees were shaking and my eyes were three times their size. I was so scared I didn't know where to go, not having a foxhole . . . I started to dig with my hands and feet. The sweat was rolling off me like a fountain. I was in a daze. I was ready and I thought, that was the end. I prayed and prayed to God and asked him to forgive me for all my sins and I swore if I ever got home alive and safe I would never gamble again and as much as I like to gamble, that is my promise. Just as soon as I step on home ground. You may not believe this but it is true, every word of it. This is just a little chapter of my experience on Saipan Island.

By the way I meant to ask you, do you save these letters? I hope so!

Here is hoping for a wonderful New Year . . . Answer soon.

Love always,
Your Henry ∎

when he learned that a powerful enemy fleet was approaching the Marianas from the west. "The Japanese are coming after us," he told officers aboard his flagship U.S.S. *Indianapolis* on June 16. Spruance sent Mitscher's task force to fend off the approaching fleet—which included nine aircraft carriers and more than 400 warplanes—but instructed Mitscher to remain close enough to Saipan to keep his aircraft within range of that island. Spruance did not want his carriers drawn into a hazardous pursuit that would divert them from the Fifth Fleet's primary mission: protecting the troops who had landed on Saipan a few days earlier and would soon invade nearby Tinian and Guam.

Mitscher found himself on the defensive because his aircraft had a shorter range than warplanes launched by the Japanese fleet, which struck first. Radar gave the American pilots ample warning of that attack, however, and their opponents were not nearly as well prepared as Japanese naval aviators had been in 1941, when they were among the best in the world. Many now had only a few months' training, and their lightly armored Mitsubishi Zeros—once dreaded for their prowess in combat—were now fatally vulnerable to faster, sturdier fighters like the Grumman F6F Hellcat. In a rout remembered as the "Great Marianas Turkey Shoot," nearly 300 Japanese warplanes were downed on June 19, many of them by seasoned American pilots from the task force, who lost just 30 of their own aircraft. Mitscher's ships emerged intact while submarines dispatched by Admiral Lockwood attacked the Japanese fleet and sank two carriers.

Plowing ahead, that battered fleet was spotted 250 miles from Mitscher's task force on the afternoon of June 20, putting it within range of his aircraft. Although his pilots had no chance of returning to their carriers before nightfall, Mitscher received permission from Spruance to launch an attack, during which Americans sank a third aircraft carrier, damaged two more, and shot down 65 fighters before turning back at dusk. Many were running out of fuel when they glimpsed their own carriers in the distance, lit up at night like cruise ships to guide them home. Some ditched in the sea or crashed on deck, but most landed safely, amid what one pilot dazzled by the light show described as "a Mardi Gras setting fantastically out of place here, midway between the Marianas and the Philippines." Having lost nearly all its warplanes, the Japanese fleet withdrew. Some critics faulted Spruance for not taking greater risks to destroy it. But in this crucial Battle of the Philippine Sea, he had in fact turned Operation Z—the desperate Japanese pursuit of a decisive victory at sea—into a staggering defeat for his foes while fulfilling his primary task of landing troops on the Marianas and shielding them until their task was fulfilled.

Saipan was defended by some 25,000 Japanese troops, and they did not yield easily. The Marines who launched the assault there on June 14 faced an ordeal that would prove far longer and costlier for them and the Army troops who followed in their wake than the bitter battle for Tarawa. "We looked at each other, and our glances formed a common pool of anxiety," recalled Sgt. David Dempsey, whose Marine platoon landed in one of more than 700 amtracs amassed for this operation. "In a few minutes, our tractor grumbled up onto the reef. Lurching tipsily we crawled over it, giving us the feeling, for the moment, that we were very naked and exposed."

Casualties were steep on that first day, but the sheer weight of the invasion overwhelmed the defenders. By nightfall,

20,000 Marines held a beachhead nearly a mile wide. Within a week, the Japanese were outnumbered nearly four to one and had fallen back to Mount Tapotchau, midway up the island. By month's end, Marines and soldiers had clawed their way around that mountain, seizing Tanapag Harbor to the north and isolating Lt. Gen. Yoshit-

> "We deeply apologize to the Emperor that we cannot do better."
>
> Lt. Gen. Yoshitsugu Saito, who died by his own sword on Saipan when facing defeat

sugu Saito and several thousand of his surviving troops on the high ground. Six days later, Saito sent his last message to Tokyo: "We deeply apologize to the Emperor that we cannot do better." Then he died by his own sword in a ritual called seppuku, or hara-kiri, long performed by samurai who faced defeat. His troops met death the next day by launching a hopeless banzai (suicide) charge on their foes at Tanapag Harbor. "The Japs just kept coming and coming," one soldier there said afterward. "I didn't think they'd ever stop." In the final act of the tragedy on Saipan, several hundred Japanese civilians who had settled there before the war and had been told that Americans would treat them brutally leaped from cliffs at the northern end of the island and drowned rather than submit to the enemy.

The defeat of Japanese naval forces in the Philippine Sea and the fall of Saipan—followed by the capture of Tinian and Guam—left Japan's leaders with little hope of averting disaster unless they surrendered. Shortly after the Marines landed on Saipan, Emperor Hirohito warned General Tojo that if his troops lost that island, "repeated air attacks on Tokyo will follow. No matter what it takes, we have to hold there." Indeed, American construction crews soon transformed Saipan and Tinian into launching pads for B-29s that posed a mortal threat

Ground crewmen load 500-pound bombs into a Boeing B-29 Superfortress, dubbed Dauntless Dotty, at Isley Field on Saipan.

to Tokyo and other Japanese cities. Tojo resigned, but Hirohito was not ready to admit defeat and end the deadly struggle. Instead, he and his chiefs remained intent on achieving a "decisive victory" and prolonged a conflict that was becoming suicidal for Japan.

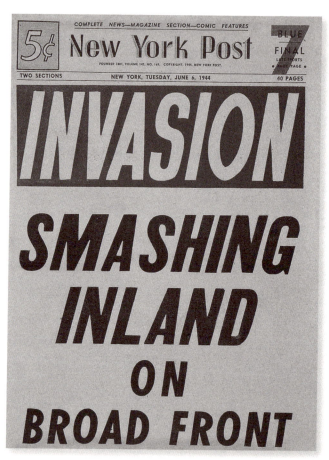

First reports of the landings on D-Day reached the U.S. during the night in time for newspapers to break the news with banner headlines.

CHRONOLOGY

AUGUST 25, 1940
Britain begins bombing Berlin.

OCTOBER 30, 1942 British sailors seize the Enigma key from a boarded German U-boat.

MARCH 6, 1941 Churchill acknowledges the beginning of the Battle of the Atlantic.

THE WESTERN FRONT

FROM THE BATTLE OF THE ATLANTIC TO D-DAY

At the same time the Allies were fighting with Japan for dominance in the Pacific, they were involved in another naval war, this one with Germany for control of Atlantic shipping. Like Japan, the island nation of Great Britain was heavily dependent on imported goods and highly vulnerable to attacks on its maritime supply lines. Winston Churchill was keenly aware that these wartime shipments of food, fuel, and munitions from America helped keep his country fighting, and he feared defeat if German submarines severed Britain's transatlantic lifeline. "The U-boat attack was our worst evil," wrote Churchill in later years. "It would have been wise for the Germans to stake all on it."

Fortunately for the Allies, Hitler did not invest heavily in submarines until after the war began. Much of Germany's

FEBRUARY 20–25, 1944 "Big Week" in which U.S. bombers ensured Allied air supremacy in advance of the invasion of Normandy.

JUNE 6, 1944 D-Day

JUNE 5, 1944 General Eisenhower gives the final go-ahead for the invasion.

industrial might as war loomed went to producing tanks, aircraft, and impressive but vulnerable naval blockbusters like the battleship *Bismarck,* which lasted only a few weeks in the open Atlantic in 1941 before succumbing to warships and carrier-launched warplanes of the Royal Navy's superior surface fleet. Meanwhile, Germany's submarine force, which entered the conflict with only 55 U-boats, was surpassing expectations under the keen direction of Vice Adm. Karl Dönitz, who deployed them in groups directed by radio—dubbed "wolf packs" by the British—to attack Allied convoys. "The Battle of the Atlantic has begun," declared Churchill in March 1941 as Germany stepped up submarine production. "The U-boat at sea must be hunted, the U-boat in the building yard or in dock must be bombed."

> "The U-boat at sea must be hunted, the U-boat in the building yard or the dock must be bombed."
>
> Winston Churchill

In April 1941, President Roosevelt extended the Pan-American Security Zone—in which the U.S. Navy protected merchant ships against attack—far across the Atlantic to the vicinity of Iceland, where the Royal Navy took charge of escorting convoys to Britain and wolf packs gathered to attack them. In October 1941, two American destroyers escorting merchant ships were torpedoed near Iceland: the U.S.S. *Kearny,* which lost 11 men but stayed afloat, and the U.S.S. *Reuben James,* which went down with most of its crew after being hit by the German sub *U-552* on October 31, just a little more than five weeks before Pearl Harbor. "America has been attacked," declared Roosevelt, who continued to aid Britain and uphold America's right to navigate the Atlantic freely.

Soon after Germany declared war on the United States in December, Admiral Dönitz ordered his U-boats to attack ships along the Atlantic coast and the Gulf Coast and in the Caribbean. The offensive, code-named Operation Drumbeat, was launched by five long-range Type IX U-boats that set out from Lorient, France, and wreaked havoc off American shores, where authorities had failed to organize coastal convoys or order blackouts, leaving ships dangerously silhouetted against city lights. This was a "happy time" for U-boat captains and a fearful time for those they targeted. The captain and several crewmen of the tanker *Cities Service Empire,* torpedoed off the coast of Florida, perished when their life raft was consumed by burning oil, reported a survivor, who "last saw the captain going into a sheet of orange flame."

In May 1942, Dönitz reinforced Operation Drumbeat by sending out large Type XIV subs, known as "milk cows," that were designed to refuel and resupply other U-boats and extend their patrol time. By then, the U.S. Navy had begun to run convoys along the East Coast, but the losses continued. In six months, Drumbeat sank 397 ships at a cost of just seven U-boats.

RESCUED FROM A WATERY GRAVE

The Battle of the Atlantic claimed many victims, including sailors who survived attacks at sea but died in the water or in lifeboats before help arrived. Under international law, naval forces were supposed to aid opposing sailors who survived shipwrecks. The British did so by rescuing German survivors of the sunken battleship *Bismarck* in May 1941. Admiral Dönitz officially abandoned such rescue efforts by his U-boat fleet, however, following an incident in September 1942 when the

Margaret Latimer Straight
A Wartime Summer in Galveston

German U-boats operated not just in the open Atlantic and Pacific but also in the Gulf of Mexico, where they did their best to disrupt the oil supply critical to the Allied war effort, attacking U.S. shipping in general and tankers in particular. In 1942, 10-year-old Margaret Latimer got a little too close for comfort when she spent the summer with her family in Galveston, Texas.

In the spring of 1942 I was a 10-year-old Kansas girl with two long blond braids. I knew about World War II only from my diligent reading of Life magazine and from overhearing my parent's conversations. Almost every morning my father, who was fluent in both English and German, would arise very early and listen on his shortwave radio to the BBC and German stations—sometimes even picking up Axis Sally [a female radio personality broadcasting Axis propaganda]. Towards the end of that spring my father accepted a position as visiting professor of anatomy at the University of Texas medical school in Galveston to help train doctors for the war effort.

The car trip without air-conditioning was long and hot.

Young Margaret Latimer gives the Girl Scout salute.

We arrived in Galveston after dark and drove toward our lodging. But it was so dark! All the street lights were out. There were no cars and no people. I sensed my parents' growing anxiety.

Suddenly there was an angry policeman at my father's driver side window. He told us we were breaking the law by using our car headlights. Only parking lights were allowed within six blocks of the ocean due to the fact that there were German U-boats lurking in the water just off the coast. Because we were completely unfamiliar with the town we had no idea how to find our accommodations. My father politely explained the situation and asked for the officer's assistance. Gruffly, the policeman pointed towards what he said was a motel restaurant on our side of the seawall. Though we couldn't even see the building, my father slowly eased the car forward, using only the dim glow of our car's parking lights to avoid hitting anything. It was quite dangerous. So much so, that we narrowly avoided being involved in a violent collision that happened just in front of us.

We settled into our Galveston summer house, just six short blocks from the beach. I loved to walk to the ocean with my father after he returned from work. Sometimes we could not swim due to globs of tarlike oil on the sand and on the boulders at the base of the seawall that indicated that another submarine had been destroyed. I always hoped that it was one of the German U-boats which then freely roamed the Gulf of Mexico and not an American boat!

A special treat we enjoyed was picnicking with friends on the beautiful beach south of the seawall protecting Galveston. But as the sun started to go down everyone scurried to pack up. Every night, a jeep loaded with our armed soldiers drove slowly north up the beach toward us announcing that anyone remaining on the beach on their return would be shot. My parents had read an article in the paper about this actually happening so we believed them. More troublesome than the fear of getting shot by our own soldiers was the fear that under the cover of darkness Germans could attack the military installation at the south end of Galveston Island.

That summer there was a pervasive anxiety. The war was going very badly for us and we were in a very vulnerable location. Though we loved our summer in Galveston, we were all a bit relieved to head back to the inland safety of Kansas. ■

submarine *U-156* sank the British troopship *Laconia* off West Africa and then came to the aid of survivors—many of them Italian POWs—along with other U-boats and a Vichy French cruiser. During that rescue effort, an American plane bombed *U-156,* killing survivors from the *Laconia* in a lifeboat towed by the submarine and forcing it to submerge, which doomed other survivors clinging to the U-boat's deck. Afterward, Dönitz prohibited U-boat captains from making any further efforts to aid survivors of ships they torpedoed—a policy of unrestricted submarine warfare like that pursued by the United States and Japan in the Pacific.

The chief victims of U-boat attacks were Allied merchant mariners. Their chances of being rescued if a torpedo or mine wrecked

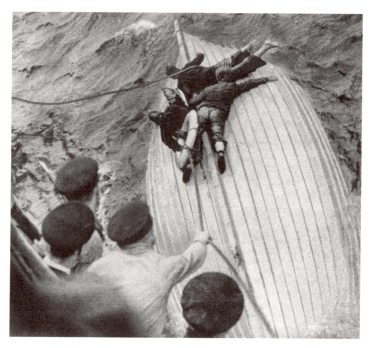

Crewmen aboard the French cruiser Gloire *aid survivors of the British troopship* Laconia, *clinging to an overturned lifeboat.*

their ship had been poor even before Dönitz issued his order. Many who abandoned sinking vessels drowned, burned, or suffocated in clinging fuel oil or died from exposure in the icy North Atlantic. Those who managed to reach a lifeboat or raft were by no means assured of survival. Allied merchant ships risked being torpedoed if they stopped to help survivors, and Allied warships escorting convoys had to concentrate on seeking and destroying U-boats. Not until late in the war were rescue ships assigned to convoys to aid survivors.

For all the perils merchant seamen faced, few abandoned their task. "Those who have been torpedoed and rescued ship right out again as soon as they can get out of the hospital," one reporter noted. "That takes plenty of nerve, but the merchant seamen have it." The ranks of American merchant mariners swelled from about 55,000 to 250,000 by the end of the war—despite casualties amounting to nearly 20,000 men killed, wounded, or missing in action.

> "Those who have been torpedoed and rescued ship right out again as soon as they can get out of the hospital. That takes plenty of nerve, but the merchant seamen have it."
>
> A reporter covering the toll the Battle of the Atlantic took on civilian seamen

SAFETY IN NUMBERS

Adopting a tactic developed during World War I to reduce depredations by German U-boats, Allied naval commanders organized convoys of merchant ships escorted by warships. At any one time, there were about a half dozen fully loaded outbound convoys destined for Britain and a similar number of empty convoys returning to America. They sought to avoid wolf packs, whose movements were often revealed by intercepted radio messages between U-boats and German naval headquarters, encoded on Enigma machines and deciphered by Allied cryptanalysts.

Normally a convoy sailed in a rectangular formation, with escort ships at the perimeter, seeking to detect U-boats before they came within torpedo range. The workhorses of convoy defense were the Royal Navy's Flower-class corvettes. Adopted by both the U.S. Navy and the Canadian Royal Navy, they were tough, compact, and lightly armed, using depth charges to force an attacking submarine to dive and remain down. Kills were usually made by warships that were somewhat larger and more heavily armed, such as the Royal Navy's River-class frigates and the U.S. Navy's destroyer escorts, which had sonar detection equipment and both stern- and side-launched depth charges. As the war progressed, convoys were also protected by escort carriers, whose aircraft searched for surfaced U-boats and attacked them.

A merchant ship in a convoy was far safer than one traveling alone, but convoys had drawbacks. It took time for them to assemble, and they traveled at the speed of their slowest ships, taking from 15 to 20 days to make crossings that fast ships could make in five. Upon reaching their destination, convoys clogged ports, causing delays in unloading cargo. The greatest problem was that wolf packs penetrating convoy defenses had a wealth of targets. When the Kriegsmarine (German Navy) equipped its U-boat fleet with an improved Enigma in early 1942 and code breakers lost track of wolf pack movements, Allied losses in the Battle of the Atlantic increased alarmingly. Churchill recalled, "I was even more anxious about this battle than I had been about the glorious air fight called the Battle of Britain."

The Allies owed their ultimate victory in the Battle of the Atlantic in part to quick work by British sailors aboard the destroyer H.M.S. *Petard* in the eastern Mediterranean. On the night of October 30, 1942, they boarded the German submarine *U-559* after forcing it to the surface with depth charges and retrieved keys to Enigma settings as the U-boat sank, taking two daring British crewmen down with it. It was the second such coup by the Royal Navy (the first occurred in May 1941 when *U-110* was forced to the surface and was boarded) and enabled Allied code breakers to solve the advanced Enigma adopted by the U-boat fleet in early 1942.

That was a big intelligence breakthrough, but Allied tactical and technological advances also helped overcome the U-boat peril and scatter the wolf packs. High-frequency direction finders—designated HF/DF, or "Huff Duff"—allowed radio listeners at Allied stations to plot the positions of U-boats without decoding their messages. That helped convoys take evasive action and provided guidance for long-range B-24 Liberator reconnaissance bombers, which closed a gap in the mid-Atlantic left uncovered by earlier land-based bombers. Those and other Allied gains, including improved radar and depth charges, more than offset German increases in submarine production and the launching of larger Type IXC U-boats with greater range and torpedo capacity.

Allied shipping losses in the Atlantic fell from over seven million tons in 1942 to three million tons in 1943. Meanwhile, U-boat losses were mounting. In May 1943—"Black May" for the Germans—34 U-boats went down, causing Admiral Dönitz to suspend anticonvoy operations and withdraw U-boats from the North Atlantic, where his hunters had become the hunted.

JANICE MARTIN BENARIO
ULTRA

*Beginning in 1942, the U.S. military recruited graduating
seniors from seven prestigious women's colleges for jobs in cryptology,
including the Ultra secret work managing intercepted
German Enigma messages.*

I was a senior [at Goucher College] 1942-43. Everyone at the college by that time was doing something for the war. Girls were rolling bandages, going to USO parties and such. Everybody's mind was on the war, and everybody wanted to do something to help because this was a war which we had to win . . . One day an English Professor stopped me in the hall [and said] . . . Janice will you come into my office. And so I go in, sit down. She comes in and closes the door, stands in front of the door and tells me about a course that the Navy is giving in cryptology . . . and she was inviting me to take it . . . she said this is very secret, you don't tell anyone. So I talked it over with my family, decided to accept her invitation . . .

Two others from Goucher, one from Radcliffe, I believe, and I were assigned to Op 20G, and our branch of the office was that which was reading the German Naval Enigma traffic, that is, the traffic from the German High command to the U-boats and back. The four of us were cleared to handle top secret Ultra material. None of our friends, no one, none of the public knew that there was such a level because Ultra was the word which Churchill had applied to the decoding of this German Naval Enigma traffic . . . We were told you do not talk, do not breathe a word of what goes on in that office. In wartime it would be treason, and you know the punishment for treason is death . . .

The messages came in just strips of letters. The translators had to divide it into German words and translate it from German to English then we had specially chosen enlisted people in the office to do the typing and other chores. The messages were typed then were handed to the senior watch officer . . . there were also people who worked just in the daytime on research, and material was given to them. Then it was passed to our desk. We were the junior watch officers . . . There was a big board wall map of the Atlantic Ocean and the United States and Europe, and we had pins for every submarine that we knew about. Because this was 1943, our office had collected lots of material on all the German Subs and people on them. They knew a lot of what I called Navalese words, and so this helped the translators. We had a pin for every submarine, and we had a pin with a paper flag on it for every convoy, and one of our main jobs was to keep that board up to date because that material was used by those who were studying what was going on. And another job every morning . . . at 7:30 each day we prepared an envelope for Downtown containing all the messages which had been translated that day. There was a neutral shipping report, and research people wrote a couple of sheets with big red letters on the top—TOP SECRET ULTRA—and so that meant this envelope was limited to where it could go. Every morning an armed carrier came with a locked pouch. We took our envelope to the door (obviously he could not come in), signed it over to him. He put it in his locked pouch, carried it out front to his car, drove it down to the main Navy department where it went up to the United States submarine tracking room and Admiral King, the COMINCH [commander in chief]. So we were one step below the top. Ultra secret all the time. ■

"Ultra secret all the time."

Crewmen on the deck of the U.S. Coast Guard Cutter Spencer *watch as a depth charge explodes during an attack in the North Atlantic on the German submarine* U-175 *on April 17, 1943.*

Attacks on convoys later resumed, and improved U-boats were introduced, but as Dönitz conceded: "We had lost the Battle of the Atlantic." By war's end, 785 of 1,162 U-boats had gone down, along with more than 30,000 crewmen—the highest casualty rate of any armed service in World War II.

AIR WAR OVER EUROPE

After Hitler invaded the Soviet Union in 1941, the Allies resolved to open a second ground front on Germany's western flank—a task not fully accomplished until troops landed in Normandy in June 1944. Yet Allied offensive action from the air had begun as early as 1940 when British bombers struck Berlin and intensified in 1942 when the United States joined the punishing air campaign, which continued until Germany lay devastated and defeated.

Advocates of strategic bombing had long argued that wars could be won by sending masses of bombers against enemy cities and industries. Critics questioned the morality and utility of that doctrine, and early in the war, the British Royal Air Force (RAF) often struck at precise military targets such as German battleships or U-boat bases. Precision bombing had to be carried out in daylight, increasing the risk that aircraft would be spotted and shot down. Lack of support from RAF fighters, which were busy defending Britain against German attacks, made such daytime raids even costlier, and poor bomb-sights rendered them largely ineffective even when visibility was good. But after German bombers blasted cities such as Rotterdam, attacked in May 1940, Allied leaders came to view strategic bombing as justifiable. Beginning with the Battle of Britain, both the RAF and the Luftwaffe conducted deadly raids on enemy cities.

When Air Marshal Arthur Harris took charge as chief of the RAF Bomber Command in February 1942, he stated his goals as "the destruction of German cities, the killing of German workers, and the disruption of civilized life throughout Germany." Instructed to destroy the "morale of the enemy civil population," he mounted massive nighttime air raids on German cities involving as many as 1,000 bombers. The first such attack was launched on May 30, 1942, against Cologne, where more than 4,500 people were killed or wounded and 13,000 homes were destroyed. The British had suffered similar losses during German air raids on London, Coventry, and other cities and felt that such reprisals were warranted. Aside from scourging the populace, attacks on cities disrupted the German economy and war effort by damaging factories, government offices, ports, and other facilities.

The workhorses of Harris's command were the heavy Handley Page Halifax bomber and the heavier Avro Lancaster, which was introduced in 1942 and had greater range and a larger bomb load than its predecessors. Technology kept pace with the requirements of nighttime bombing. Radar beams from two stations were used to pinpoint British bombers in flight and guide them to their targets in the dark. Bomber crews dropped small, thin, aluminum foil strips known as chaff (also called Window) to reflect and confuse the German radar that guided antiaircraft batteries. Path finders in twin-engine Mosquito fighter-bombers led the way during attacks, dropping flares or incendiaries to mark targets for bomber pilots, one of whom recalled that his illuminated target looked "like a huge shovelful of hot ashes which someone had flung on the ground."

AMERICANS SEIZE THE DAY

The U.S. Eighth Air Force began flying from Britain against German targets in France in May 1942, marking the opening of the American daylight precision-bombing campaign. Commanders hoped that masses of heavily armed B-17 Flying Fortresses and B-24 Liberators, flying in formation with each bomber providing cover to its neighbors, could overcome German air defenses and wreck

"By bombing the devils around the clock, we can prevent the German defenses from getting any rest."

Maj. Gen. Ira Eaker to Winston Churchill

German war industries. On their first missions over France, American bombers were escorted by RAF fighters. But Maj. Gen. Ira Eaker, who took charge of the Eighth Air Force in December 1942, wanted to attack Germany's industrial heartland, which was beyond the range of fighter escorts—and to do so daily while the RAF blasted German cities by night. "By bombing the devils around the clock," he wrote to an appreciative Winston Churchill, "we can prevent the German defenses from getting any rest."

Eaker's airmen conducted their first raid on Germany in late January 1943, bombing naval yards at Emden and Wilhelmshaven. By mid-1943, they were delving deep into Germany, far beyond the range of fighter escorts, and imposing heavy losses on German fighters. The toll would have been even higher had they

B-17s of the U.S. Eighth Air Force's 390th Bombardment Group, based in Britain, head out to blast German war industries on August 12, 1943, accompanied part of the way by fighters at higher altitude, leaving contrails in their wake.

lacked stout defenses of their own. Their mainstay was the Boeing B-17, which was manned by a crew of 10 and bristled with .50-caliber machine guns. Unescorted B-17s flew in tight formations of squadron "boxes," staggered vertically so that their machine guns could provide overlapping fields of fire. Their secret weapon for precision bombing was the Norden bombsight, a gyroscopically stabilized telescopic sight linked electronically to the B-17's automatic pilot to deliver bomb loads on target. Conditions in those unpressurized bombers at altitudes approaching 30,000 feet were brutal, forcing crewmen to don oxygen masks and wear bulky flight suits. "We were always afraid when we flew missions, every one of us," said a B-17 tail gunner, who added that without that fear, "I think every one us would have been lost."

Even with fighting capabilities, these aircraft were woefully vulnerable. In August 1943, the Eighth Air Force launched raids on targets essential to the Luftwaffe and closely guarded by its fighters, including Messerschmitt plants in Regensburg and ball-bearing factories at Schweinfurt. During one raid on Schweinfurt, 60 of 250 B-24s went down. The Mighty Eighth could not afford such losses and sorely needed fighter escorts. But even advanced Allied fighters like the P-47 Thunderbolt and the RAF's Spitfire lacked the range to accompany bombers deep into Germany.

The aircraft that came to their rescue was a splendid example of Anglo-American teamwork, commissioned by the British Air Ministry and designed by the North American Aviation Corporation. Known as the Mustang and designated Mark I by the RAF and P-51 by the U.S. Army Air Force (USAAF), its streamlined frame and advanced wing design reduced drag and eliminated the control problems plaguing earlier high-performance fighters.

The P-51B, introduced in December 1943, had a Packard-built version of the Spitfire's Rolls-Royce Merlin V-12 engine and a top speed of 445 miles an hour. Its exceptional range of 2,200 miles, facilitated by 150-gallon drop tanks that could be jettisoned when empty, made it an ideal escort for long-distance bombers.

Mustangs outmatched German fighters in the air and pounded them on runways. "If they wouldn't come up into the air," said Capt. Don Salvatore Gentile, he and other Mustang pilots would "shoot them up on the ground . . . kill them, trample them down." Bolstered by P-51s, the Eighth Air Force and the 15th Air Force, based in Italy, dealt a crushing blow to the Luftwaffe during "Big Week"—seven days of relentless attacks in February 1944 that disrupted German aircraft production and downed nearly 600 enemy fighters, ensuring Allied air supremacy when troops landed in Normandy in June.

Although USAAF bombers focused their attacks on German war industries, they also joined the RAF in conducting saturation bombing raids on German cities that caused massive civilian casualties. Some American commanders objected, including General Eaker, who warned that such assaults would convince "Germans that we are the barbarians they say we are." But Allied leaders were committed to the strategic bombing of cities in Germany as well as Japan until those opponents surren-

> "It was very still in the city after these attacks. The concentration camp inmates took the dead away . . . they threw them on the ruins. And the mountain got higher and higher."
>
> Horst Sinske on the bombing of Berlin

dered. Incendiaries dropped by Allied bombers on Hamburg, Germany, in July 1943 and Dresden in February 1945 kindled horrendous firestorms—hurricanes of flame that incinerated or asphyxiated tens of thousands of people. Other German

A blackened statue atop the Dresden town hall overlooks ruins after Allied aircraft firebombed the city in mid-February 1945, killing as many as 25,000 people.

cities like Berlin suffered similar losses over months as a result of repeated bombing raids. "It was very still in the city after these attacks," recalled Horst Sinske of Berlin. "The concentration camp inmates took the dead away . . . they threw them on the ruins. And the mountain got higher and higher."

Allied air strikes alone did not win the war or deprive the enemy of the will to fight. They did, however, force Luftwaffe and German civil defense commanders to divert scarce personnel, antiaircraft batteries, and fighter planes from military to civilian targets. Allied airmen who blasted Dresden and other German cities in the war's last months did not know how long the struggle would last and were prepared to keep up the pressure until it ended. "We thought we had a lot of fighting left to do," one of them said. Ultimate responsibility for prolonging Germany's suffering lay with Hitler, who refused to yield even after Allied troops overran his borders. "We may be destroyed," he said, "but if we are, we shall drag a world with us—a world in flames." Hundreds of thousands of civilians died in the flames and rubble as he dragged Germany down with him.

OPERATION OVERLORD

By the spring of 1944, a million and a half American soldiers were stationed on British soil, preparing for what Allied Supreme Commander Dwight Eisenhower called "the greatest amphibious assault ever attempted." The war in North Africa and Italy, the Battle of the Atlantic, and the sustained around-the-clock bombing of Germany had prepared the ground for that landing in Normandy, code-named Operation Overlord, which would launch the liberation of France and the invasion of Germany. Some in Britain complained that their own country had already been invaded—by the boisterous Yanks, caricatured as "overpaid, oversexed, and over here." But Eisenhower was careful not to let resentments at high levels threaten the Anglo-American alliance on which the success of Over-lord depended. Even stern critics like British army chief Alan Brooke gave him credit for promoting that transatlantic partnership. As D-Day approached, Brooke wrote privately that Ike was "just a coordinator, a good mixer, a champion of inter-Allied cooperation, and in those respects few can hold a candle to him."

> "[Ike was] just a coordinator, a good mixer, a champion of inter-Allied cooperation, and in those respects few can hold a candle to him."
>
> British army chief Alan Brooke

What Brooke considered a small matter—nurturing and strengthening the alliance—was in fact the supreme task of the supreme commander, a job demanding military, diplomatic, and executive skills that were rarely combined in one war leader as they were in Eisenhower. Among the strong-willed subordinates he had to harness and hold in line were talented and troublesome generals like his countryman George Patton and Britain's Bernard Montgomery, whom Winston Churchill called "indomitable in retreat, invincible in advance, insufferable in victory."

Monty could indeed be insufferable, but he was a logical choice to command Allied troops in Normandy until they broke out of their beachhead and Eisenhower set up headquarters in France. Ike recognized that the British were entitled to have one of their own serve as field commander under the American supreme commander—and that Monty's arrogant and abrasive manner toward men of high rank was outweighed by his proven

A massive Krupp 380-mm coast artillery gun juts from a newly constructed concrete casement on the French coast, one of hundreds of coast artillery batteries placed on the Atlantic Wall.

ability to inspire soldiers and lead them to victory. He earned the respect of his troops by planning operations meticulously and mustering all the strength he could before placing their lives at risk. His thorough, deliberate approach to battle had been vindicated in late 1942 at El Alamein, where he had defeated Erwin Rommel, who was now responsible for defending the northern coast of France between Normandy and Calais, where the English Channel was its narrowest. Although the German High Command considered Normandy a less likely target for the Allies than the area around Calais, which offered invaders both a shorter crossing and a shorter path to Germany, Rommel recognized that Normandy was vulnerable to attack, and he was strengthening its coastal defenses. "We'll have only one chance to stop the enemy," he said, "and that is when he is in the water. Everything we have must be on the coast. The first 24 hours of the invasion will be decisive. For the Allies as well as Germany, it will be the longest day."

> "We'll have only one chance to stop the enemy and that is when he is in the water."
>
> Field Marshal Erwin Rommel

Montgomery was well suited to plan and implement the landing at Normandy because he respected Rommel without being intimidated by him. Rommel was an "energetic and determined commander," Monty remarked, and he had made "a world of difference" since taking charge of the coastal defenses. But Allied commanders had no reason to fear defeat, he insisted, if they strengthened their attack in response to Rommel's measures and instilled in their troops "infectious optimism, and offensive eagerness. Nothing must stop them. If we send them into battle in this way—then we shall succeed." Montgomery and Eisenhower agreed that the original plan for Overlord, which called for landing three divisions across a 30-mile-wide front, was inadequate to overcome Rommel's defenses. The revised plan broadened the front to 50 miles and boosted the initial assault force to five infantry divisions, three divisions of paratroopers, and several brigades of commandos and other forces. In all, more than 150,000 soldiers would land in Normandy in the first 24 hours, a feat requiring a prodigious armada of 5,000 warships, transports, and landing craft.

Obstructions that Rommel's engineers had placed along the beaches prevented landing craft from reaching shore at high tide, which meant that the first wave of troops would have to land when the tide was lower and advance farther under fire from German artillery and machine-gun posts overlooking the beaches. Demolition squads operating at great peril would have to clear obstructions and mines before landing craft could safely disgorge tanks to join in the attacks. Monty wanted armor up front during the invasion and turned to his innovative countryman Maj. Gen. Percy Hobart, who designed floatable tanks called Duplex Drives (DDs), driven by propellers in water and by tracks on land. Some of Hobart's tanks were rigged with devices that could clear mines, allowing armor to lead the way in assaults and shield oncoming infantry. American commanders were skeptical of Hobart's "Funnies," as those strange vehicles were known, and made less use of them on D-Day than the British did, but Eisenhower later doubted that his "assault forces could have firmly established themselves without the assistance of these weapons."

Eisenhower's genial exterior masked the gritty determination of a leader who had grown tougher and more demanding as his responsibilities increased. Earlier, in North Africa, he had in fact been "just a coordinator," overseeing a campaign managed by his more experienced subordinates. Now he was fully in command. On issues of vital importance, he bowed to no one—not even Churchill, who opposed drawing troops away from Italy to launch Operation Anvil, an invasion of southern France that was supposed to coincide with the landings at Normandy. Eisenhower preserved Anvil over Churchill's objections by agreeing to delay the operation until after Overlord, which allowed the Italian campaign to achieve a major objective—the capture of Rome on June 5.

Another high-level dispute arose when Churchill joined top Allied air commanders in opposing Ike's plan to shift the brunt of their bombing campaign from Germany to France, where railways, depots, and bridges would be targeted to isolate enemy troops in Normandy and block efforts to reinforce them. Inevitably, many French civilians would die in those air raids, and Churchill denounced such "cold-blooded butchering" of people whom Overlord was meant to rescue. Churchill urged Franklin Roosevelt to intervene, but the president trusted in Eisenhower and the plan went ahead. Among those who backed the supreme commander's decision was Maj. Gen. Pierre Koenig, whose Free French forces in England were preparing to join Allied troops and members of the French Resistance in liberating their country. "This is war and it is expected that people will be killed," Koenig said of the air raids. "We would take twice the anticipated loss to be rid of the Germans."

No call made by the supreme commander was more difficult or fraught with peril than his final decision to proceed with the invasion. Originally planned for early May, Overlord was put off until June 5 to allow for a larger assault, which required more landing craft and other equipment. Stormy weather over the English Channel in early June then forced Eisenhower to postpone the launch until June 6. His chief meteorologist, Group Capt. R. M. Stagg of the Royal Air Force, predicted that the weather would improve that day. Seas would remain rough and clouds might obscure targets for pilots, but waiting longer for ideal conditions could be costly. If the invasion was not launched during the lull that Stagg forecast, it would have to be postponed for at least two weeks, when there would once again be a bright, moonlit night—required for operations by airborne troops—followed by a low tide at dawn for the amphibious assaults. The consequences of such a lengthy postponement, wrote Eisenhower, were "almost too bitter to contemplate." The greatest risk was that secrecy would be lost, allowing the Germans to mass forces at the point of attack.

Weighing the hazards of delay against the danger that conditions would prove worse than predicted and doom the landings, Eisenhower chose to trust in Stagg and his staff, who had proven accurate in trials when asked to forecast weather over the landing zone. After one last briefing before dawn on June 5, Ike confirmed the decision he had reached the night before. "OK. We'll go," he announced. Later that day, he drafted a press release to be issued if the invasion failed. "The troops, the air force and the navy did all that bravery and devotion to duty could do," he wrote. "If any blame or fault attaches to the attempt it is mine alone."

> "If any blame or fault attaches to the attempt it is mine alone."
>
> General Eisenhower in a press release to be issued if the D-Day invasion failed

Like Eisenhower, tens of thousands of troops who embarked for Normandy by sea and by air on the eve of D-Day were hoping for the best but preparing for the worst. Pvt. Harold Baumgarten and other men of the 116th Infantry Regiment, 29th Infantry Division, had already been informed by their colonel that they would be among the "first forces into the second front in Europe, and that two out of three of us aren't expected to come back." At a briefing before they shipped out, they learned that their target was the beach code-named Omaha, the most heavily defended of the five amphibious landing sites in Normandy. They were shown aerial reconnaissance photos of "Germans preparing the defenses," recalled Baumgarten. Afterward, he wrote to his sister in New York City, asking her "to get the mail before my parents, and to break the news gently to them when she received the telegram that I was no longer alive." In the event, Baumgarten survived, sparing his sister her devastating task.

DECEPTION AND DOUBLE CROSS

Nothing in the Allied arsenal could have averted disaster if German generals—who commanded 11 armored and 50 infantry divisions in France—had anticipated the landing at Normandy and concentrated forces there, so it was critical for the Allies to make sure they were focused elsewhere. After selecting Normandy as the landing site, British and U.S. officers conducted elaborate deceptions to keep the Germans guarding other possible targets across a wide area—from the Mediterranean to Norway—before leading them to the conclusion that the invasion would most likely occur at Calais. Collectively, those deceptions were labeled Operation Bodyguard for a remark made by Winston Churchill: "In wartime, truth is so precious that she should always be attended by a bodyguard of lies."

Among those who helped guard the truth by feeding lies to the enemy were agents recruited by the Abwehr (German military intelligence) to spy on the British, who then turned them against their German handlers. That high-stakes spy game began in 1939 when MI-5 (British counterintelligence) arrested Arthur Owens, a Welsh agent working for the Abwehr. Owens helped MI-5 catch other German spies who parachuted into Britain in 1940. By 1941, they had all been turned by MI-5 and were feeding false intelligence to the Abwehr by radio from a secret detention center in London. The operation was so sensitive that a top-flight committee of British intelligence officers called Double Cross (XX) was formed to handle it.

As the landings at Normandy loomed, double agents controlled by the Double Cross Committee played a big part in the ultimate Allied deception, dubbed Operation Fortitude, designed to reinforce German expectations that invasion forces would cross the Strait of Dover (Pas de Calais). "Never did we say anything directly about the Pas de Calais," remarked one double agent afterward. Instead, they offered vague hints of a buildup of men and materiel around Dover.

Anticipating that the Germans might try to confirm those reports by conducting reconnaissance flights, the Allies placed dummy aircraft, inflatable rubber tanks, and other props that looked suitably convincing from a distance on airfields and bases near Dover. Radio operators there broadcast false signals from imaginary divisions of the fictitious FUSAG (First U.S. Army Group), and hundreds of soldiers were given sleeve insignia for those divisions to wear on leave. As a final flourish, General Pat-

*Soldiers at a camp in Yorkshire heft an inflatable M4 Sherman tank,
one of several dummy weapons created by American and British intelligence
services as part of Operation Fortitude to fool aerial observers.*

ton—well known to the Germans after his hard-charging advance across Sicily—was put in charge of the phony FUSAG. Meanwhile, the real commander of the Normandy invasion forces, General Montgomery, was impersonated by an actor who made appearances around the Mediterranean to conceal Monty's whereabouts and intentions.

Patton's presence in England was publicized to bolster the hoax, but he nearly lost his commission as the phony leader of FUSAG—and the real commander of armored forces slated to land in Normandy after D-Day—when he gave a foolish speech in April stating that it was "the evident destiny of the British and Americans to rule the world." Ike was furious, but kept him on after sending a public relations officer to shut him up. That officer translated Ike's curt message into polite language, but Patton insisted on knowing what his boss had really said, to which the messenger replied: "He said that you were not to open your goddamned mouth again publicly until he said you could!"

It didn't take long for the Allies to confirm their ruse was working. The same unwitting diplomat whose intercepted communication had tipped off Washington to an imminent Japanese attack in December 1941 was now, according to U.S. Army chief George Marshall, the Allies' main informant "regarding Hitler's intentions in Europe." Lt. Gen. Hiroshi Oshima, Japan's ambassador to Germany, was described by correspondent William Shirer as "more Nazi than the Nazis." A confidant of German foreign minister Joachim von Ribbentrop and top German generals, he was allowed to tour the Atlantic Wall, which guarded the west coast of occupied Europe against an Allied invasion. In late 1943, Oshima had reported to Tokyo by radio that Normandy was lightly defended by the Germans. Now Oshima's deciphered dispatches confirmed the success of Allied efforts to make the Germans expect an invasion at Calais and concentrate forces there.

Final confirmation of Operation Fortitude's success came on D-Day itself, when German forces in France were concentrated around Calais. Rommel had not only been fooled into expecting the invasion at Calais, but had also discounted the possibility of an attack of any kind in such bad weather and had returned home to visit his wife on her birthday and to confer with Hitler, who was sleeping late this morning and would not be awakened until 10 a.m. Other German officers serving in France under Rommel were off conducting war games on June 6 in anticipation of an invasion in the weeks or months to come. Long after the invasion of Normandy began, Hitler believed that it was a diversion and held back panzer divisions to meet the anticipated threat at Calais, which never materialized.

ARMING THE RESISTANCE

Starting well in advance of the invasion of Normandy and ready now to play their part in the battle to come, British and American spy agencies had teamed up with the Free French and the Resistance to undermine the ability of the Germans to defend their occupied territory in France. In July 1940, British authorities had created the Special Operations Executive (SOE), a shadowy organization assigned to strike back at Germany by conducting a secret war in Axis-occupied territories. The SOE worked in close cooperation with Lord Mountbatten's Combined Operations Headquarters, an organization tasked with harassing the enemy through commando raids and combined naval and army amphibious operations. While the commandos of Combined Operations raided enemy outposts in coastal areas, ranging from islands off Norway to German radar sites on French beaches, highly trained SOE teams were dropped behind enemy lines to conduct sabotage operations and organize guerrilla units. The SOE's American counterpart was the Office of Strategic Services (OSS), created by President Roosevelt in June 1942 and directed by Col. William "Wild Bill" Donovan. The OSS was meant to be America's primary intelligence-gathering organization, and its field teams also worked closely with the SOE to penetrate occupied Europe.

Technicians and scientists working for the SOE and OSS devised unique weapons and equipment for clandestine operatives, including James Bond–worthy coins with tiny swivel-out knife blades, a gun that looked like a tobacco pipe, fuses that looked like pencils, and shoes with concealed knife blades. The SOE pioneered the use of plastic explosives, and both the OSS and SOE developed compact shortwave transceivers; the SOE version weighed less than 40 pounds and looked like an ordinary suitcase. In preparation for Operation Overlord, Royal Air Force bombers dropped weapons and supplies to the French Resistance, providing arms for nearly half a million fighters. OSS and Free French agents formed two-man Sussex teams to gather intelligence about German troop movements. Coinciding with the invasion, Jedburgh teams made up of OSS, SOE, and Free French officers would launch a guerrilla campaign throughout France, including wide-ranging bombing raids, hit-and-run attacks by French Resistance fighters on phone lines and other means of communication, and artful deceptions including dropping thousands of dummies fitted with parachutes to simulate airborne assaults far from the actual attack. General Eisenhower later praised those secret efforts, stating that the disruption of enemy communications and the "increasing strain placed on German security services throughout occupied Europe by the organized forces of Resistance, played a very considerable part in our complete and final victory."

DAY OF DECISION

Shortly before midnight on June 5, hundreds of planes filled with airborne troops—their faces blackened to avoid being spotted at night and loaded with equipment weighing 70 pounds or more—began taking off from runways in southern England. Civilians roused from sleep by the roar of engines overhead realized that a momentous new day in their long struggle against Germany was about to dawn. "It seemed as if every aircraft in the world was in flight, as wave followed upon wave without intermission," recalled John Keegan, who witnessed that stirring scene as a boy and went on to become a military historian.

Troops involved in this massive airborne assault faced a rough landing in Normandy, whether they parachuted from C-47 transports or descended in gliders that plowed into fields with a bone-jarring impact that could leave men dazed and battered before they even began to fight. Their targets lay at either end of the Allied landing zone, bounded by Utah Beach to the west and Sword Beach to the east—between which lay Omaha, Gold, and

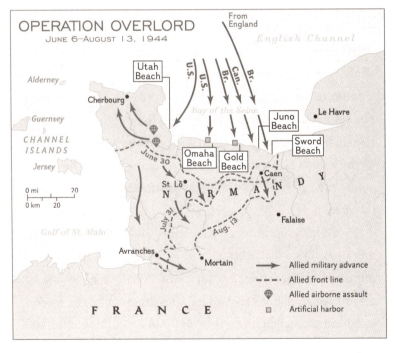

Preceded by airborne troops, Allied infantry landed on the beaches of Normandy on the morning of June 6, 1944. U.S. forces landed at beaches code-named Omaha and Utah; British and Canadian forces landed at Gold, Juno, and Sword Beaches.

Juno Beaches. The U.S. 82nd and 101st Airborne Divisions came down behind Utah Beach, which, like neighboring Omaha Beach, would be assaulted around dawn by American troops arriving by sea. The British Sixth Airborne Division landed behind Sword Beach, which, like Gold and Juno Beaches, would be stormed by British Commonwealth forces, including two brigades of Canadians.

Men of the Sixth Airborne, led by Maj. John Howard, were assigned to seize two vital bridges situated between Sword Beach and the city of Caen, an enemy stronghold that General Montgomery hoped to capture on the first day of the battle. Descending in gliders around 12:30 a.m. on June 6, they were the first Allied troops to enter battle on D-Day. "Crash-landing was the big fear," Howard remarked. "My other worry was that we were all carrying grenades that were already primed. If one of those went off and exploded, it would have blown all the ammunition in the glider." Fortunately, no such blasts occurred, but hard landings killed some of the pilots—who came down remarkably close to their targets—and wounded others. Most of the troops emerged intact and took the bridges by storm before their startled foes could detonate charges and demolish the spans.

Few Allied paratroopers who landed in Normandy were as quick to achieve their objectives as Howard's men. The weather improved, as predicted, but their task remained daunting. In the American sector behind Utah Beach, much of the terrain consisted of marshes or fields that had been flooded by the Germans to impede landings. Accuracy was essential, but pilots of the C-47 transports had difficulty maintaining formation as they flew in and out of cloud banks over the English

Channel and drifted farther apart when they encountered heavy flak over the coast of Normandy and began ducking and weaving. "We could see tracers coming up from many angles," recalled one pilot. "There was a tremendous racket such as experienced when flying through hail." Unnerved by the flak, some pilots sped up before reaching their drop zones, subjecting paratroopers to a dangerous "prop blast" that stunned them as their parachutes jerked open. Many landed far from their intended targets. Robert Flory of the 82nd Airborne looked down after jumping and "went into a state of shock. I was over water. My first thought was that the SOB pilot had dropped us over the English Channel. I looked to the right and saw a herd of dairy cows grazing. About that time I landed in water up to my chest. I was in a salt marsh." Weighed down by cumbersome gear, many paratroopers who landed in water as he did drowned, but Flory managed to reach dry land. "All this time, the gun fire was deafening, and the planes kept going over," he remarked." I saw one plane take a direct hit and explode in midair."

The main objective of the 82nd Airborne was the town of Ste.-Mère-Église, a vital crossroads a few miles inland from Utah Beach. Some ill-fated paratroopers drifted down in the center of town, where the glare from a burning building made them easy targets for German troops stationed there. One American was incinerated when he fell into that "flaming building, chute and all," related a fellow soldier. "He was burnt up so bad that he broke in two."

After killing or capturing a few dozen other paratroopers who descended in their midst, the Germans holding Ste.-Mère-Église mistakenly concluded that the battle was over. In fact, hundreds of men with the 505th Parachute Infantry Regiment had landed safely near the town along with bundles containing bazookas. Those heavy weapons were handled by two-man teams, including Bill Dunfee, a veteran of the Sicily campaign, and his partner, Jim Beavers. "By the time Jim joined me I had the bundle unrolled and the bazooka and ammo out," Dunfee related. "We loaded up and headed for Ste.-Mère-Église. It was easy to locate. That's where most of the fire was coming from."

They were held in reserve while other paratroopers led by Lt. Col. Edward Krause overpowered the small German garrison there. Then they dug in at the outskirts of town "to await the counterattack that came all too swiftly," Dunfee recalled. "The enemy really socked it to us with 88s and Screaming Meemies," so-called for the shrill sound those rockets made. Among the victims were three paratroopers, one of whom had a grenade in his pocket when a rocket hit and was blown apart as Dunfee looked on: "His head, chest, and right arm were all that remained intact. One of our men remarked, 'That's what you call going to hell in a hurry.' He wasn't being callous or unfeeling; his statement seemed appropriate at the time." Their commander, Krause, was wounded twice but refused to be evacuated and remained with his men until the Germans fell back and Ste.-Mère-Église was safely in hand.

"That's what you call going to hell in a hurry."

An American paratrooper, after a fellow soldier was blown apart

For Maj. Gen. Maxwell Taylor, commander of the 101st Airborne Division, the battle for Normandy began as a frustrating search for his paratroopers, scattered across the countryside. "I landed alone in a field surrounded by the usual high hedges

On June 5, 1944, General Eisenhower encourages men of the 502nd Parachute Infantry Regiment, 101st Airborne Division, as they prepare to depart for a predawn descent on Normandy on D-Day.

and trees with a few cows as witnesses," he related. His men were equipped with noisemakers called "crickets," whose clicking sounds helped them distinguish friend from foe in the dark, but it took hours for the far-flung paratroopers to gather in bands large enough to fight effectively. Taylor rounded up about 30 followers, many of them officers. "Never in the field of human conflict have so few been commanded by so many," he said ruefully.

Though most German commanders had their eyes far from the ball on June 6, one notable exception was Gen. Erich Marcks, who remained at his headquarters in St.-Lô, 20 miles inland from Utah Beach. When informed that paratroopers were landing along the coast, Marcks promptly alerted the 352nd

Infantry Division, whose troops guarded Utah and Omaha Beaches. They held strong positions at Omaha but were vulnerable to attack at Utah—and were not reinforced there on D-Day because large elements of Taylor's 101st Airborne coalesced before dawn and seized roads and causeways behind that beach, isolating the German defenders. Nearly 2,500 of the 13,000 American paratroopers who went into action on D-Day were killed, wounded, or captured, but their sacrifices enabled troops arriving by sea to take Utah Beach and secure the Allies' western flank at a cost of just 200 casualties—a toll that astonished planners who feared losing as many as 10,000 lives in the landings at Normandy.

Other factors contributed to the successful outcome at Utah, including good luck and dynamic leadership by 57-year-old Brig. Gen. Theodore Roosevelt, the eldest son of the late president Theodore Roosevelt. Although he walked with a cane and had a weak heart, he secured permission to land with the first wave from Lt. Gen. Omar Bradley, who led the American troops sent to Normandy as commander of the U.S. First Army. "It will steady the men to know I am with them," Roosevelt insisted. After wading ashore, he discovered that the first wave had landed more than a mile off course—a fortunate mistake, he realized, because the area was sparsely defended and close to a causeway held by the 101st Airborne. Rather than divert his troops laterally to their intended landing zone, he sent them rushing inland to link up with the paratroopers. "We'll start the war right here," he declared. Roosevelt's war would end a month later when he died of a heart attack, but what he accomplished

> **"It will steady the men to know I am with them."**
>
> Brig. Gen. Theodore Roosevelt, explaining why he wanted to land with his men even though he was in poor health

at Utah Beach rivaled his father's celebrated charge up San Juan Hill in Cuba.

Schoolbook tales of heroism in battle did little to prepare troops of the U.S. First and 29th Infantry Divisions for the horrors awaiting them on Omaha Beach. Unlike most of the men of the 29th who were entering their first battle on D-Day, many in the Big Red One had fought in North Africa and Sicily. But none had faced an ordeal as trying as this assault, which proved deadly even before they came under fire from heavy German artillery on cliffs overlooking Omaha, or from machine guns and rifles protruding from slits in concrete pillboxes set in dunes along the beach, or from tanks half-buried in the sand with their barrels pointed menacingly at obstructions, mine-fields, and barbed wire through which troops would have to struggle before they reached shore.

The mayhem began far from land when Rear Adm. Alan Kirk anchored the transports before dawn a dozen miles from Omaha Beach—safely beyond the range of the big German guns there but perilously exposed to heavy seas—and troops on those ships piled into landing craft that were pitching wildly. Several of those craft sank before coming under fire, drowning hundreds of men. Landing craft that were carrying artillery or conventional tanks also went down, as did more than two dozen float-able DDs, which could not withstand high surf and sank with their crews. Few armored vehicles made it onto the beach to support the infantry in the first wave. "Everyone in my tank was praying," recalled J. C. Friedman whose battalion came under attack as it approached shore in a landing craft. "I kept thinking: is this the end of me? Will I ever see my family again? God give me strength to go on and see this day through. There was

constant shelling and shrapnel flying off the tanks." Many crewmen who survived did so by abandoning their shattered vehicles
and wading ashore on foot.

Preliminary bombardment of the German defenses had little
impact on gunners in the sturdy pillboxes, many of them veterans
of hard fighting on the Eastern Front. Unlike Friedman and his
tank crew, infantrymen approaching Omaha Beach in landing craft
had no armor to shield them. "About 200 to 300 yards from shore
we encountered artillery fire," recalled Sgt. Bob Slaughter of the
116th Regiment, which led the way for the 29th Infantry. Shaken
by the shelling, the sailor piloting the craft was reluctant to bring
the troops any closer to shore. "These men have heavy equipment,"
Sgt. Willard Norfleet told him. "You *will* take them all the way in."
When the sailor protested that they would all be killed, Norfleet
drew his pistol, put it to the man's head, and shouted: *"All the way
in."* Like many others in that heaving landing craft, Slaughter was
seasick: "I had given my puke bag to a buddy who already had filled
his. Minus the paper bag, I used my steel helmet." When the ramp
went down, the water was still treacherously deep for soldiers
wearing 60-pound packs. "Many were hit in the water and
drowned," Slaughter said. "There were dead men floating in the
water and live men acting dead, letting the tide take them in."

Demolition crews were among the first to land and the first to
fall as they attempted to remove mines and obstructions on
Omaha Beach. Sgt. Roy Arnn tried to unload his mine detector
from its box "but couldn't because the lid was jammed. There was
no place to hide in the open, and a sniper shot me." Moments
later, he was hit by shrapnel in the leg and was unable to move as
the tide rose around him. He was saved from drowning by a
lieutenant who dragged him to the high-water mark and was

wounded as he did so. As Arnn prayed to God for deliverance, he could hear another stricken soldier nearby "crying and asking for his parents."

Private Baumgarten of the ill-fated 116th Regiment expected to die—and considered defeating the Nazis who were targeting his fellow Jews in Europe a cause worth dying for. But he survived several staggering wounds, the first of which occurred just moments after he descended from his landing craft: "Fragments from an 88-millimeter shell hit me in my left cheek. It felt like being hit by a baseball bat, only the results were much worse. My upper jaw was shattered, the left cheek was blown open . . . Blood poured from the gaping wound." Those who made it to the beach intact entered an arena of appalling carnage and chaos. "People were yelling, screaming, dying," said Sgt. Felix Branham of the 116th. "Men were bleeding to death, crawling, lying everywhere, firing coming from all directions."

> "People were yelling, screaming, dying. Men were bleeding to death, crawling, lying everywhere, firing coming from all directions."
>
> Sgt. Felix Branham, 116th Infantry Regiment, Omaha Beach

Many of the 3,000 casualties that American troops at Omaha suffered occurred in the first few desperate hours when the living huddled among the dead and the assault appeared doomed. The sparks that revived the attack and got those who were still able to fight moving came from officers who braved the terrors with their men and would not let them rest until they had achieved their goal—sergeants, lieutenants, and colonels like Charles Canham, who had warned his regiment that two of every three men might be lost here. "Colonel Canham was screaming at us to get across the beach," recalled Branham. "Back in training we used to call Colonel Canham everything not fit to print . . . We thought

ENSIGN JOSEPH VAGHI
BEACHMASTER ON D-DAY

Vaghi landed on the "Easy Red" sector of Omaha Beach with Platoon C-8, Sixth Naval Beach Battalion, to serve as a beachmaster, directing the movement of men and equipment.

Coming in with the first wave, heavily loaded soldiers of the 16th Regiment, First Infantry Division, wade ashore under fire at Omaha Beach on D-Day.

My first awareness that what we were doing was for real was when an 88-mm shell hit our LCI [landing craft] and machine-gun fire surrounded us. The Germans were in their pillboxes and bunkers high above the beach on the bluff and had an unobstructed view of what we were doing.

The atmosphere was depressing. The top of the bluff behind the beach was barely visible; the sound of screeching 12 and 14-inch shells from the warships, the *USS Texas* and *USS Arkansas*, offshore were new sounds never heard by us before; the stench of expended gunpowder filled the air and rocket

> "[T]he stench of expended gunpowder filled the air and rocket launchers mounted on landing craft moved in close to the shore and were spewing forth hundreds of rounds at a time onto the German defenses."

launchers mounted on landing craft moved in close to the shore and were spewing forth hundreds of rounds at a time onto the German defenses. The sea was rough. Purple smoke emanated from the base of the beach obstacles as the UDT [underwater demolition team] prepared to detonate another explosive in the effort to clear a path through the obstacles to the dune line—this was the state of affairs as the Platoon made its way to the dune line oh, so many yards away.

Using the obstacles as shelter, we moved forward over the tidal flat under full exposure to machine-gun fire as we finally reached the dune line. All C-8s made the long trek, including Commander Carusi. God was with us!

Having reached the high-water mark, we set about organizing ourselves and planning the next move as we had done so many times during our training period. The principal difference was that we were pinned down with real machine-gun fire with very little movement to the right or the left of our position and absolutely NO movement forward.

Because the UDT had opened gaps through the underwater obstacles into Easy Red, most of the personnel and vehicles came ashore on my beach with the result that we were very crowded and became "sitting ducks" for the enemy fire. ■

he would be another rear-echelon commander. After seeing him in action, I sure had to eat a mess of crow." Col. George Taylor, commander of the 16th Regiment, First Infantry, provided similar prodding to his men, pinned down at the far end of Omaha. "Two kinds of people are staying on this beach," he shouted, "the dead and those who are going to die. Now let's get the hell out of here!" Brig. Gen. Norman Cota of the 29th Infantry put it more bluntly to troops shuddering in the sand: "No sense dying here, men. Let's go on up the hill and die."

Some soldiers made daring assaults on German strong points, notably men of the Second Ranger Battalion who scaled a 100-foot-high cliff and seized a battery at great cost, only to discover that the massive 155-mm howitzers they were sent to capture had been removed by the Germans. More damage to enemy batteries and pillboxes was done by Navy destroyers that ventured perilously close to shore at midmorning and succeeded where the earlier bombardment had failed. That pounding helped clear the way for troops who had been trapped below the cliffs and dunes to push inland through ravines that were shrouded in smoke from blazes ignited by shellfire. By late afternoon, some units had advanced more than a mile and were battling Germans from house to house in the town of Colleville-sur-Mer. Behind them, reinforcements were pouring in by the thousands. "The entire beach was a mass of men, supplies, and equipment," one witness stated. Enemy guns continued to pound Omaha periodically, but the Germans would never again be as close as they were that morning to driving their foes back into the sea.

Most of the Allied forces who landed east of Omaha on Gold, Juno, and Sword Beaches fared better initially, with the exception of Canadian troops destined for Juno, who lost many of their landing craft to mines or artillery fire. Those low beaches were not as forbidding or as stoutly defended as the high ground above Omaha, and both the Canadians and the British troops who landed on either side of them had pushed several miles inland by midafternoon.

Commandos led by the Scottish nobleman Lord Lovat came ashore at Sword Beach marching to the tune of his piper, Bill Millen. Brigadier Lovat was "a typical aristocrat who would walk calmly with his head held high while the rest of us would be ducking and diving to avoid shells," Millen remarked. As they advanced beyond the beach, the shooting stopped, and French civilians, among whom were refugees from various European countries under Nazi rule, gathered along the road to applaud the commandos. Entranced with Millen's bagpipe and kilt, one little girl tried to join the procession and had to be dissuaded by the piper, who knew that trouble lay ahead. Their assignment was to link up with Major Howard's Sixth Airborne paratroopers, who were fighting to hold the bridges they had seized long before dawn that morning. "The bridge over the Orne River was coming under sniper fire as we approached it," Millen said. "Lovat made a wave of his hand, telling us to go on and for me to continue playing." Some were shot as they crossed the bridge, but Millen and the bulk of Lovat's men came through unscathed and were heartily embraced by the battle-weary paratroopers.

Montgomery's hopes of occupying Caen on D-Day—the objective for which Howard's men had seized the bridges—were dashed a few hours later when the powerful 21st Panzer Division advanced from that city and drove a wedge between the British forces pushing inland from Sword Beach and the Canadians at Juno. "We were to make a strong thrust directly to the coast, wipe out the enemy, and take over the beaches to prevent further landings," reported Lt. Franz Grabmann, who had fought against the British in North Africa. "We met little resistance and drove on until we could actually see the sea, and then we met stiffening opposition." Late in the day, Grabmann learned that "some of our troops and tanks had actually reached the beach, which was heartening news. Then, like a thunderbolt from the sky, came a great aerial column of planes and gliders." That column consisted of 250 transport planes towing gliders filled with reinforcements for the embattled British Sixth Airborne. Fighters shielded the transports and swooped down to strafe German tanks and antiaircraft batteries. By nightfall, Gen. Edgar Feuchtinger, commander of the 21st Panzers, had lost nearly half his tanks and decided to pull his forces back to Caen rather than have them pinched off by "heavily concentrated airborne troops."

Had the Germans brought more armored forces to bear against their foes on D-Day, they might have altered the outcome. But Hitler did not approve sending two panzer divisions to support the 21st until late that afternoon, and once they began moving toward Caen, they were subject to air strikes that delayed them and did considerable damage.

The decisive factor in the battle for the beaches was Allied air supremacy. While the battered Luftwaffe had little impact on the fighting, British and American airborne operations proved crucial in securing Sword and Utah Beaches and shielding the flanks of the amphibious assault forces. By the time Rommel returned to his headquarters in France late that night, he had lost his chance

LSTs (landing ships carrying tanks and other vehicles) clog Omaha Beach on June 8, 1944, as an American tank-destroyer battalion moves inland in the foreground. Barrage balloons like those aloft here were moored by cables that deterred low-flying enemy aircraft.

to stop his opponents in the water before they had established a beachhead. The pivotal 24-hour struggle he called "the longest day" would be remembered as the finest day for those fighting to loosen Hitler's deadly grip on Europe.

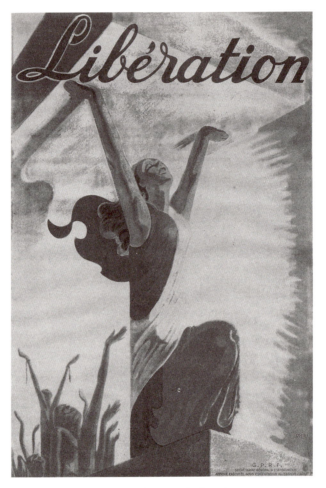

A French poster depicts the spirit of Liberty freeing captives by lifting the lid from the sarcophagus of Nazi oppression.

CHRONOLOGY

JULY 25, 1944 Allies break out in Normandy and begin advancing toward Paris.

AUGUST 25, 1944 Germans abandon Paris.

AUGUST 15, 1944 Allied troops land on the French Mediterranean coast.

DECEMBER 16, 1944 Battle of the Bulge begins.

VICTORY OVER GERMANY

THE LAST YEAR OF THE THIRD REICH

Allied commanders had known that landing on the coast of Normandy would be risky, but few anticipated how treacherous the next step in their campaign would be. Beyond the beaches lay *bocage,* the traditional Norman patchwork of low fields and woodlands, with property lines delineated by tall hedgerows, long banks of earth covered with dense thickets in which snipers and machine gunners could lurk unseen. "We were flabbergasted by the bocage," wrote Maj. Gen. Elwood Quesada. Infantrymen were "paralyzed" by small-arms fire from the hedgerows, he added, and tanks became snagged there and fell prey to artillery or rocket launchers. Stubborn German defenders exploited that terrain to the utmost and made breaking out of the beachhead in Normandy far costlier for the Allies than landing there.

JANUARY 27, 1945 Soviet troops liberate Auschwitz.

MARCH 1945 Allied troops cross the Rhine and advance into Germany.

MAY 7–8, 1945 Germany surrenders and Allies celebrate victory in Europe.

FEBRUARY 4–11, 1945 Roosevelt, Churchill, and Stalin meet at Yalta in Crimea to discuss how to organize Europe when the war is over.

APRIL 30, 1945 Hitler commits suicide as Soviet troops overrun Berlin.

The only way around the bocage for troops seeking to advance eastward to Germany lay through Caen, where Rommel concentrated the bulk of his armor. British and Canadian forces dispatched by Montgomery tried repeatedly to puncture German defenses in and around Caen before finally entering that city on July 9 after blistering Allied bombing raids that killed several thousand civilians there. "The dead lay everywhere," one witness reported, "not corpses, just the remains, fingers, a hand, a head, pathetic personal belongings." Many soldiers on both sides perished as well in the attack, which forced the Germans back a few miles but failed to achieve a breakout. Monty was criticized for taking more than a month to seize an objective he had planned to capture on the first day of the campaign. Among his detractors was Churchill, who considered him overcautious and worried that "we were descending into a bitter 'trench warfare' situation similar to that of World War I." Yet Montgomery's ponderous assault on Caen pinned down some of the strongest German divisions in France while Bradley's American troops advanced westward up Normandy's Cotentin Peninsula against less formidable opposition.

By late June, Bradley had captured the port of Cherbourg, where Lt. Gen. Karl Wilhelm von Schlieben had orders from Hitler to "leave the enemy not a harbor but a field of ruins." His engineers wrecked the place so thoroughly that it took months to clear mines, sunken ships, and other obstructions and render the port fully operational. In the meantime, the Allies relied on two artificial harbors on the Normandy coast. Marvels of engineering, they helped boost Allied strength in Normandy to 1.5 million troops and 300,000 vehicles by late July. But importing enough fuel and other supplies to keep those forces moving became a big concern as the campaign progressed.

Taking Cherbourg had been no easy task for American forces. Although their foes included some demoralized recruits from Poland and other occupied countries who chose to fight for Germany rather than be sent to prison camps, strongholds like Fort du Roule, overlooking the harbor, were stoutly defended by German troops and were attacked at great risk by Allies wielding grenades and other explosive devices. One officer, Col. Carlton McNeely, was devastated by the sight of the Americans who died taking that fort. "It tears me up to see so many of our fine young men being killed like that," he told Capt. George Mabry, who urged him to steel himself when fellow soldiers fell in battle by focusing on the enemy. "The only way I can do it," Mabry added, was to say: "You German SOBs killed my buddies, I'm going to get ten more of you for that."

Men like McNeely who took the cruelties of war to heart soon became hardened to battle as the campaign intensified. After securing Cherbourg and the Cotentin Peninsula, American infantry and airborne troops—who advanced on foot after landing in Normandy—turned eastward toward the heart of France and entered the worst of the bocage, held by tough German veterans who yielded ground grudgingly. The struggle began in earnest on July 3 when Bradley's forces set out to seize the towns of Coutances and St.-Lô, beyond which lay open country that contained few barriers to armor and motorized infantry. If Americans broke out there, they could launch a blitzkrieg of their own and might bring the war to a swift conclusion. Mindful of that threat, Germans defended the bocage as if fighting for their home ground.

War correspondent Ernie Pyle described the combat: "The fields were surrounded on all sides by immense hedgerows— ancient earthen banks, waist high, all matted with roots, and out of which grew weeds, bushes, and trees up to twenty feet high. The Germans used these barriers well. They put snipers in the trees. They dug deep trenches behind the hedgerows and covered them with timber, so that it was almost impossible to get at them . . . They even cut out a section of the hedgerow and hid a big gun or tank in it, covering it with brush . . . Our men didn't go across the open fields in dramatic charges such as you see in the movies . . . They went in tiny groups, a squad or less . . . The attacking squads sneaked up the sides of the hedgerows while the rest of the platoon stayed back in their own hedgerow and kept the forward hedge saturated with

American troops cross a road under fire near St.-Lô after bombers blast a hole in the German defenses on July 25, 1944.

bullets. They shot rifle grenades too, and a mortar squad a little farther back kept lobbing mortar shells over onto the Germans . . . This hedgerow business was a series of little skirmishes like that clear across the front, thousands and thousands of little skirmishes . . . Added up over

> "The fields were surrounded on all sides by immense hedgerows— ancient earthen banks, waist high, all matted with roots, and out of which grew weeds, bushes, and trees up to twenty feet high."
>
> Ernie Pyle, war correspondent, in Normandy

the days and weeks, however, they made a man-sized war—with thousands on both sides getting killed."

Among the soldiers caught up in those deadly skirmishes was Sgt. Bud Warnecke, Company B, 508th Parachute Infantry Regiment, 82nd Airborne Division. On July 4, he and another sergeant were "standing behind a hedgerow being briefed" by Lt. Homer Jones when a German machine gunner targeted them. One bullet grazed Warnecke, who "went down as if hit by a sledgehammer" but was not seriously wounded. Another hit Jones in the neck. "Blood was squirting out both sides and he was in terrible pain," Warnecke related. "We called for a medic. Jones was saying, 'Let me die! Let me die!' and Sgt. Roland Fecteau who was nearby, immediately stuck two fingers in the lieutenant's neck and plugged the holes." That prompt action helped save Jones, but he and many others in the company who were not killed outright while struggling through the bocage had to be evacuated. "By the time the fighting stopped for us on July 9," Warnecke said, "we in B Company, which started with 148 troopers, were down to 33."

By mid-July, Bradley's First Army had suffered more than 40,000 casualties and had yet to achieve its objectives. Coutances remained beyond his grasp, but his troops finally entered St.-Lô on July 18 after it was reduced to rubble. "We sure liberated the hell out of this place," one soldier remarked. As they did at Caen, Germans fell back to the outskirts of town but kept the Allies hemmed in. To shatter the enemy line and break out decisively, Bradley called for a massive bombing raid on German armor and infantry west of St.-Lô. Montgomery, who remained in command of all Allied troops in Normandy, approved Bradley's proposal and supported it by launching a preliminary attack by British and Canadian forces near Caen. Monty's enthusiastic reports as that offensive unfolded gave Eisenhower and his staff in England the impression that a breakout at Caen was imminent. When the attack there sputtered, pressure increased on Ike at headquarters to relieve Montgomery. Instead, he accepted Monty's assurances that his Commonwealth troops would continue to do their part by keeping powerful German forces tied down near Caen while Bradley prepared to deliver the big blow near St.-Lô.

Ike's forbearance allowed Montgomery to fulfill that pledge. Six of eight panzer divisions in Normandy remained engaged near Caen when Bradley's attack opened on July 25 with a terrific aerial bombardment by more than 1,500 B-17s and B-24s. American troops had pulled back from the front there to avoid being hit—but not far enough. Hundreds were killed or wounded when bombs went astray. Yet the carnage was far worse among the Germans, who had advanced when their foes pulled back and were dreadfully exposed. "My front lines looked like the face of the moon," reported Maj. Gen. Fritz Bayerlein, whose panzer division bore the brunt of the bombing. "At least 70 percent of my troops were out of action—dead, wounded, crazed or numbed.

"My front lines looked like the face of the moon."

Maj. Gen. Fritz Bayerlein, whose panzer division was hit by Allied bombers on July 25

All my forward tanks were knocked out, and the roads were practically impassable."

Bradley's infantry poured through the gap, followed by tanks, some of which had steel blades attached up front to cut through hedgerows. Within days, the Americans had broken out of the bocage. To exploit that opening, Eisenhower sent in Patton's Third Army, led by fresh armored divisions that raced eastward across open country and threatened to cut off German forces who were falling back from Caen toward the town of Falaise. Field Marshal Gunther von Kluge, who had taken charge of all Axis forces in France in July after Rommel was wounded and returned to Germany for treatment, warned Hitler that the situation was critical. "As a result of the breakthrough of the enemy armored spearheads," Kluge reported on August 1, "the whole Western Front has been ripped open."

That alarming news could not have come at a worse time for Hitler, who had narrowly escaped assassination on July 20 when a bomb exploded at the Wolf's Lair, his headquarters in East Prussia. The conspirators, who included several high-ranking officers, had hoped to topple the Nazi regime and make peace with the Allies before they conquered Germany. An existing German contingency plan known as Operation Valkyrie called for the Territorial Reserve Army to impose order in the event of civil unrest. A group of senior army officers, including Gen. Friedrich Olbricht, Maj. Gen. Henning von Tresckow, and Col. Claus von Stauffenberg, chief of staff of the Reserve Army, planned to use those forces to disarm the SS and arrest the Nazi leadership once Hitler was dead.

On July 20, 1944, Stauffenberg attended a meeting with Hitler and others at the Wolf's Lair, the führer's command post in East

*Col. Claus von Stauffenberg stands at attention at far left as Hitler
arrives at the Wolf's Lair on July 15, 1944.*

Prussia, and placed a briefcase containing a time bomb under the
conference table before excusing himself. At 12:42 p.m., the
bomb detonated, injuring Hitler and fatally wounding four others. Stauffenberg flew to Berlin to implement Valkyrie, but the
plot collapsed with the news that Hitler was still alive. Stauffenberg and Olbricht were arrested and shot the same day. Hitler
then eliminated proven conspirators as well as suspected enemies.

More than 7,000 Germans were arrested, and nearly 5,000 were executed or forced to commit suicide. Hitler believed that he had been spared by fate for "the task imposed upon me by Providence" and continued with that ruinous task until he died by his own hand. Among those who paid with their lives after that plot collapsed was Erwin Rommel, who had met with conspirators beforehand and favored removing Hitler but not assassinating him. Rommel committed suicide in October 1944 to avoid being arrested and executed.

Although few German commanders actively defied Hitler, many had lost faith in him after D-Day as their country faced defeat on two fronts. A massive onslaught by two million Soviet troops that summer pushed German invaders out of the Soviet Union and back toward their own border. Unable to shift any more divisions from his imperiled Eastern Front to repair his crumbling Western Front, Hitler ordered a desperate counterattack by forces caught in the Falaise pocket, surrounded by Canadian, Polish, British, and American forces. Kluge dutifully complied, but his panzers were pounded by Allied warplanes and stopped dead in their tracks. "No matter how many orders are issued," Kluge informed Hitler in mid-August, German troops had no chance against such opposition and would be annihilated if not withdrawn from the pocket.

Kluge set that withdrawal in motion without Hitler's permission and began extricating tens of thousands of men who would otherwise have been killed or captured when the pocket closed around them. Suspecting Kluge of treachery, Hitler recalled him to Germany. On August 19, Kluge committed suicide by swallowing a cyanide capsule after writing a letter to Hitler in which he urged him to end the war. "The German people have suffered so unspeakably that it is time to bring the horror to a close," he pleaded. Kluge praised Hitler for his "iron will" but pointed out that willpower alone could not turn defeat into victory. "If fate is stronger than your will and your genius, then that is destiny," Kluge wrote. "Show now that greatness that will be necessary if it comes to the point of ending a struggle which has become hopeless."

> **"The German people have suffered so unspeakably that it is time to bring the horror to a close."**
> Letter to Hitler written by Field Marshal Gunther von Kluge before he committed suicide

His plea was futile, for Hitler lacked the greatness that Kluge attributed to him. Having thrust his forces into a disastrous war on two fronts, he had no intention now of surrendering to spare Germans or their opponents further suffering.

While German troops in the Falaise pocket were being battered and blasted, the Allies struck another blow against Hitler by landing in southern France. On August 15, the long-delayed Operation Anvil unfolded between Nice and Marseille on the Mediterranean coast, where nearly 100,000 men came ashore by day's end. Commanding the assault was Maj. Gen. Lucian Truscott, who had distinguished himself in Italy and brought several American divisions from that campaign with him to Anvil. They were bolstered by Allied forces from many countries, including Frenchmen who were returning to their homeland after fleeing Nazi rule. They were among the first to land on the coast and enter Marseille, a major port that would help supply Allied armies as they advanced.

French liberators were hailed in the city that gave birth to their national anthem, the "Marseillaise," but several thousand German troops remained holed up there for a week before surrendering. As French tanks went from one street to the next, wrote their commander, he did not know whether they would be covered with flowers "by pretty, smiling girls or fired at by an 88-mm shell." While the French took Marseille, Americans hurried north to close a gap along the Rhône River through which Germans were squeezing to avoid being cut off. Some escaped there, as many did from the Falaise pocket, but tens of thousands were captured or killed on clogged roads below the gap. As one witness recalled, shattered tanks, trucks, and bodies formed "an inextricable tangle of twisted steel frames and charred corpses . . . through which only bulldozers would be able to make a way."

By late August, the infectious spirit of liberation had spread to the French capital, where Parisians were up in arms against the hated German occupiers. Eisenhower worried that sending Allied troops to secure Paris might have ruinous consequences. Indeed, Hitler had ordered Maj. Gen. Dietrich von Choltitz to destroy Paris if his forces could no longer hold it. "On the departure of the Wehrmacht, nothing must be left standing, no church, no artistic monument," Hitler insisted. Choltitz, a ruthless commander known to his men as "Hard Guy," found this order abhorrent and thought Hitler was crazy. Meanwhile, Gen. Charles de Gaulle and other Frec French officers were urging Eisenhower to let their forces intervene in the ongoing uprising by the Resistance against the Germans in Paris and free that city. "I guess we'll have to go in," said Ike, who concluded that the danger of a bloody and chaotic rebellion was now greater than the risk of committing troops there.

Maj. Gen. Jacques Leclerc's French Second Armored Division led the way, followed by the U.S. Fourth Infantry Division. Choltitz tried to hold them off at the city's outskirts, but when Allied forces broke through and entered the capital in large numbers on August 25, he defied Hitler's order and surrendered Paris

Young girls with bouquets wait in the street of their war-ravaged town to welcome Free French leader Charles de Gaulle, who returned to France from exile in Britain on August 20, 1944, as Allied troops advanced toward Paris.

intact. Bells tolled, wine flowed, and jubilant Parisians thronged the streets as the liberators marched in. "I have never seen in any face such joy as radiated from the faces of the people of Paris this morning," wrote war correspondent Charles Wertenbaker. Four days later, they were still celebrating when the U.S. 28th Infantry Division paraded down the Champs-Élysées. "My feelings as we marched along in the parade were that surely the war must be nearly over," remarked one soldier who took part, Ralph Johnson. "I could not have been more wrong. So many of my friends and comrades would be killed before that happy moment would arrive. Hitler just would not give up."

THE BATTLE OF THE BULGE

"I have just made a momentous decision," Hitler informed his top commanders on September 16. "I shall go over to the counterattack!" Pointing on a map to Germany's border with Belgium and Luxembourg, he added: "Here, out of the Ardennes, with the objective—Antwerp!" The announcement startled Field Marshal Wilhelm Keitel, chief of the Wehrmacht, and others in attendance, who were struggling to defend their country against invasion by foes who appeared unstoppable. Since taking Paris, Allied troops had advanced northward into Belgium and seized the vital port of Antwerp, but it remained closed to shipping because the Schelde Estuary between Antwerp and the North Sea was mined and menaced by big German naval guns. Once the Allies secured that estuary, they could use Antwerp to supply troops preparing to invade northern Germany. Until then, supplies unloaded at more distant ports like Cherbourg and Marseille moved slowly along roads that were heavily congested because the French rail network had been shattered by Allied bombers. Trucks hauling those supplies consumed precious petroleum, depriving tanks and other military vehicles of the fuel needed to continue advances made by armored divisions since the breakout in July. Hitler planned to exploit this situation by massing armor and infantry in the Ardennes and sending his forces barreling across Belgium to Antwerp. If successful, the surprise attack would recapture that strategic port and divide Allied forces to the south from those to the north.

> **"I have just made a momentous decision. I shall go over to the counterattack!"**
>
> Adolf Hitler, informing top commanders on September 16, 1944

Hitler's plan was reminiscent of the stunning German blitzkrieg in 1940, when panzers emerged from the Ardennes and raced to Dunkirk, stranding hundreds of thousands of Allied troops in Belgium and Holland and dooming France. Since then, however, Hitler had added two great powers, the United States and the Soviet Union, to his roster of enemies. His long war against formidable opposition had taken a heavy toll on the Wehrmacht and on Hitler himself, who was visibly shaken by the worsening military situation and the recent attempt on his life. Subject to insomnia and stomach ailments, he was now addicted to dangerous drugs administered by his physician, Theodor Morell. Hitler "had suddenly grown old," wrote his aide and diarist, Maj. Percy Schramm: "He often stared vacantly, his back was bent, and his shoulders sunken . . . The most frightening impression, however, was the tremble of his hands, which had become more pronounced during the last few months."

Yet Hitler was still capable of sizing up his foes and sensing their weaknesses, as he demonstrated by recognizing that Allied forces in France and the Low Countries were overextended and vulnerable to a counterattack. But his plan had an air of desperation that alarmed his commanders. To strengthen his offensive, he would drain German reserves of armor and manpower. All able-bodied males between 16 and 60 would be subject to military service. He even proposed shifting divisions temporarily from the Eastern Front to bolster the counterattack in Belgium. That would be inviting disaster, protested the army's chief of staff, Gen. Heinz Guderian, who had waged war on both fronts and knew that Soviet forces were not only more numerous than their Western Allies but also more dangerous, having suffered a cataclysmic invasion of their homeland that they were now poised to avenge. Hitler proposed to meet that threat by dealing the Americans and British such a crippling blow that he could then move the bulk of his forces eastward and repel the oncoming Soviets—a scenario his commanders considered fanciful, given Allied air supremacy. "This plan hasn't got a damned leg to stand on," said Field Marshal Walter Model when briefed by those who met with Hitler. Model proposed a limited offensive in Belgium by his Army Group B that promised smaller gains at less risk. Hitler would have none of it. He was prepared to stake everything—including the welfare of his nation, which faced a bitter reckoning in the east—on one last gamble in the west.

Three months elapsed before Hitler's decision could be translated into action on the battlefield. During that time, several factors combined to make Eisenhower's forces more vulnerable to attack. Ike's plan for invading Germany consisted of two thrusts—one northward through Belgium and Holland and across the Rhine into the Ruhr, Germany's industrial core; and the other eastward across the Moselle and Saar Rivers below the Ardennes. Shortages of fuel and other supplies meant that one of those thrusts would have to receive priority. Ike, who had set up headquarters in France and assumed operational command there on September 1, gave priority to the drive northward because he needed Antwerp and was under pressure to capture German bases along the North Sea from which two fearsome new strategic weapons were being launched at Britain: the V-1 (a guided missile that flew around 400 miles an hour and could be shot down) and the V-2 (a much faster ballistic missile against which there was no defense). Montgomery led that advance into the Low Countries with British and Canadian forces and Lt. Gen. Courtney Hodges's U.S. First Army. Patton's Third Army was assigned to push eastward. But Patton, whose armored columns had made great progress since entering

France in July, did not receive enough supplies to sustain that momentum. He railed against Ike for favoring Monty and

pleaded in vain for more fuel, even if that meant reducing shipments of food. "My men can eat their belts," he said, "but my tanks have gotta have gas."

The controversy would soon have ended had Montgomery succeeded in punching his way into Germany that fall. But after taking Antwerp, he attempted to reach that goal in one quick leap by landing airborne troops in Holland in late September and capturing bridges over the Rhine. That overly ambitious plan, known as Operation Market Garden, went awry when two panzer divisions surprised the British First Airborne near the Rhine and tore up that division, which lost three-fourths of its 10,000 men. The failure of Market Garden was all the more bitter for Eisenhower because the operation delayed efforts to secure the Scheldt Estuary and open the port of Antwerp, a task that Ike urged Monty to focus on more intently. Not until late November were the coastal batteries neutralized and the last mines removed, allowing supply ships to reach Antwerp. As the weather worsened, Allied troops in France and Belgium struggled to make dents in Germany's fortified western frontier, known as the West Wall or Siegfried Line. In a letter to his wife, Mamie, Eisenhower disparaged premature claims of victory in Europe: "You can be certain that this war is not 'won' for the man that is shivering, suffering and dying up on the Siegfried Line . . . My whole time and thought is tied up in winning the bloody mess."

In fierce fighting that October, men of the U.S. First Infantry Division, heavily engaged in North Africa, Sicily, and Normandy over the past two years, enhanced the reputation of the Big Red One by penetrating the West Wall and blasting their way into the historic German border city of Aachen. Hitler was so attached to Aachen—the medieval capital of Emperor Charlemagne, touted by Nazis as founder of the first German Reich—that he instructed the commander there to hold out to the last man and, if necessary, "allow himself to be buried under its ruins." That officer ultimately surrendered, but not before Aachen was reduced to rubble. "The city is as dead as a Roman ruin," wrote one witness who walked through streets strewn with corpses, "but unlike a ruin it lacks the grace of gradual decay."

Such gains were costly for Americans who would soon bear the brunt of Hitler's counterattack. Hardest hit were those fighting in the dismal Hürtgen Forest south of Aachen, where soldiers who eluded shots fired by entrenched Germans risked being impaled when trees struck by shells shattered explosively. One in every four Americans in action there was killed, captured, wounded, or hospitalized with "combat fatigue," a deceptively tranquil term for a condition we now call posttraumatic stress, which caused some men to go "berserk, screaming and yelling," as one sergeant put it. Soldiers of the 28th Infantry, who had marched in triumph through Paris a few months earlier, took such a beating in the Hürtgen Forest that the division was pulled out in November and sent to rest and refit in a quiet sector of the front where no trouble was expected—the Ardennes.

A few hours before dawn on December 16, U.S. troops holding an 80-mile-long line in the snow-covered Ardennes came under intense bombardment. "All hell broke loose with artillery shells landing all over," recalled Sgt. Ben Nawrocki of the 99th Infantry

Division, who occupied a dugout with his platoon at the northern end of the line. "We could not stick our heads up. Trees and branches fell all over, and shrapnel whined around." When the bombardment ceased, German infantry attacked, guided by searchlights that allowed some men to find gaps in the American line but made others easy targets: "We kept mowing them down," Nawrocki said. "In many places, the Germans piled up on top of one another like cordwood."

> "All hell broke loose with artillery shells landing all over. We could not stick our heads up. Trees and branches fell all over, and shrapnel whined around."
>
> Ben Nawrocki of the
> 99th Infantry Division

Those attackers were hastily trained Volksgrenadiers (People's Infantry), including boys in their teens, men in their 50s, and transfers from the navy, air force, or noncombat duty who knew little about soldiering. Rushing forward recklessly, they suffered heavy casualties, but the sheer weight of their assaults wore down the outnumbered Americans, many of whom were new to combat or battle-weary veterans like those in the 28th Infantry Division who held the center of the line. As the day wore on, seasoned panzer divisions equipped with giant Tiger tanks moved in to exploit breakthroughs by the Volksgrenadiers.

By December 17, panzers had pushed the 28th back five miles to the town of Clervaux, Luxembourg, where Col. Hurley Fuller's 110th Regiment was badly in need of help. "We've got twelve Tigers sitting on the high ground east of town, looking down our throats," radioed Fuller, whose corps commander, Maj. Gen. Troy Middleton, had issued a stand-fast order to prevent retreat from turning into a rout. "Sorry, Fuller, one battery is all I can give you," he was told. "Remember your orders. Hold at all costs. No retreat." Fuller and his troops—a

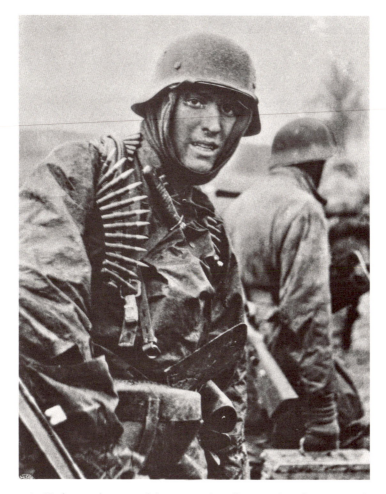

An SS photographer snapped this picture of a well-equipped machine gunner of the First SS-Panzer "Leibstandarte Adolf Hitler" Division, on the road near Poteau, Belgium, on December 18, 1944, the third day of the Battle of the Bulge.

few hundred men, including cooks and clerks armed for combat—were badly mauled by the oncoming Tigers but held out until the following day, when he and other survivors were captured. Heroic resistance by his regiment, which suffered casualties of over 80 percent, helped slow the enemy advance toward the city of Bastogne, where roads the Germans relied

Pfc. James Morris
Frozen Feet and Shell Shock

*Private Morris joined the 87th Infantry Division in 1944
and saw his first combat in grueling conditions when his division
attacked the southern flank of the Bulge in late December.*

So we got to our destination, we got to the road crossing. And we tried to dig in but there was no way to dig it because the ground was froze, snow on the ground and we just couldn't dig in a hole. So I got down behind that big tree. There's a tree right in the forks of the road off to the left and I got down behind this big tree . . . in the snow and tried to keep my head down because the next morning I knew we was gonna catch it. So sure enough the next day, we caught mortar fire, we caught rifle fire, machine gun and about all we could do is just keep down.

We didn't get much chance to fight. And I noticed on this big tree where I was laying the bark was knocked off of that tree about six or eight inches above

Wearing waterproof boots called "shoepacs" to guard against trench foot, Sgt. Tommy Lyons leans exhausted on a snowbank after a week on the front lines during the Battle of the Bulge.

my head. That's how close I came to right there getting killed and finally our tanks come up behind us. And by the way, we were pinned down there

> "I remember shaking so much
> from the cold that my chest was so sore
> I couldn't hardly touch it."

for three days. Three days we couldn't get up to eat or nothing. I had a little piece of chocolate bar, and a piece of cheese, and a C ration left over that I ate during those three days. After the tanks came up, why they mowed everything down just like you cutting bushes in a thicket. And, of course, the Germans moved on . . .

And there was some of our men, I know of at least three, their feet froze and swelled in their boots to where they couldn't get their boots off. And others, their hands would get so cold you couldn't hardly work your rifle. I remember shaking so much from the cold that my chest was so sore I couldn't hardly touch it. And I might mention too that after we left there and went on into the Rhineland there were men that . . . had been shelled so much, even though they were coming back to the hospital to be treated, they were like wild men. They just looked wild out of their eyes. Their nerves were so bad they couldn't sleep. They said that they jumped out of bed at night just in a dream of what they'd been through. They were so nervous they couldn't sleep. I didn't get to that point but I have woke up during the night dreaming and have to get up and walk around to get over it. And I remember there in England after I got back to that little hospital there, I had some terrible dreams of battles and the places I'd been through. ∎

on converged. Without taking Bastogne or St.-Vith, another vital crossroads to the north, they would be hard-pressed to break out of the Ardennes.

Although many American troops fought hard and withdrew grudgingly before the enemy onslaught, some panicked and fell back in disarray. "It was a case of every dog for himself," remarked Maj. Donald Boyer of the U.S. Seventh Armored Division, whose tanks pushed forward through a chaotic mass of retreating Yanks to defend St.-Vith. "It wasn't orderly; it wasn't military; it wasn't a pretty sight," he added. "We were seeing American soldiers running away." Adding to the confusion and alarm were Germans who had orders from Hitler to terrorize their foes. Lt. Col. Otto Skorzeny, leader of the daring raid that rescued Mussolini from prison in 1943, sent German commandos disguised as American soldiers to commit sabotage and sow panic behind Allied lines.

> "It was a case of every dog for himself. It wasn't orderly; it wasn't military; it wasn't a pretty sight. We were seeing American soldiers running away."
>
> Maj. Donald Boyer, Seventh Armored Division, Battle of the Bulge

Worse deeds were committed by troops of the Waffen-SS (the military wing of the brutal Nazi Schutzstaffel) who massacred American prisoners of war and Belgian civilians. The worst incident occurred on December 17 near the town of Malmédy, where more than 80 American POWs were slaughtered. Sgt. Kenneth Ahrens lay wounded there among the dead as SS troops fulfilled their grim task: "Each time they would hear somebody moan, they would shoot him . . . Every once in a while a tank or a half-track would roll by and turn their guns on us, just for a good time." Ahrens and others who feigned death got away and spread word of the massacre, which enraged U.S. troops and incited some to show no mercy to Germans who tried to surrender. "If they wore the black uniforms of the SS, they were shot," remarked one American soldier, who was seemingly unaware that black uniforms were worn by men in armored units of both the Waffen-SS and the regular German Army.

On December 19, Eisenhower met with top Allied commanders. "The present situation is to be regarded as one of opportunity for us and not disaster," he insisted. Since September, they had been assaulting fortified German troops along the West Wall with little success. Now their foes were out in the open, where they would be highly vulnerable to attack when their advance faltered. "Hell," Patton burst out, "let's have the guts to let the sons of bitches go all the way to Paris. Then we'll really cut 'em off and chew 'em up." Ike would not allow the Germans anywhere near Paris and planned to stop them short of the Meuse River in Belgium. But he did give Patton the opportunity to cut them off at Bastogne, which lay at the heart of this bitter struggle—known as the Battle of the Bulge for the salient formed by the Germans as they dug deep into Allied territory.

Although bad weather prevented Eisenhower from launching air strikes against German forces bearing down on Bastogne or landing paratroopers there, he rushed 11,000 men of the 101st Airborne Division in by truck to hold that crossroads as a fortress with troops of the 10th Armored Division until relieved. By December 21, they were surrounded by the enemy. Patton hurried armor north to break that siege, but his tanks were several days away. On December 22, German officers carrying a white flag delivered an ultimatum to Brig. Gen. Anthony McAuliffe of the 101st, demanding that he surrender Bastogne "to save the

"If you don't understand what 'Nuts' means, it is the same as 'Go to hell.' "

Col. Joseph Harper, 101st Airborne Division, rejecting a German demand that Americans surrender Bastogne

encircled troops from total annihilation." McAuliffe's one-word reply, delivered by Col. Joseph Harper, summed up the defiant spirit of embattled Americans: "Nuts!" "If you don't understand what 'Nuts' means," Harper told the Germans, "it is the same as 'Go to hell.' "

Desperate fighting ensued, culminating on Christmas morning in a predawn attack by German tanks, which crushed troops under their tracks and reached the outskirts of Bastogne before being blasted by antitank battalions lying in wait for them with artillery and bazookas. Although the weather remained frigid, the skies cleared, allowing supplies to be airlifted to the besieged city and dropped by parachute. When one of the C-47 transports was shot down, Schuyler Jackson of the 101st recalled, "I took a fleece-lined jacket from the body of one of the crew. It sounds terrible, but he had no more use for it. There was a bridge in front of us. We had planted explosives, but the detonator froze when they hit us on Christmas Day. Their infantry rode on the tanks and we were picking them off. I got myself a bazooka and hit one in the motor. The crew came out fighting. They did not surrender. We had to shoot them." Dead soldiers from both sides "lay frozen stiff where they had fallen," remarked another soldier defending Bastogne. "Burial details had problems putting them on stretchers . . . But in spite of the shells from the Germans, we managed to guide in enough supplies to fight off the enemy. It was great Christmas present delivered by air."

On December 26, Patton's Fourth Armored Division approached Bastogne. Heavy fighting the day before had cost the

Fourth nearly a dozen tanks. But Lt. Col. Creighton Abrams, who would one day become chief of the U.S. Army, radioed headquarters and asked if Patton would authorize a risky end run into Bastogne around a German strongpoint south of town. "I sure as hell will!" Patton replied. Led by Lt. Charles Boggess in a Sherman M4A3 Jumbo tank nicknamed *Cobra King,* the assault force left the main highway and dashed into Bastogne on a side road. "We were going through fast, all guns firing," Boggess recollected, "straight up that road to bust through before they had time to get set." At day's end, they lifted the siege by linking up with McAuliffe, whose refusal to yield Bastogne had been backed up triumphantly by his troops.

Some panzers skirted Bastogne and advanced to within a few miles of the Meuse River, where the U.S. Second Armored Division stopped them in their tracks in late December. Hitler's offensive was now literally running out of gas. Unlike the Americans, who airlifted fuel to Belgium to keep their tanks running, the Germans depended on capturing Allied fuel depots, most of which remained beyond their grasp. At the northern end of the bulge, they seized St.-Vith after a lengthy struggle but failed to reach Liège, a big Allied supply base on the west bank of the Meuse. As their tanks ran dry, they lost the protection of cloud cover and came under attack by warplanes.

On New Year's Day 1945, Hitler sent most of what remained of his Luftwaffe to target enemy air bases. That so-called Great Blow did significant damage to the Allies but greater harm to the Germans, who lost 300 planes and were left without air support as the tide turned against their ground forces. In mid-January, Patton's armor drove north from Bastogne toward St.-Vith, forcing Germans to pull back toward their border to avoid being trapped. At month's end, Allied troops finally closed off the bulge and won the battle. For American forces, who did most of the fighting and suffered a staggering 80,000 casualties, it was a harrowing ordeal that would haunt veterans for years to come. One soldier who returned home to Maine afterward could not stand being in the woods

"There was something ominous about the evening in the country. It echoed of faint screams and the crash of shell fire."

One veteran's recurring anxiety after the Battle of the Bulge

there after dark. "There was something ominous about the evening in the country," he wrote. "It echoed of faint screams and the crash of shell fire."

The toll of battle would have been much worse without the merciful efforts of doctors, nurses, and medics who tended to the wounded and kept the vast majority of them alive. Most Americans who died in action during the war were killed instantly or perished before medical help reached them. Of those wounded who received treatment, just 4 percent died— half the death rate of World War I. Miracle drugs such as penicillin saved numerous victims, but their survival on the battlefield depended largely on medics who risked their own lives to deliver first aid and evacuate them to field hospitals. Nearly 2,000 medics were killed in the line of duty in Europe during the war. Doctors and nurses at field hospitals were at less risk, but some worked perilously close to the front lines at makeshift surgical wards. Dr. Henry Hills of the U.S. Medical Corps volunteered to parachute into besieged Bastogne in December 1944 but ended up landing there in a glider. He operated without a gown or mask in a dimly lit garage filled with 800 wounded men, many of them suffering from gangrene and requiring amputations. One officer objected that he was removing limbs "right and left" and questioned whether all those operations were necessary. "So I picked up a limb and handed it to him," Hills related. "He just about passed out. He never said another word."

U.S. Army nurse Mary Breeding worked at a French hospital that was overwhelmed with wounded during the Battle of the Bulge. Patients requiring extended treatment were transferred overseas. Those who remained under her care were given little respite once they recovered. "Much to my sorrow," she said, they were sent "back to duty." As the war drew to a close, most of her patients were wounded German POWs. They were in "terrible shape," she observed. "Severed cords, paralysis . . . Our boys did a number on them to be sure. We cared for them not as prisoners, but as we would take care of our own in hopes that their side was doing the same for our personnel." Those grateful POWs honored her daily in proper military fashion: "When I entered the ward every morning, I would hear this loud command in German, 'Achtung!' " All the patients would stand or sit upright at attention until she gave them the order "at ease" in German. "What a shock it was for me at first," she said, "not being used to this type of respect."

DIVIDED AND CONQUERED

The Battle of the Bulge proved doubly disastrous for Germany. On the Western Front, Hitler's gamble succeeded only in delaying the Allied invasion for a few months while depleting German forces along the border and depriving them of reinforcements. On the Eastern Front, Soviet troops exploited Hitler's decision to risk nearly all his reserves on a breakthrough in Belgium by sweeping across Poland in January 1945 and invading East Prussia, the first German state to suffer the terrors of Soviet occupation. After entering Germany, one Soviet soldier wrote home: "We are proud to have made it to the beast's lair. We will take revenge, revenge for all our sufferings."

Unarmed parties of German civilians fleeing westward were overtaken by the Red Army and attacked. Many women and girls were raped by Soviet troops, who continued those assaults as they advanced toward Berlin. In the town of Potsdam, near Berlin, young Ingrid Schuler was spared because her parents hid her from soldiers, but a baker and his wife who lived on her street were less fortunate. "The Russians had gone into their house intending to rape the baker's wife," she related. "Her husband, who happened to be at home, stood in front of her and tried to protect her." He was shot dead by the intruders, who then raped his defenseless wife. Some Soviet officers tried to prevent such atrocities, but others looked the other way or took part in the mayhem.

The territorial gains the Red Army made as the Western Allies were beating back Hitler's counterattack in the Ardennes had a profound impact on the Yalta Conference—the last meeting between Stalin, Churchill, and Roosevelt, who was in poor health when the Big Three convened at that Crimean city in February and would die two months later. The major Allied powers had already agreed in principle to divide conquered Germany into occupation zones. The Soviets would occupy eastern Germany and the eastern sector of Berlin, located within their zone. The Western Allies would occupy western Germany and western Berlin. What remained to be determined was the political status of countries occupied by the Red Army—notably Poland. The United States, Britain, and France supported the Polish government-in-exile in London, which had launched an ill-fated uprising in Warsaw in 1944 while the Germans still held Poland. Stalin had withheld support from that uprising and waited until it was brutally crushed by the Nazis to invade that country and install Polish collaborators loyal to Moscow as the country's new rulers. "We drew the sword for Poland against Hitler's brutal attack," Churchill said. "Never could I be content with any solution that would not leave Poland as a free and independent state."

In the end, however, Churchill and Roosevelt settled for Stalin's empty promise that Poland would be "free, independent, and

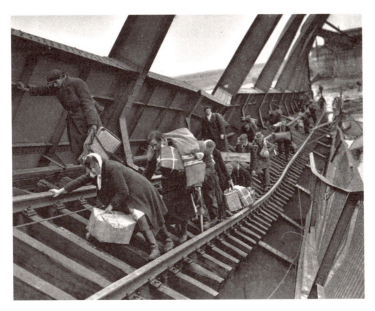

Frightened German civilians, fearing reprisals by Russian troops advancing from the east, carefully make their way westward across the Elbe River on a damaged railroad bridge at Tangermünde, Germany, shortly before the war's end.

powerful." His pledge to allow democratic elections would not be fulfilled in Poland or in other eastern European countries that were occupied by the Red Army and became Soviet satellites. Privately, Churchill may have suspected what the British diplomat Hugh Lunghi, who served in Moscow, already knew—that "there was not a chance in hell that Stalin would allow free elections in those countries when he didn't allow them in the Soviet Union." But Churchill and Roosevelt had little

leverage at Yalta when Stalin's forces were within 50 miles of Berlin and their own troops were struggling to get beyond the West Wall. As U.S. diplomat James Byrnes put it: "It was not a question of what we would *let* the Russians do, but what we could *get* the Russians to do."

The big push into Germany by Eisenhower's forces began on February 8 while the Yalta Conference was under way. German engineers slowed the advance by opening dams on the Rur River and flooding large areas along the border. Punishing air raids by the British and Americans—who blasted Berlin and firebombed Dresden in February, killing tens of thousands of civilians—stiffened the resolve of German troops defending their western frontier. Yet they were now heavily outnumbered and outgunned, for Hitler had recently shifted most of his panzer divisions eastward to meet the dire Soviet threat. By early March, Allied troops had shattered the West Wall and reached the Rhine River, the last big natural barrier on their path to victory. Most of the bridges across that river were blown by retreating Germans, but one was captured intact at Remagen by troops of the First Army, whose commander Hodges reported that coup to his boss, Bradley, at

Ducking to avoid enemy fire, men of the U.S. 89th Infantry Division cross the Rhine River in an assault boat near Oberwesel, Germany, on March 26, 1945.

the 12th Army Group headquarters. "Hot dog, Courtney, this will bust 'em wide open," Bradley replied. "Shove everything you can across!" The bridge at Remagen, weakened by German attacks, lasted only 10 more days before it collapsed. There and elsewhere along the Rhine, however, Allied engineers hastily built new spans to carry troops, tanks, and artillery into the heart of Hitler's doomed Reich.

Eisenhower likened the crossing of the Rhine to the invasion of Normandy and launched a massive airborne assault in late March that landed more than 20,000 troops on the far side of that river. One Allied pilot noted that German prisoners seized in that operation appeared resigned to their fate: "A short time before, when they had their weapons, they fought like hell trying

JAMES JOCHEN,
89TH INFANTRY DIVISION
INJURED

On Easter Sunday, 1945, a few days after crossing the Rhine River, James Jochen was seriously injured as the 89th Infantry Division traveled by truck convoy to support the Fourth Armored Division.

The 4th Armored Division had made a successful thrust many miles eastward, and there was immediate need for infantry to back them up to protect their rear areas from counterattack. We loaded into a truck convoy and set out just as darkness fell. It was raining, cold, and miserable. Naturally on these convoy operations in "questionable" areas, there were no tops on the trucks, so that the troops could bail out of the vehicles as quickly as possible when fired on. Sometime after midnight, the convoy halted briefly, having encountered a roadblock of tree trunks and utility poles which had been constructed by the enemy. The tanks of the armored division had simply blown a hole in it and proceeded. Experience with similar situations had taught that enemy troops often permitted strong forces to pass through their defenses, then returned to defend against subsequent traffic which might not be as formidable. We, therefore, were on high alert as we approached this suspicious area. I had got up from my seat, kneeling on it with one leg over the sideboards of the truck, in preparation for going "over the side" if need be. I felt the truck lurch, and felt an impact of something hitting me, and then nothing. I was out cold. I didn't know it, of course, but my war was over.

I regained my senses the next day. I was in a medical tent fastened to a stretcher. When a nurse noticed I was awake, she spoke with me briefly to make sure I was able to respond. I asked what my situation was, and she replied that I was in an evacuation facility, that I had head injuries and a compound fracture of my left leg between the knee and ankle. She reassured me that in all probability, while the damage was severe, no permanent impairment would result. She gave me a shot of morphine, and I went back to sleep. The next time I awakened, it was dark again, but I saw what I thought was a figure I recognized . . . It was Captain Lucius Curry . . . I asked him what had happened to me. He said the information they had was that one of the trucks had driven over a land mine and that there had been others injured, but they had been treated and released with very minor injuries. It was Captain Curry's duty, as personnel officer of the battalion, to see that home folks were notified of deaths or injuries to troops, and to write a brief letter of explanation when the injuries were serious, or when the victim was a fatality. He assured me that he would tend to this promptly, and urged me to write home as soon as I was able. About 50 years later, upon being reunited with John Searle, one of my comrades of that Easter night in 1945, I learned what really happened to me. Apparently as our truck, with me astride the sideboards, passed through the partially demolished roadblock, the truck sideswiped a portion of it, colliding me with it, and knocking me back into the truck. A medical aid man happened to be in the truck with us. He stopped the bleeding, immobilized the broken leg using my carbine as a makeshift splint, and gave me a shot of morphine to lessen the effect of possible shock and to keep me unconscious. When the convoy stopped to refuel, I was transferred to a medical jeep and transported back to the evacuation facility in which I woke up the next day. Of course, Captain Curry did his duty faithfully, and my parents received the customary form telegram, followed by his letter of inaccurate information. ∎

> **"I didn't know it, of course, but my war was over."**

to kill you. Now with no weapons they were as docile as cows and seemed to sense that they had lost the war."

THE HOLOCAUST

Allied forces advancing into Germany encountered appalling evidence of the evil that lay at the heart of Hitler's Reich. Horrified GIs liberated emaciated survivors of concentration camps, most of them Jews seized throughout Nazi-ruled Europe and conveyed to those killing grounds in freight cars like cattle. Some survivors were so "weak and listless," said one soldier, "that they were difficult to distinguish from the dead which lay everywhere." The Allies uncovered a vast system of forced labor and mass murder, designed to enslave and ultimately eradicate all Jews under German authority and others who had no place in Hitler's malevolent New Order.

The Holocaust (a word of German origin meaning "consumed by fire") had been kindled early in Hitler's reign—with prison camps known as concentration camps established soon after he took power in 1933—but it was nine years before the Nazis developed the efficient and systematic program of genocide known as the Final Solution, complete with gas chambers masquerading as showers. Nazi terror in the early part of the war was far less sanitized.

The conquest of Poland in September 1939 left millions of Jews and Slavs at the mercy of Nazi authorities, who terrorized the country. Thousands of Polish leaders, including government officials, teachers, and priests, were rounded up and shot to death. Hundreds of thousands of Slavs were driven from their homes to make room for German settlers. Many of those evicted were forced to labor for the Reich, and some were sent to concentration camps. Polish Jews were uprooted and crowded into dismal ghettos in Warsaw and other cities, where they were subjected by taskmasters to a policy of "destruction through work" and died by the thousands of mistreatment, malnutrition, and disease. Hans Frank, the Nazi governor of Poland, remarked, "I ask nothing of the Jews except that they should disappear."

Ultimate responsibility for the Holocaust lay with Hitler and SS chief Heinrich Himmler, who left the task of implementing mass murder to his eager chief deputy, Reinhard Heydrich. Shortly before the invasion of the Soviet Union in June 1941, Heydrich had formed SS Einsatzgruppen ("action groups") to execute Jews, Communists, and other presumed enemies of the

An uprising by Jews in the Warsaw ghetto in 1943 was crushed by German forces, who deported the occupants to death camps. Avraham Neyer—shown in a dark coat being led away from the burning ghetto with female relatives—was the only member of his family to survive.

Reich in occupied areas of the Soviet Union as German troops advanced. German police were recruited to assist the SS in detaining, shooting, and disposing of thousands of victims at a time. Local civilians motivated by anti-Semitism or anticommunism also took part in those massacres.

Ukrainian collaborators helped German executioners round up more than 30,000 Jews living in and around Kiev, who were shot to death in a ravine called Babi Yar in late September 1941. "The corpses were literally in layers," one witness reported. "A police marksman came along and shot each Jew in the neck with a submachine gun." Hitler knew of such massacres and hoped that they would frighten and demoralize his Soviet foes. He said to Himmler and Heydrich in October 1941, "It is good if our advance is preceded by fear that we will exterminate Jewry."

On January 20, 1942, Reinhard Heydrich met with senior German officials at the Berlin suburb of Wannsee to lay out the Final Solution, as approved by Hitler, and implement the plan, which called for the extermination of all Jews, Romanies (Gypsies), Slavs, Communists, homosexuals, mental patients, and others whom Nazis considered unfit to live. Those able to work would serve as slaves until they collapsed and died or were put to death, ensuring that none would survive to "constitute the germinal cell for the re-creation of Jewry." Others, particularly women, children, and the infirm and elderly, would be promptly exterminated.

The Final Solution required a new kind of concentration camp—known as a death camp, or killing center—and a new method of extermination. At Auschwitz in Poland, three camps were in operation by 1942, one of which (Auschwitz-Birkenau) served as a killing center. Many prisoners were sent there soon after they arrived, told to remove their clothes for a shower, and put to death in one of four gas chambers, where as many as 6,000 people were killed each day using Zyklon-B tablets, which released an odorless gas containing cyanide. "We had two SS doctors on duty at Auschwitz to examine the incoming transports of prisoners," stated Auschwitz commandant Rudolf Höss. As prisoners marched by, those doctors "would make spot decisions," he added. "Those who were fit for work were sent into the [labor] camp. Others were sent immediately to the extermination plants."

Prisoners sent to labor camps lived in unheated barracks swarming with vermin. Disease, overwork, and starvation combined to kill many inmates or so weaken them that they were sent to the gas chambers. "We used to search for a potato peel and fight over it," one prisoner recalled. Inmates were beaten, tortured, and experimented on by SS overseers, whose aim, one survivor said, was "to destroy our human dignity, to fill us with horror and contempt for ourselves and our fellows."

As Allied troops closed in on concentration camps, SS guards tried in vain to conceal evidence of mass murder by demolishing gas chambers and removing inmates. When Soviet troops advanced from the east and reached Auschwitz in January 1945, they found several thousand emaciated prisoners—left behind when most inmates were removed—and incriminating items taken from murdered victims, including huge piles of men's and women's garments and more than 14,000 pounds of human hair.

Allied forces who entered Germany from the west a few months later came upon massive evidence of genocide, including

PRIMO LEVI
DEPORTATION FROM ITALY TO AUSCHWITZ

Italian chemist Levi was arrested by Italian Fascists as a partisan in 1943 and deported by Germans with other Jews to the concentration camp at Auschwitz in February 1944.

Pictured in the spring of 1945 after Allied troops entered Buchenwald concentration camp, inmates there stare bleakly through barbed wire, haunted by their harrowing ordeal under the Nazis.

They loaded us on to the buses and took us to the station of Carpi. Here the train was waiting for us, with our escort for the journey. Here we received the first blows—and it was so new and senseless that we felt no pain, neither in body nor in spirit. Only a profound amazement—how can one hit a man without anger?

There were twelve goods wagons [freight cars] for six hundred and fifty . . . in mine we were only forty-five, but it was a small wagon. Here then, before our very eyes, under our very feet, was one of those notorious transport trains, those which never return, and of which, shuddering and a little incredulous, we had so often heard speak . . . closed from the outside, with men, women and children pressed together without pity, like cheap merchandise . . .

The doors had been closed at once, but the train did not move until evening. We had learnt of our destination with relief, Auschwitz—a name without significance for us at the time, but it at least implied some place on this earth.

The train traveled slowly, with long unnerving halts. Through the slit, we saw the tall pale cliffs of the Adige Valley and the names of the last Italian cities disappear behind us . . . We suffered from thirst and cold—at every stop we clamored for water, or even a handful of snow, but we were rarely heard—the soldiers of the escort drove off everybody who tried to approach the convoy. Two young mothers, nursing their children, groaned night and day, begging for water. Our state of nervous tension made the hunger, exhaustion and lack of sleep less of a torment. But the hours of darkness were nightmares without end . . .

Through the slit, known and unknown names of Austrian cities, Salzburg, Vienna, then Czech, finally Polish names. On the evening of the fourth day the cold became intense—the train ran through interminable black pine forests, climbing perceptibly. The snow was high. It must have been a branch line as the stations were small and almost deserted, during the halts, no one tried any more to communicate with the outside world—we felt ourselves by now "on the other side."

There was a long halt in open country—the train started up with extreme slowness, and the convoy stopped for the last time, in the dead of night, in the middle of a dark and silent plain. That dark and silent plain was Auschwitz. ■

> "Two young mothers, nursing their children, groaned night and day, begging for water . . . the hours of darkness were nightmares without end."

10,000 unburied corpses at Bergen-Belsen, where prisoners evacuated from other camps recently had been held with little food or water. Another 13,000 people died there after the camp was liberated, despite the efforts of Allied doctors. Many survivors were scarred mentally as well as physically by their ordeal. "It will take time for them to become human beings again," said one doctor. Soldiers who thought they had been through hell in battle confronted an even worse inferno, where innocent victims had been tortured and burned. After witnessing one camp, a U.S. Army chaplain wrote to his wife, "This was a hell on earth if there ever was one." By war's end, six million of Europe's nine million Jews had been killed, along with hundreds of thousands of others the Nazis condemned. Including victims who died of mistreatment as forced laborers or POWs, Hitler's murderous regime claimed well over 10 million lives.

> **"This was a hell on earth if there ever was one."**
>
> U.S. Army chaplain in a letter to his wife after seeing a Nazi death camp

THE END OF THE WAR IN EUROPE

By early April, Eisenhower's overwhelming forces had pushed all the way eastward to the Elbe River, within 60 miles of Berlin. Soviet troops were preparing to advance on that city, but nothing in the Yalta accord or other Allied pacts prohibited Eisenhower from crossing the Elbe and entering Berlin before the Soviets got there. His reluctance to do so was based partly on his desire to eliminate pockets of German resistance in western Germany. He also knew that the political fate of eastern Germany had already been decided at high levels and that sending American and British

*The skeletal remains of murdered camp inmates fill two ovens
in the crematorium at Buchenwald in Germany.*

troops to smash their way into Berlin would not alter that outcome. Bradley estimated the cost of seizing the capital at 100,000
casualties and called that "a pretty steep price to pay for a prestige
objective . . . especially when we've got to fall back and let the
other fellow take over." Churchill, now deeply concerned by
Soviet advances and fearful that Stalin would renege on his promises, urged Ike to try for Berlin. "I deem it highly important that
we should shake hands with the Russians as far east as possible,"
Churchill wrote.

The question of whether Eisenhower should cross the Elbe and
target Berlin became moot when the Soviets launched a massive
offensive against that city on April 16. The battle for Berlin provided a brutal climax to a war that devastated Europe and left the
continent in crisis for decades to come. The cost of seizing the
capital was three times higher than Bradley had estimated, and

GERDA KERNCHEN DREWS
THE BATTLE FOR BERLIN

In 1945, as the war was drawing to a close, Gerda Kernchen Drews, a Berlin teenager, was well aware that Germany was about to lose. This excerpt from an interview given to her daughter-in-law, Canadian author Elinor Florence, begins as Gerda is traveling home to be with her family for the inevitable Soviet conquest of Berlin.

When I left the soldiers to turn towards my neighborhood, I saw one of my relatives pushing a baby carriage towards me with her two little girls. She was trying to make it to her parents to stay with them. She yelled at me as she passed: "Watch out! Watch out! They are shooting at us!" There were shells landing all around us.

I made it to our cottage in Wittenau, a suburb on the northwest edge of the city. The door was locked and nobody was home. I let myself in with my key and went into the cellar we used as an air raid shelter, and locked myself in.

Suddenly the trap door opened, and it was my father! My family—my parents and little sister—had moved into the nearby bunker, or bomb shelter. They were convinced I had been killed. My father came

Teen Gerda Kernchen faced almost unspeakable challenges in Germany as Soviet troops took control.

to see if the house was still standing.

At first we couldn't make it back to the bunker because the shelling was too heavy. Finally there was a break, and we ran all the way to the bunker.

There we stayed for days while the fighting raged outside. We didn't know what would happen to us. We were also worried about my older brother Heinz, who was fighting with the German Army on the eastern front.

We remained inside the bunker for days, but we didn't have enough food for everyone, so three men from the bunker snuck out and came back with a bag of flour. I decided to try to get flour from the nearby bread factory. When I left the bunker, I realized that the Russians were on the roof of a nearby school—I could hear the bullets whistling past.

I made it to the factory and the owner gave me a small bag of flour and I brought it back to the bunker. When I think about it today, I can't believe how stupid I was.

Finally, on May 5th, the shooting outside stopped. We were terrified. Russian soldiers battered down the door and entered the bunker.

They said two words in German: "Women, come!" Then our neighbor's mother was raped. It was horrible. They kept several women inside the bunker, but while they were preoccupied, some of us, including my family, managed to escape.

We thought we would be shot the minute we went through the door. There were bodies lying everywhere, both German and Russian.

We ran across a field towards our house. Everywhere there were trenches dug by the German defenders. At the entrance to our neighborhood, there was a huge trench that we had to crawl through. But we reached home safely and my father hid us in the cellar, and covered the trap door with rugs and blankets.

However, there was no escape. I prefer not to talk about what happened when the Russians arrived at our house and discovered us, because it is too painful.

The front-line Russian troops who did the fighting—as a woman, you didn't have to be afraid of them. They shot every man they saw, even old men and young boys, but they left the women alone.

It was the ones who came afterwards, the second echelon, who were the worst. They did all the raping and plundering. They went through all the houses and took whatever they wanted. They stripped homes of every single possession, right down to the toilets. ∎

A Russian soldier waves the red flag of the victorious Soviets over fallen Berlin.

those Soviet casualties were matched by steep losses among the city's defenders, who included women and children. "They should be placed in the second line," advised Nazi propaganda minister Joseph Goebbels, "then the men in the front will lose all desire to withdraw." Goebbels remained with the führer in his Berlin bunker to the bitter end and shared his fate. On April 30, Hitler committed suicide rather than face capture and punishment for his crimes—the worst of which were now fully exposed as Allied troops liberated the survivors of Nazi concentration camps and death camps. Soon Soviets troops raised their red flag over the ruins of Berlin.

On May 7, Hitler's successor, Adm. Karl Dönitz, surrendered unconditionally to the Allies. For many people on both sides of the Atlantic, V-E Day—celebrated on May 8—was a joyous occasion, but the mood at Allied headquarters was subdued. Eisenhower found it hard to savor victory in this great struggle, which he considered necessary and just but also found abhorrent. As he said afterward: "I hate war as only a soldier who has lived it can, only as one who has seen its brutality, its futility, its stupidity."

The Chicago Daily Times *hailed the war's end late on August 14, 1945, as gas rationing ceased and Hirohito came under MacArthur's authority.*

CHRONOLOGY

OCTOBER 20, 1944 U.S. troops led by Gen. Douglas MacArthur land on Leyte in the Philippines.

FEBRUARY 19, 1945 U.S. Marines land on Iwo Jima.

OCTOBER 24–25, 1944 Battle of Leyte Gulf

MARCH 8–9, 1945 American B-29s launched from the Marianas firebomb Tokyo.

VICTORY OVER JAPAN

FROM LEYTE GULF TO NAGASAKI

On October 12, 1944, as U.S. troops commanded by Gen. Douglas MacArthur prepared to land on the island of Leyte and retake the Philippines, another event with potentially devastating consequences for Japan occurred on distant Saipan in the Marianas. Seized three months earlier at a cost of more than 16,000 American casualties, Saipan was now ready to receive the prize for which that island had been captured—the mighty B-29 bomber, whose exceptional range and capacity would enable it to reach Tokyo, some 1,500 miles from Saipan, and rain destruction on Japan's political and industrial core. Construction crews had been laboring mightily to complete the 8,500-foot-long runway required for takeoffs by fully loaded B-29s and were not quite finished with that task when the first of those Boeing Superfortresses arrived. Dubbed *Joltin' Josie,* it was piloted by Brig. Gen.

APRIL 1, 1945
U.S. forces invade Okinawa.

AUGUST 14–15, 1945 World War II ends as Emperor Hirohito announces the surrender of Japan to the Allies in Tokyo, prompting V-J Day celebrations in the United States.

AUGUST 6–9, 1945 Atomic bombs dropped by American airmen devastate Japanese cities of Hiroshima and Nagasaki.

Haywood Hansell, whose 21st Bomber Command would carry out repeated attacks on Tokyo and other Japanese cities. A boisterous crowd of servicemen gathered to greet Hansell and his gleaming aircraft, the largest, fastest, highest-flying bomber in America's arsenal. As they "surged across the coral rubble toward the new landing strip and the idling B-29," wrote one observer, a jubilant sergeant entranced by that imposing warplane shouted above the din of its four huge prop engines: "Look at 'er, look at 'er, look at 'er!"

The B-29 was a potent symbol of America's military and industrial might, which had increased greatly since December 1941 when a nation still suffering the effects of the Great Depression and wary of foreign entanglements was thrust reluctantly into a global conflict. Roused by that challenge, the United States was now capable of committing millions of troops to battle in both Europe and the Pacific while producing technological marvels on the home front like the Superfortress, a multibillion-dollar project that coincided with other defense programs requiring huge investments of capital, labor, and brainpower.

When the B-29 entered service in 1944, few Americans were aware that it might eventually be used to deliver an awesome new superweapon—the atomic bomb, which was being developed in strict secrecy by some of the world's top scientists and a dedicated workforce of hundreds of thousands of people at various sites across the country. Military chiefs who were informed of that "Manhattan Project" had no way of knowing if it would succeed in providing them with a means to end the war. They proceeded on the assumption that Japan would have to be defeated by other methods, including conventional bombing raids launched from Saipan and other islands in the Marianas, as well as costly amphibious assaults on Japanese troops holding occupied territory in the Pacific that shielded their home islands from invasion. Lt. Gen. Tadamichi Kuribayashi, commanding Japanese forces on Iwo Jima—located roughly midway

> "Every man will resist until the end, making his position his tomb."
>
> Lt. Gen. Tadamichi Kuribayashi, Japanese commander on Iwo Jima

between Saipan and Tokyo—vowed to defend that desolate island and its vital air base as he would his native ground. "Every man will resist until the end," he promised his superiors, "making his position his tomb."

How to overcome such fierce opposition and conquer Japan was a matter of intense debate among American commanders. Hansell and his boss, Lt. Gen. Henry "Hap" Arnold, chief of the U.S. Army Air Forces, believed that strategic bombing alone could win the war if enough B-29s were deployed against Japan and its air defenses were neutralized. They favored seizing Iwo Jima and its air base, which threatened their bombers. But they hoped to avoid further amphibious landings—which were sure to result in heavy casualties for American troops—by targeting Japanese cities and industries and forcing Emperor Hirohito to surrender or see his nation reduced to rubble. Adm. Chester Nimitz, in charge of all naval and ground operations in the Pacific except those in MacArthur's theater, proposed following up the assault on Iwo Jima with an invasion of Okinawa, situated near Japan's home islands and a potential staging ground from which to invade them.

MacArthur, for his part, saw no road to victory that did not run through the Philippines, having vowed to return there. During a meeting with President Roosevelt in mid-1944, he insisted that the United States had a moral obligation to free

Filipinos from Japanese occupation and warned his commander in chief bluntly not to abandon them: "American public opinion will condemn you, Mr. President. And it would be justified." In targeting the Philippines, MacArthur and the admirals supporting him would bring only a portion of America's naval power to bear—but that would be enough to cope with the once mighty Imperial Japanese Navy, reduced now to desperate and often suicidal attacks.

Nations without America's vast resources had to make tough choices when considering how to defeat their foes. But the United States was capable of following various paths to victory and forcing the enemy to defend against multiple threats, as American troops did in Europe by continuing to fight in Italy while others landed in Normandy and southern France and invaded Germany. In the Pacific, all options that might contribute to the downfall of imperial Japan were vigorously pursued, beginning with MacArthur's landing in the Philippines, continuing with a conventional strategic bombing campaign against Japan from the Marianas and amphibious assaults on Iwo Jima and Okinawa, and concluding with the use of devastating nuclear weapons against the cities of Hiroshima and Nagasaki.

That the United States could wage war successfully on various fronts in the Pacific while at the same time securing victory over Germany was something that few Japanese commanders had anticipated when the fighting began—with the exception of shrewd observers like the late Adm. Isoroku Yamamoto who had visited America before the war. Another officer who foresaw America's rise as a superpower was the ill-fated defender of Iwo Jima, General Kuribayashi, who toured the United States as a military attaché in the depths of the Depression, marveled at its resilience and resourcefulness during that crisis, and wrote prophetically in 1931: "The United States is the last country in the world Japan should fight."

RETURN TO THE PHILIPPINES

On the morning of October 20, 1944, MacArthur's troops came ashore on Leyte, nestled between Mindanao, at the southern end of the Philippines, and the populous northern island of Luzon, MacArthur's ultimate objective. Japanese commanders had expected him to target Mindanao and had fewer troops on Leyte, most of whom withdrew into the island's rugged interior before the landings occurred. Facing little opposition on the beaches, MacArthur himself went ashore that same day. When his landing craft was prevented from coming all the way in to the crowded beach, he proceeded to wade in—a determined gesture that made a fine picture for cameramen on hand to record the event. Technicians of the U.S. Army Signal Corps set up a radio microphone on the beach to broadcast MacArthur's words to Filipinos, including thousands of guerrillas prepared to join American forces in ousting the Japanese. "People of the Philippines, I have returned," he proclaimed. "The hour of your redemption is here . . . Rally to me . . . As the lines of battle roll forward to bring you within the zone of operations, rise and strike."

> "People of the Philippines, I have returned. The hour of your redemption is here."
>
> Gen. Douglas MacArthur

By portraying this campaign as his personal crusade, MacArthur gave Filipinos a prominent figure to rally around. But the battle to reclaim the Philippines was in fact a massive undertaking by hundreds of thousands of troops and naval forces, some of them

This leaflet, produced by the U.S. Army's Southwest Pacific Area Psychological Warfare Branch, announced to Filipinos that General MacArthur had returned to the Philippines as promised in October 1944 along with that country's president, Sergio Osmeña.

not under MacArthur's command. Nimitz sent the U.S. Navy's potent Third Fleet, commanded by Adm. Bull Halsey, to bolster Vice Adm. Thomas Kinkaid's less formidable Seventh Fleet, known as "MacArthur's Navy" because it was under the general's authority and covered his amphibious operations. Reporting to separate bosses, Halsey and Kinkaid did not communicate directly with each other. That nearly proved disastrous when Adm. Soemu Toyoda committed what remained of Japan's Combined Fleet to a crucial naval battle waged in and around Leyte Gulf, off the island's east coast, soon after MacArthur's forces came ashore there. Toyoda, whose objective was to cut off those troops and doom their invasion, was taking a huge gamble. But he and other Japanese naval commanders were determined to make a heroic last stand against the oncoming enemy. All they asked, stated one admiral, was the chance to risk everything for their homeland and emperor and "bloom as flowers of death."

Toyoda's plan of attack reflected what his subordinate, Vice Adm. Takeo Kurita, called the fleet's "suicide spirit." Kurita would approach Leyte from the west with a seemingly formidable task force, including the superbattleships *Yamato* and *Musashi,* encased in thick armor and equipped with monstrous guns that could strike targets more than 25 miles away. No battleship was invincible, however, when detected by aircraft carriers beyond the range of its guns and targeted by their warplanes. Halsey's fleet alone was far superior in airpower to Toyoda's—so much so that the Japanese commander decided to use his few remaining aircraft carriers as decoys, hoping to lure Halsey away from Leyte Gulf in pursuit of that Northern Force while Kurita's Center Force and a weaker Southern Force, commanded by Vice Adm. Shoji Nishimura, converged on Kinkaid's Seventh Fleet.

Even if Halsey took the bait and left Kinkaid exposed, Toyoda's fleet would require air support to have any chance of prevailing in battle. To that end, the Japanese prepared to launch warplanes from bases on Luzon and Formosa. Some pilots would employ a fearsome new tactic that epitomized the suicide spirit—kamikaze attacks, which called on them to crash planes loaded with heavy bombs into American warships and die in a blaze of glory. Devoted young pilots like 23-year-old Isao Matsuo felt honored

> "I have been given a splendid opportunity to die . . . I shall fall like a blossom from a radiant cherry tree."
>
> Isao Matsuo, Japanese kamikaze pilot

to be chosen for that task. "Please congratulate me," he wrote his parents. "I have been given a splendid opportunity to die. This is my last day. The destiny of our homeland hinges on the decisive battle in the seas to the south where I shall fall like a blossom from a radiant cherry tree."

The showdown that loomed in Leyte Gulf would indeed prove decisive and historic—the last great naval contest of World War II and one of the largest battles ever fought at sea. Japanese hopes rested largely on the hefty Center Force of Admiral Kurita, who knew that the odds were against him but told his officers that desperate times required desperate measures. "Would it not be a

BATTLE OF LEYTE GULF
OCTOBER 1944

Northern Force (Ozawa)

Third Fleet (Hasley)

Southern Force (Shima)

Luzon

P H I L I P P I N E

Philippine Sea

20°N

15°N

South China Sea

MANILA ★

San Bernardino Strait

Center Force (Kurita)

Mindoro

Sibuyan Sea

Samar

Panay

Leyte
Leyte Gulf

Carrier Force (Sprague)

Southern Force

Negros

Surigao Str.

U.S. Seventh Fleet

10°N

Palawan

Sulu Sea

Battle Force (Oldendorf)

Southern Force (Nishimura)

Mindanao Sea

Mindanao

→ Path of American naval forces

→ Path of Japanese naval forces

120°E

Celebes Sea

125°E

0 mi   100   200
0 km   100   200

In October 1944, Adm. Soemu Toyoda divided the Japanese Combined Fleet into three forces, as shown on this map, and challenged the U.S. Third and Seventh Fleets, which were stationed in Leyte Gulf covering MacArthur's invasion of Leyte.

shame to have the fleet intact while our nation perishes?" he asked them. "I think that Imperial General Headquarters is giving us a glorious opportunity . . . You must remember that there are such things as miracles. What man can say that there is no chance for our fleet to turn the tide of war in a decisive battle?"

Kurita needed a small miracle to escape detection as his hulking warships threaded straits above Leyte to reach that island's east coast, where the Third and Seventh Fleets stood guard. Straits through which Japanese ships passed frequently were favorite hunting grounds for U.S. submarines. In the early hours of October 24, the submarines U.S.S. *Darter* and U.S.S. *Dace* spotted Kurita's force, alerted Halsey by radio, and stalked the warships until dawn. At first light, they torpedoed two Japanese cruisers, including Kurita's flagship, *Atago.* "She was belching flame from the base of the forward turret to the stern," recalled Cmdr. David McClintock of the *Darter,* who watched through his periscope. "She was plowing ahead, but she was also going down by the bow . . . She was finished."

Kurita abandoned the *Atago* and resumed command aboard the superbattleship *Yamato,* but greater trials lay ahead for him. Halsey had yet to detect the Northern Force that was meant to decoy him. When he learned of the approaching Center Force, he launched most of his carrier-based fighters, dive-bombers, and torpedo planes against Kurita in the Sibuyan Sea. Crewmen aboard the *Yamato* and *Musashi* thought that their big ships could withstand anything the enemy threw at them. "The *Musashi* is unsinkable," sailors said. "If it sinks, Japan will sink with it." Like proud heavyweights in prime condition, those twin giants appeared invulnerable and emerged from the first round of their bout with Halsey's airmen unscathed, but warplanes attacking in the second and third waves delivered staggering blows. Around noon, a torpedo struck near the *Musashi's* bow, buckling its armor and sending water flooding into its forward compartments. Subsequent attacks compounded that damage and wounded the *Yamato,* hit by a 1,000-pound bomb that punctured its deck and detonated deep below the waterline. It survived that strike, but the *Musashi* keeled over and sank at day's end, a catastrophe

"Trusting in divine guidance, resume the attack."

Adm. Soemu Toyoda to Vice Adm. Takeo Kurita, Battle of Leyte Gulf

that claimed a thousand lives and cast a pall over Kurita's battered force. As that great ship foundered, he reversed course and debated with his staff whether to prolong what looked increasingly like a hopeless suicide mission. Kurita concluded that he was duty-bound to proceed toward Leyte Gulf, and a message from Admiral Toyoda confirmed his decision: "Trusting in divine guidance, resume the attack."

Prospects for Toyoda's offensive went from bad to worse late that night when warships of Kinkaid's Seventh Fleet shattered Admiral Nishimura's Southern Force as it entered Leyte Gulf from the south through Surigao Strait. Toyoda's plan had called for Kurita to attack from the north at the same time. But when Kurita was delayed by the punishing air strikes Halsey launched on October 24, Nishimura forged ahead and entered a trap laid for him by Vice Adm. Jesse Oldendorf, who crossed Nishimura's "T"—a classic maneuver in which a fleet lined up perpendicular to an oncoming column of warships and delivered converging fire on them with devastating impact. One American officer who took part in that coup said afterward: "We were in the ideal position, a position dreamed of, studied, and plotted in War College maneuvers and never hoped to be attained." Nishimura went down with the stricken battleship *Yamashiro,* and the remnants of his force retreated.

Shortly before dawn on October 25, Kurita's Center Force emerged from San Bernardino Strait, north of Leyte Gulf. Kurita fully expected to be challenged by Halsey's fleet and was startled to find the coast clear. During the night, Halsey had taken the bait and darted off in pursuit of the Northern Force, whose commander, Vice Adm. Jisaburo Ozawa, had finally succeeded in attracting his attention. Halsey did not know that Ozawa's carriers were decoys, with few warplanes on their decks, and he could not be faulted for pursuing them after receiving a report that Kurita had reversed course under fire. But he would indeed be faulted for not leaving a task force behind to guard San Bernardino Strait and the northern approach to Leyte Gulf.

Lacking direct communication with Halsey, Kinkaid knew only what he gleaned from a radio message he intercepted between Halsey and his fleet captains, which gave the false impression that Halsey had indeed left warships to guard the strait. Kinkaid had no inkling that his northernmost carrier group, commanded by Rear Adm. Clifton Sprague, was now exposed to attack by Kurita's oncoming force. "This was indeed a miracle," wrote Kurita's chief of staff. "Think of a surface fleet coming up on an enemy carrier group. Nothing is more vulnerable than an aircraft carrier in a surface engagement." What Kurita and his staff did not know was that Sprague's group contained the most vulnerable of all flat-tops—small escort carriers converted from merchant ships to support amphibious landings and officially designated CVEs, an acronym that sarcastic crewmen took to mean "Combustible, Vulnerable, and Expendable." Kurita had more reason than he realized for the hopeful message he sent to headquarters as battle loomed: "By heaven-sent opportunity we are dashing to attack enemy carriers."

Sprague and his men proceeded to demonstrate that the spirit of sacrifice was not confined to the Japanese. They threw everything they had into a battle that they expected to lose but had to fight to shield MacArthur's troops and their beachhead. The warplanes on Sprague's six escort carriers lacked armor-piercing bombs. Some delivered torpedoes, and others simply strafed or buzzed Kurita's warships in an effort to distract and deflect them. With no time to fuel up, Lt. William Gallagher took off from the carrier U.S.S. *Gambier Bay* with a nearly empty tank, released a torpedo at a Japanese battleship, and plunged to his death moments later.

Similar sacrifices were made by men on Sprague's destroyers, whose task was to protect the carriers at all cost. The captain of the destroyer U.S.S. *Johnston,* Cmdr. Ernest Evans, who hailed from Oklahoma and was part Cherokee, took as his motto the defiant words of Revolutionary War hero John Paul Jones: "I intend to go in harm's way." As Kurita's force closed in, Evans did just that. After first laying down a smokescreen to shield the carriers, he advanced under withering fire and unleashed torpedoes that crippled the

"I intend to go in harm's way."

Cmdr. Ernest Evans, U.S. Seventh Fleet, quoting John Paul Jones

cruiser *Kumano*. His own ship and crew emerged from that attack battered and bloodied, but Evans, who lost two fingers, remained at the helm and refused treatment. "Don't bother me now," he told the ship's doctor. "Help some of those guys who are hurt." He continued to fight—and draw fire away from the carriers— until the *Johnston* was pounded into oblivion. Evans and 60 of his 330 men went down with the ship, and only about half those

Two Japanese battleships make evasive moves to avoid bombs dropped by U.S. carrier-based aircraft, one of which casts a shadow at lower right.

who jumped overboard survived. Just one of the American destroyers and destroyer escorts assigned to protect the carriers survived this desperate battle. Stunned by his determined foes, Kurita worried that he might soon face an even greater challenge from Halsey's Third Fleet, summoned to aid Sprague in an urgent, uncoded message that Kurita intercepted. Around 9:30 that morning, he withdrew, much to the astonishment of his adversary. "I could not believe my eyes," said Sprague, "but it looked as if the whole Japanese fleet was indeed retiring." Victory came as a shock for an admiral who had resigned himself to defeat, if not death. "At best, I had expected to be swimming by this time," he remarked.

In addition to the destroyers that went down, Sprague lost the *Gambier Bay* to Kurita and another escort carrier later that day when the U.S.S. *St. Lo* fell victim to a kamikaze attack. But American casualties were far outweighed by the massive damage inflicted on the Japanese fleet during the sprawling, two-day struggle known as the Battle of Leyte Gulf. Bull Halsey's all-out pursuit of Ozawa's Northern Force led to the destruction of the aircraft carriers *Zuikaku* and *Zuiho,* among other warships, in a rout dubbed the Battle of Bull's Run. The Japanese also lost three battleships in and around Leyte Gulf as well as 18 cruisers and destroyers. In pursuit of a miraculous victory, Admiral Toyoda had suffered a momentous defeat that all but demolished his fleet and left the U.S. Navy in command of the Pacific.

ADVANCING ON MANILA

Victory in Leyte Gulf sustained MacArthur's campaign by ensuring that his troops on shore would continue to receive supplies and reinforcements. But his opponents were bolstered as well by Japanese convoys arriving at the port of Ormoc on Leyte's west coast. Preoccupied with securing Leyte Gulf, U.S. naval forces were not in position to attack those convoys until November, by which time enemy strength on Leyte had increased from 20,000 to more than 40,000. To reach Ormoc and cut the Japanese supply line, American troops followed roads winding through treacherous mountain passes like Breakneck Ridge, fiercely defended by opponents who held the high ground. For several weeks, the U.S. 24th and 32nd Infantry Divisions battled the elite Japanese First Division there in torrential rains and deep mud. American casualties approached 1,500, but the toll on the Japanese, who came under heavy artillery fire, was far higher. Lt. Tatsuhide Yasuda lost three-fourths of his company and greeted two soldiers sent to him as replacements fatalistically. "We are glad you are going to die with us," he told them.

> "We are glad you are going to die with us."
>
> Lt. Tatsuhide Yasuda, addressing two soldiers sent to him as replacements on Leyte

As the year drew to a close, MacArthur's troops on Leyte gained the upper hand. On December 7, three years after the attack on Pearl Harbor, the U.S. 77th Infantry Division made a daring amphibious landing south of Ormoc, which fell to American forces three days later. Japanese troops on the island were now stranded, but they remained dangerous and defiant. That did not stop MacArthur from declaring that his foes had suffered "the greatest defeat in the annals of the Japanese Army." The campaign for Leyte was "closed," he announced, except for some "minor mopping up."

It was not the first time that MacArthur had proclaimed victory when there was still hard fighting to be done. "Often these pronouncements produced bitterness among combat troops, and with considerable cause," wrote Lt. Gen. Robert Eichelberger, whose Eighth Army was charged with "mopping up" Leyte. "I was told that there were only six thousand Japanese left on the island," he noted, an estimate that fell far short of the actual number: "It took several months of the roughest kind of combat to defeat this army. Between Christmas Day and the end of the campaign we killed more than twenty-seven thousand Japanese." Eichelberger's experience was much like that of Australian commanders whose troops were left to mop up on New Guinea when MacArthur moved on to the Philippines. "If there is another war," Eichelberger stated, "I recommend that the military, and the correspondents, and everyone else concerned, drop the phrase 'mopping up' from their vocabularies. It is not a good enough phrase to die for."

> "I recommend that the military, and the correspondents, and everyone else concerned, drop the phrase 'mopping up' from their vocabularies. It is not a good enough phrase to die for."
>
> Lt. Gen. Robert Eichelberger

MacArthur's triumph on Leyte was not as quick or complete as he claimed, but he had good reason to press ahead promptly to Luzon and strike while he had the advantage. The Japanese army commander on Luzon, Gen. Tomoyuki Yamashita, found himself in a plight similar to MacArthur's when the Japanese had invaded that island and taken Manila three years earlier. Yamashita had more than 250,000 men, but many were in poor condition, and they would receive little support from Japanese naval or air forces. U.S. warplanes from Halsey's carriers and bases on Leyte and Mindoro—a small island near Luzon occupied by American forces in mid-December—pounded Clark Field and smashed enemy aircraft there in attacks reminiscent of those carried out by the Japanese in late 1941 when they appeared unstoppable. Now they were reduced to launching kamikaze assaults on MacArthur's fleet as it entered Lingayen Gulf, north of Manila, to clear the way for his invasion forces. On January 6, 1945, Japanese planes crashed into a dozen warships there and killed hundreds of sailors. But those desperate attacks failed to deter landings that brought 60,000 troops ashore on January 9, with many more to follow. MacArthur repeated his dramatic gesture on Leyte

When MacArthur landed at Leyte, Gen. Tomoyuki Yamashita took his depleted
forces into the Luzon Mountains and did not come down to surrender
until the war ended.

by wading onto the beach at Lingayen Gulf as photographers
recorded the event. "The decisive battle for the liberation of
the Philippines and the control of the Southwest Pacific is at
hand," he declared.

Yamashita did not contest the landings. Many of his troops
withdrew into the mountainous recesses of northern Luzon,

where they would hold out for months. Others opposed MacArthur's advance on Manila or defended Corregidor, the stronghold at the entrance to Manila Bay where he had come under siege before escaping to Australia. A combined assault there by U.S. paratroopers and amphibious forces in mid-February trapped several thousand Japanese soldiers, holed up in tunnels. That showdown ended explosively when they first tried to blast their way out and then detonated a massive powder keg in a suicide attack that killed dozens of Americans and most of the remaining Japanese. "I have never seen such a sight in my life," remarked an American officer who was sent sprawling by that eruption. "Utter carnage, bodies laying everywhere—*everywhere.*"

> "I have never seen such a sight in my life. Utter carnage, bodies laying everywhere—*everywhere.*"
>
> An American officer on the aftermath of a Japanese suicide attack on Corregidor

Worse sights awaited U.S. troops who fought their way into Manila. Yamashita ordered his forces to abandon the city as Americans closed in, but the Japanese naval commander there, Rear Adm. Sanji Iwabuchi, had more than 15,000 men and chose to resist to the bitter end. His defiant stand placed civilians at great risk. MacArthur's troops, who liberated emaciated prisoners of war left behind in the Philippines after most of the POWs had been shipped to Japan, also succeeded in freeing 4,000 American, British, and other foreign civilians held in squalid conditions at Santo Tomás University in Manila. Less fortunate were Filipinos trapped in the embattled city, where as many as 100,000 residents perished. Some were killed by vengeful Japanese troops, retaliating for assaults by Filipino guerrillas. Others were caught in the crossfire as fighting raged from street to street and buildings collapsed.

The bodies of Filipino civilians and Japanese soldiers were "strewn over the streets, in gutters, on lawns," recalled Tom Howard, whose tank battalion led the way into Manila for troops of the 37th Infantry Division. Attempts to remove the dead "were met with sniper fire," he said, "so instead of removal, when dusk came the bodies were covered with quicklime to hasten their deterioration and to stifle the smell." He and other soldiers found more Japanese casualties when they entered shattered buildings to clear out snipers: "To keep from being tricked by a sniper pretending to be dead, we pulled all the bodies to the wall and sat them up leaning against the wall. We proceeded to shoot each one in the forehead regardless of whether they were already dead . . . It was a grotesque, gruesome picture to see these row-by-row bodies along the walls. These were the day-by-day necessities to survive one day more."

The searing battle for Manila ended in March 1945 when U.S. troops stamped out the last embers of Japanese resistance in the capital. MacArthur's mission was still not accomplished, however. Fighting to secure Luzon and other Philippine islands continued until Japan surrendered. Much like the Allied campaign in Italy, which contributed indirectly to Germany's defeat by tying down and chewing up enemy forces, reclaiming the Philippines did not force Japan to yield, but it helped achieve that outcome by sapping its strength and morale. "If we occupy the Philippines," one Japanese admiral had assured Emperor Hirohito before his forces attacked U.S. bases there in December 1941, "it will be easier for our navy to carry on the war." Three years later, that navy was crushed at Leyte Gulf, and the Philippines became a graveyard for Japan's hopes and hundreds of thousands of its troops.

THE BATTLE FOR IWO JIMA

The bloody toll paid by U.S. ground forces as they reclaimed one island after another from diehard Japanese soldiers made the prospect of achieving victory through the air all the more compelling. But the initial results of the strategic bombing campaign launched from the Marianas in November 1944 were discouraging. B-29s, equipped with pressurized cabins that allowed the crew to operate at an altitude of 30,000 feet without oxygen masks, flew above the range of antiaircraft batteries but were subject to attack by Japanese fighters and buffeted by jet-stream winds that made hitting targets precisely almost impossible. One pilot, David Burchinal, recalled that on his first mission, directed against an aircraft-engine factory near Tokyo, "we were bombing as high as they could get the airplane, practically in a stall, up to 31,000 feet, scared to death of the fighters. At that altitude, we suddenly ran into these terrific jet winds that no one had run into before. They were well over 100 knots, sometimes you'd get up to 200 knots." Under those conditions, there was no way for the bombardier to get a fix on his target, Burchinal remarked: "The bombs would fly into the fields."

Maj. Gen. Curtis LeMay, a tough veteran of strategic bombing campaigns in Europe and China who took command at Saipan in January 1945, concluded that so-called precision bombing from high levels was too imprecise and ineffective to bring Japan to its knees. He laid plans for low-level, saturation bombing of urban and industrial areas, using incendiaries of the sort that caused firestorms in Dresden and other German cities. Those raids would expose B-29 crews to greater risk of attack, and LeMay stepped up efforts to protect them and save those whose planes were too badly damaged to make it back to the Marianas. To that end, he urged the Navy and Marines to seize Iwo Jima, from which Japanese warplanes menaced B-29s in the air and on the ground. Once in American hands, that island could serve as a rescue station for stricken bombers and a base for fighters, which did not have sufficient range to escort B-29s to Japan from the Marianas but could do so from Iwo Jima.

The attack on Iwo Jima would be followed by a massive assault on Okinawa, which lay close to Kyushu, Japan's southernmost home island. If strategic bombing from the Marianas did not achieve victory, Okinawa would serve as a base for air strikes and amphibious landings on Kyushu, from which U.S. troops would then invade Honshu, the main island containing much of Japan's population and its capital, Tokyo. The cost of that ultimate invasion was almost too dreadful for American commanders to contemplate. Japan's home defense forces included three million soldiers of varying capabilities and vast numbers of civilians, who were being trained for combat in schools and workplaces using bamboo spears and other crude weapons. Girls were instructed to "guard their honor like samurai" when the Americans invaded and join in the suicidal defense of their country. "If you don't kill at least one enemy soldier," they were told, "you don't deserve to die!"

"If you don't kill at least one enemy soldier, you don't deserve to die!"

Instructions given to Japanese girls in preparation for an American invasion

Japanese troops defending Iwo Jima were prepared to give their lives in exchange for a heavier toll in American blood. Their commander, General Kuribayashi, rejected suggestions from naval officers that he fortify the beach and try to repulse the landings. Reports of previous battles in the Pacific convinced him that American firepower, delivered by ships, planes, and artillery, would soon shatter coastal defenses, allowing U.S. troops to break through and score a quick victory. Instead, he planned a defense in depth, embedding his 20,000 men in pillboxes, tunnels, and caves throughout the island, which was only five miles long and two miles wide. His most imposing bastion was on Mount Suribachi, a 500-foot-high extinct volcano overlooking the beach, but dozens of other strongholds, covered in earth and sand and barely recognizable except for the guns protruding from them, awaited the oncoming Marines elsewhere on Iwo Jima. Kuribayashi hoped to prolong the battle and make it as costly as possible for his foes, but he did not expect to prevail or survive. "I am sorry to end my life here, fighting the United States of America," he wrote his wife, "but I want to defend this island as long as possible and to delay the enemy air raids on Tokyo." As invasion forces outnumbering his troops more than three to one approached Iwo Jima, he sent a parting letter to his son: "The life of your father is like a flicker of flame in the wind . . . There is no possibility of my survival. Therefore, you must be the central figure of our family and help Mother."

In keeping with Kuribayashi's orders, his troops allowed thousands of Marines to land on Iwo Jima on the morning of February 19, 1945, before targeting them with mortars and rockets. Caught under the deadly barrage in soft, black volcanic sand, men with heavy packs who tried to run had the nightmarish sensation of being stuck in place. Most clung to the beach, attempting to burrow into the sand and find shelter.

"One of the first sights I saw was a Marine blown in half."
Capt. LaVerne Wagner, at Iwo Jima

"One of the first sights I saw was a Marine blown in half," recalled Capt. LaVerne Wagner, who landed with his company after the Japanese opened fire. "The beach was crowded with Marines as far as I could see. Enemy artillery fire was very hot and it seemed to me that almost half the men on the beach had been wounded and were waiting to be evacuated." Some units made inroads that first day, but for most, it was a matter of hanging on desperately until they had enough men and machinery ashore to challenge their fortified opponents.

Here as at Omaha Beach on D-Day, the impetus to advance came from battle-tested officers like Lt. Col. Charles Shepard of the 28th Regiment, Fifth Division, who made it clear to his battalion that the only way out of the fix they were in was to press forward. "Secure this lousy piece of real estate so we can get the hell off it," he urged as they launched a harrowing assault on Mount Suribachi on February 20. "There probably wasn't a man among us who didn't wish to God he was moving in the opposite

U.S. Marines of the 28th Regiment come under intense enemy fire soon after the invasion of Iwo Jima began on February 19, 1945. Japanese artillery on Mount Suribachi, looming in the background, could target much of the island.

direction," said Cpl. Richard Wheeler. "But we had been ordered to attack, so we would attack . . . Our training had imbued us with fierce pride in our outfit, and this pride helped now to keep us from faltering."

For three days, Marines grappled up the slope at great peril, blasting their foes with grenades, TNT, and flamethrowers and turning their concrete pillboxes into coffins. Finally, on the morning of February 23, men of the 28th Regiment reached the summit and raised a small American flag. Barely visible from the beach below, it was replaced later that day by a larger flag, raised by six Marines—three of whom would die in action before the war was over—as photographer Joe Rosenthal captured the moment for posterity. "I took the picture," Rosenthal said of that famous image, "but the Marines took Iwo Jima."

For many Americans, that flag raising summed up the fighting spirit of the Marines and their hard-won victory on Iwo Jima, but the battle was far from over when the Stars and Stripes rose over Suribachi. Thirty days of horrific fighting lay ahead before the last deep pockets of Japanese resistance on the island were cleaned out. One incident witnessed by a war correspondent typified that brutal struggle. As Marines took possession of two airfields in mid-island and advanced toward a third airstrip under construction at the north end of Iwo Jima, they came under fire from the entrances to caves occupied by Japanese troops.

After hurling grenades and calling in tanks to silence the gunners, Marines brought up flamethrowers and shot napalm, an inflammable gel that sticks to clothing and skin, deep into the caves, where soldiers lurked. "The Marines heard the Japs howling," the correspondent reported. "A few rushed out of the caves on fire. The Marines shot them or knocked them down and beat out the flames and took them prisoner." Japanese troops were seldom captured alive unless severely wounded, so the Marines were surprised when about 40 men who had escaped the flames emerged and gave themselves up. They turned out to be Koreans, forced to labor on Iwo Jima by the Japanese: "They said that everyone else in the caves had either been burned to death or had committed suicide." Groping through the rubble, the Marines found many bodies, "some burned into frightful black lumps . . . The smell was overwhelming and the men turned away in disgust."

Horror mingled with heroism as men on both sides made selfless sacrifices, including seven Americans who were awarded Medals of Honor after throwing themselves on grenades to save others. On Iwo Jima, wrote Admiral Nimitz, "uncommon valor was a common virtue." The battle ended in late March when Kuribayashi conceded defeat by committing suicide. Most of his men lay dead by then, with the exception of a few hundred who were captured and scattered holdouts who remained hidden in caves until long after the war ended. Kuribayashi had fallen far short of his stated objective, which was to kill 10 Americans for every man of his own who died. In fact, the Japanese death toll was roughly three times that of American forces, who had 6,000 fatalities. The Americans also suffered 25,000 wounded, however, making Iwo Jima one of the few battlefields where total U.S. casualties exceeded Japanese losses.

Medics and nurses flew in from Guam and airlifted the most seriously wounded back to hospitals there. "The worst thing you would see were burns, and men who were torn up by shrapnel," recalled nurse Norma Crotty. "The fellows were so much younger than us, 17 or 18 years old, and some looked younger than that . . .

2ND LT. IRVAN BAKER
SMOKING OUT THE ENEMY

*Baker, who joined the Marines in 1943, commanded
a rifle company at Iwo Jima that guarded against Japanese infiltrators
on Mount Suribachi, who used tunnels from which Baker's company
extracted prisoners for interrogation.*

*A Japanese soldier emerges with hands raised from a cave on Iwo Jima on April 5, 1945.
Of the more than 22,000 Japanese soldiers defending the island, only 216 were captured alive.*

This fellow, Ray Duncan, hears voices and he said, "They ain't speaking English." I can't see anybody. It's just a little fissure in a rock wall and a big boulder. So, we moved the boulder, pried it but kept our distance and we could see steps going down, so, we got a satchel charge, it's a hundred forty-four sticks of dynamite, and we could hear it go bump, bump, bump, bump and then boom, and they were still chattering. They were down that deep. So, I called down to regiment, I said, "You better send us a smoke generator, we've got a bunch of people here and we can't get to them." So, we got a smoke generator, and we poked the hose down, and everybody did everything very gingerly, you know, you didn't want to look in, straight down, because you'd get killed, and so, we smoked them. We could see smoke coming out hundreds of feet away. This was like the headquarters of this particular area, like an octopus, and all of these tunnels, and that's where they were feeding those tunnels and coming up at night and shooting at us . . . You know, these guys a minute ago were killing, trying to kill your buddies, and so they came, eight of them came out and one of them was a corporal, or a sergeant, and he had his blouse out of his pants, and another guy was brown nosing him, by tucking [that] shirt in, and I was ready to shoot him, just on general principles . . . They were escorted down to the division intelligence and I hope they got a lot of information from them . . . One day . . . we liberated a cave full of foodstuffs . . . they said, you know, "Don't touch the food, they probably poisoned it." There's a sealed can, I figured . . . why would they poison it? . . . so I opened it up with a bayonet, and little cubes of meat, evidently horse meat, had no fat, and we've been living on K rations, and so, this looked good and some of the kids said, "Lieutenant, you told us, you were a short order cook" . . . So, I got some plastic C-2, which is a plastic explosive, it burns . . . So, they found some scallions, and we rinsed them off with our canteen water, threw it in there, and the sergeant major was leaning against a rock . . . and I said, "Top, you get the first taste," and he leaned over, he took his taste, and then he keeled over. I mean, "My God, it was poisoned. I'm going to be court-martialed." Then I looked behind him, he had six bottles of sake, he got to the cave before we did, and disposed of all the sake. He was stone drunk. ∎

"So, we got a smoke generator, and we poked the hose down, and everybody did everything very gingerly, you know, you didn't want to look in, straight down, because you'd get killed, and so, we smoked them."

ENSIGN FRANCIS T. KLEBER
TWO BROTHERS AT IWO JIMA

Francis Kleber, who later went on to become a career naval officer and commanding officer of two ships, was junior assistant navigator on the U.S.S. West Virginia *during the battle for Iwo Jima. His brother was on shore with the Marines.*

After several days of gunfire support duties and retiring to an outer area at night time, our shipboard existence took on somewhat of a routine aspect. Not so with the Marines ashore, however. As reports came in, it appeared as if some of the unlucky ones would make a costly down payment with their lives before the exchange of any real estate, especially the craggy and apparently enemy-laden Suribachi . . .

I managed to take a hasty look at some of the operation orders which were received on board after our arrival. To my surprise and dismay, I discovered that my brother's regiment had been assigned the objective of capturing Suribachi . . . As a recon platoon leader, he would be taking his platoon out at night trying to determine the positions of the Japanese defenders . . . How was he faring? Was he still alive? Had he been hit by a bullet? . . . Had he killed anybody? . . . While I am sleeping on clean sheets, eating fresh food in the wardroom served by stewards and using table silverware on starched tablecloths, what is happening to my brother, Vic? . . . I visualized him in hand to hand combat with numerous "Banzai!" screaming Japanese fanatics, but I couldn't settle on an ending to such encounters. I wondered if I would ever see him again . . .

On the morning of February 23, 1945, the Troop Commander ashore notified all ships present that Old Glory was flying from the top of Suribachi as a result of a successful assault by the 28th

Marines. With the possession of this mountain, our whole endeavor to capture the entire island had been strengthened greatly. I felt extremely proud to have had something, 'though small, to do with this success, but . . . I felt more proud that my brother was in the regiment which took Suribachi. I still had no idea of whether he was alive or dead, so my emotions were mixed with joyous thoughts of the partial victory and anxiety over his wellbeing. What could I do to assist him? . . . to let him know that I was there even though in sort of a "man behind the man behind the gun" position?

I could write him a letter and let him know that I was nearby . . . At least I could do that, but how could I get it to him? . . . The next day as our OS2U "Kingfisher" float plane was catapulted from the WEST VIRGINIA, my letter was aboard carrying a three-cent stamp. One of our pilots had agreed to drop it . . . in an official message carrier designed for air drop use. When he returned, he assured me that it had landed right smack in the center of airfield #1 which was already ours and that he had seen a Marine pick it up . . .

Much to my surprise and elation, I received a letter from brother Vic after the "Wee Vee" had left Iwo Jima to prepare for the Okinawa invasion. He said that he had, indeed, received the letter in a foxhole the same day it was dropped, that it was a great source of comfort to him . . .

"What is happening to my brother?"

Years later he wrote to me: "The letter's delivery under those circumstances was nothing short of fantastic. Its loss, when the back pocket of my utility pants became torn, denied me possession of one of the most precious items ever given to me in my lifetime." While this letter meant so much to us, two brothers during war time, to others it was merely the first piece of U.S. Mail delivered on Iwo Jima before its surrender. ∎

"The feeling of closeness to these boys I didn't have again until I had children."

Nurse Norma Crotty on the soldiers she cared for on Iwo Jima

They wanted their mothers, and we sort of became their mothers and comforted them . . . The feeling of closeness to these boys I didn't have again until I had children." Many of her patients were fresh recruits, "right out of high school," she noted. "And now a lot of them were ruined for life."

NAVAJO CODE TALKERS

As brutal as the struggle for Iwo Jima was for American forces, it would have been much worse if not for the open battle communication made possible by a special group of signalmen who transformed U.S. codes just when they most needed additional secrecy. In the early Pacific contest, Americans had found that their radio and field phone communications were all too often intercepted by the Japanese, who proved adept at deciphering coded messages spoken in English or other languages they understood. Philip Johnston, a World War I veteran who had grown up as a missionary's son on Navajo reservations and was fluent in the Navajo language, offered a solution. Recalling that the Army Signal Corps had experimented with using Choctaw-speaking signalmen during World War I, Johnston believed that the complex Navajo language would be unintelligible to anyone who was not a native speaker.

In early 1942, Johnston persuaded Maj. Gen. Clayton Vogel of the U.S. Marines, commander of the Pacific Fleet's Amphibious Corps, to begin recruiting Navajo signalmen to encode, transmit, and decipher messages. That spring, the first 29 Navajo recruits began training at Camp Elliott, California, where they created a

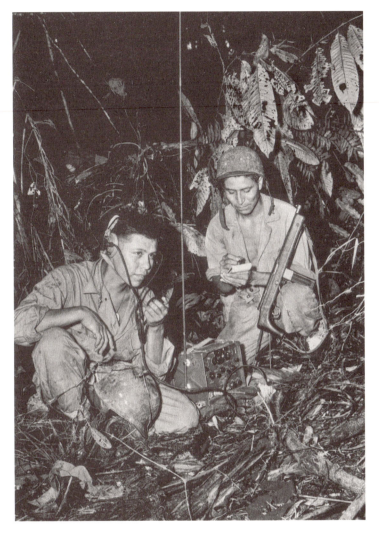

Two Navajo code talkers—one communicating by radio and the other decoding and transcribing a message—act as signalmen on the embattled Pacific island of Bougainville in 1943.

code that used Navajo words to represent military terms. Tank became "tortoise" (*chay-da-gahi*), artillery was "many big guns" (*be-al-doh-tso-lani*), and a fighter plane was a "hummingbird" (*dah-he-tih-hi*). Other English words were encoded using a

Navajo word to stand for each letter. The Navajo words for ant (*wol-la-chee*), apples (*be-la-sana*), and axe (*tse-nill*) all stood for the letter "A." Thus the word "Marine" might be spoken as *na-as-tso-si* (mouse)—*tse-nill* (axe)—*gah* (rabbit)—*yeh-hes* (itch)—*tsah* (needle)—*dzeh* (elk).

By war's end, 375 Navajos were serving with the Marines, transmitting battlefield communications by radio in a code the Japanese found impenetrable. Six of those code talkers were at Iwo Jima, where they conveyed more than 800 messages. Maj. Howard Connor of the Fifth Marine Division said afterward, "Were it not for the Navajos, the Marines would never have taken Iwo Jima."

CLOSING IN ON TOKYO

The struggle for Iwo Jima was barely over before an even deadlier battle erupted on Okinawa. "This is the biggest thing yet attempted in the Pacific," a naval intelligence officer said as the campaign there unfolded. General LeMay's bombers were called in to pound Okinawa before the invasion began on

> "This is the biggest thing yet attempted in the Pacific."
>
> A naval intelligence officer describing the invasion of Okinawa

April 1, 1945, ushered in by the largest fleet ever assembled in the Pacific, consisting of 400 troop transports and more than a thousand warships. Unlike tiny, desolate Iwo Jima, Okinawa was a populous island 60 miles long. Annexed by Japan in the late 1800s, it was defended now by some 100,000 troops, one-fourth of whom were Okinawans who had been told that Americans would brutalize them. Their opponents were U.S. Marines and Army troops under the overall command of

Lt. Gen. Simon Bolivar Buckner, Jr., son of the Confederate general who surrendered unconditionally to Ulysses Grant at Fort Donelson in 1862. A methodical Army man, Buckner possessed a numerical advantage over his foes of less than two to one and had to overcome formidable Japanese defenses at the southern end of Okinawa. That made for a slow, grueling bloodbath, which author William Manchester, a Marine lieutenant on Okinawa, likened to the punishing battles of World War I, when "two great armies, squatting opposite one another in mud and smoke, were locked together in unimaginable agony."

The landings on April 1 went unopposed, offering no hint of the ordeal that lay ahead. "Never before had I seen an invasion beach like Okinawa," wrote correspondent Ernie Pyle, who would die a few weeks later while covering this campaign. "There wasn't a dead or wounded man in our whole sector of it. Medical corpsmen were sitting among their sacks of bandages and plasma and stretchers, with nothing to do." The first few days of the operation were deceptively quiet because the Japanese commander, Lt. Gen. Mitsuru Ushijima, had pulled nearly all his troops back below his defensive line, south of the landing zone. On April 3, Vice Adm. Richmond Kelly Turner, in charge of the invasion fleet, signaled Nimitz: "I may be crazy but it looks like the Japs have quit the war at least in this section." Nimitz, who had better intelligence on Japanese intentions, fired back a message dismissing everything but Turner's first few words: "Delete all after crazy."

Fierce fighting loomed both on land and at sea as Japanese soldiers, sailors, and pilots prepared to die for their cause. On April 7, warplanes from American carriers sank the superbattleship *Yamato,* which had survived the showdown at Leyte Gulf only to perish as it steamed toward Okinawa with orders to "fight gloriously to the death." That mission was thwarted, but a greater threat followed in its wake as entire squadrons of kamikaze pilots descended on Turner's fleet in the days and weeks to come. The Japanese, who used flowery terms to glorify suicide missions, called kamikazes who died together in mass attacks at sea "floating chrysanthemums." Their assaults were dreadful enough without the menacing presence of a new suicide weapon, which the Japanese called *oka* (cherry blossom) and Americans familiar with Japanese slang dubbed *baka* (idiot). A small piloted rocket plane released from the belly of a bomber and packed with TNT, it plowed into ships at speeds of more than 500 miles an hour.

Allied soldiers and sailors were shocked by the suicide missions carried out by these pilots of Japan's Special Attack Corps. The word *kamikaze* means "divine wind," a reference to the typhoon that saved Japan from a Mongol invasion fleet during the 13th century, and those pilots were sent to their deaths as a last-ditch attempt to stem the tide of the war. Vice Adm. Takijiro Onishi, commander of Japan's First Air Fleet, was initially opposed to suicide tactics but changed his mind after the Imperial Japanese Navy lost hundreds of aircraft and pilots in the Battle of the Philippine Sea in June 1944. "In my opinion," Onishi stated, "there is only one way of assuring that our meager strength will be effective to a maximum degree. That is to organize suicide attack units composed of A6M Zero fighters armed with 250-kilogram [550-pound] bombs, with each plane to crash-dive into an enemy carrier." Kamikazes were volunteers, many of them university students, motivated by loyalty to

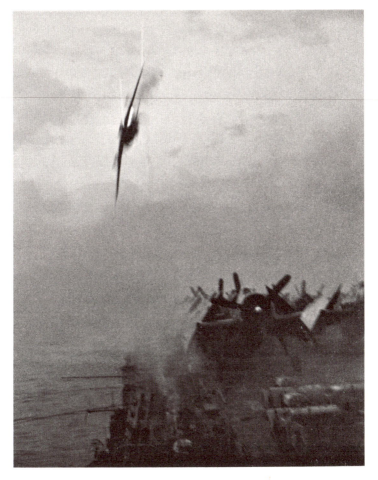

A kamikaze narrowly misses the carrier U.S.S. Sangamon
off Okinawa on May 4, 1945.

country and reverence for the emperor. They were hastily trained for a task that required more resolve than expertise. According to Admiral Onishi, their "nobility of spirit" would be enough to save Japan.

As Allied fleets closed in on Japan's home islands, kamikaze attacks increased. At Okinawa, waves of up to 300 aircraft menaced the Allied fleet. Many of the planes were shot down before they struck ships, but some did terrible damage. In mid-April 1945, the destroyer *Mannert L. Abele* was struck by a rocket plane shortly after being hit by a kamikaze and sank within minutes. The destroyer *Laffey,* blasted by six kamikazes a few days later, was left a smoldering wreck but managed to stay afloat. On May 11, the aircraft carrier U.S.S. *Bunker Hill* was attacked by two Zero fighters. The first released a bomb that smashed through the hull before the aircraft struck the flight deck. Moments later, a second Zero plunged into the flight deck near the control tower, igniting munitions and aviation fuel in a massive conflagration. The attacks killed 373 men aboard the *Bunker Hill* and wounded 264 more. The attack came out of the blue "like summer lightning without any warning rumble of thunder," a reporter wrote, and left the flight deck looking like "the crater of a volcano." Crewmen managed to control the blaze, and the crippled carrier returned to Bremerton, Washington, for repairs.

By the end of the war, the Special Attack Corps had sunk 34 Allied war vessels and damaged 368 others, inflicting 9,700 casualties at a cost of as many as 4,000 kamikaze pilots. Unlike the divine wind that saved Japan from the Mongols, these daring kamikazes failed to turn back the American onslaught. When Emperor Hirohito surrendered in August 1945, Admiral Onishi followed in the path of those doomed pilots by committing suicide in his quarters.

As kamikazes inflicted damage on ships, U.S. forces on shore were locked in a ferocious battle as they challenged Japanese troops deeply entrenched on ridges and hilltops and bolstered by heavy artillery. "Progress was being measured in yards, then feet," recalled Manchester. It was "Iwo Jima all over again, but to the nth degree." As the Americans bogged down, General Ushijima launched a futile counterattack in early May that left 6,000 Japanese soldiers dead within a few days. General Buckner then renewed his advance, but progress remained painfully slow amid drenching rains. Marines who clambered up the muddy slopes of heavily defended Sugar Loaf Hill were beaten back repeatedly. "We made eleven thrusts up that hill," reckoned Sgt. Mike Goracoff, "and fell back each time with most of our boys dead or missing." Neither side in this fiercely contested sector was able to remove their dead while the fighting lasted. "We threw mud on the corpses with our entrenching tools," one Marine recalled, but "shells came in and blew the corpses apart. There were body parts all over the place. We called it 'Maggot Ridge.'"

> "We made eleven thrusts up that hill, and fell back each time with most of our boys dead or missing."
>
> Marine Sgt. Mike Goracoff, at Sugar Loaf Hill on Okinawa

By late May, U.S. forces had secured that ridge and Sugar Loaf Hill and were targeting Shuri Castle, where Ushijima had his headquarters. Having lost more than half his troops, he fell back to a shorter defensive line near the southern tip of Okinawa and fought to the bitter end as General Kuribayashi had on Iwo Jima. Many civilians died in that war zone before Ushijima committed hara-kiri in late June and the last of his troops took their own lives or surrendered. More than 170,000 Japanese and Okinawans perished in this calamitous battle, which left 12,000 American sailors and soldiers dead—including General Buckner, one of the highest ranking Americans killed in the war—and brought the total number of U.S. casualties on Iwo Jima and Okinawa to 80,000. Based on that steep toll, it was estimated that conquering Japan's home islands could

Marine Col. Francis Fenton, an engineer with the First Marine Division, kneels by the flag-draped body of his 19-year-old son, Pfc. Michael Fenton, a scout-sniper who was killed in action on May 7, 1945, while serving with the First Battalion, Fifth Marine Regiment, on Okinawa.

cost as many as a million American casualties. "Victory was never in doubt," said Maj. Gen. Graves Erskine of the Marine Corps, which had paid a heavy price in the Pacific and faced ever greater sacrifices as it closed in on Japan. "What was in doubt, in all our minds," he added, "was whether there would be any of us left to dedicate our cemetery at the end, or whether the last Marine would die knocking out the last Japanese gun and gunner."

BOMBING JAPAN INTO SUBMISSION

By the time fighting ended on Okinawa, B-29 bombers had been blasting Japan's major cities with incendiaries for more than three months. That campaign began in earnest on March 9 when more than 300 B-29s took off from the Marianas for Tokyo. To maximize their impact, General LeMay stripped the Superfortresses of nearly all their guns and gunners and reduced the fuel load, enabling each aircraft to carry twice the usual bomb load. They would need less gas because they would not be flying in thin air at high altitudes. They would approach Tokyo just a mile or two above the ground, which would increase the accuracy of bombing but also make the B-29s more vulnerable to antiaircraft fire. "We'll get the holy hell shot out of us," one airman predicted, but LeMay shrewdly calculated that Japanese gunners would be surprised by the low-level raid and would have difficulty hitting his fast-moving bombers at night.

Pathfinder planes reached Tokyo around midnight and dropped napalm canisters that marked the target area with a blazing "X." Then each suc-ceeding B-29 added fuel to the fire by dropping up to six tons of incendiaries. A brisk wind fanned the flames,

> "In the dense smoke, where the wind was so hot it seared the lungs, people struggled, then burst into flames where they stood."
>
> Robert Guillain, describing the firebombing of Tokyo in March 1945

which spread quickly across a city made up largely of wooden buildings. Soon downtown Tokyo was engulfed in a monstrous firestorm. "This blaze will haunt me forever," said one pilot. "It's the most terrifying sight in the world and, God forgive me, it's the best." Down below, terrified civilians prayed in vain for deliverance. Robert Guillain, a French journalist, described their plight: "In the dense smoke, where the wind was so hot it seared the lungs, people struggled, then burst into flames where they stood." Thousands of men, women, and children sought refuge in the city's canals, but the water was "so hot that the luckless bathers were simply boiled alive," reported Guillain, who called the blaze "a real inferno out of the depths of hell itself." The official death toll in Tokyo was nearly 84,000, surpassing the number killed in Dresden or other German cities set ablaze by Allied bombers as the war in Europe drew to a close.

Civilian losses in later firebombings of Japanese cities were not as steep, in part because some urban areas were evacuated. Within a few months, however, LeMay's campaign had devastated the Japanese populace, leaving more than 10 million people homeless, and gutted Japanese industry, which relied heavily on small factories and workshops that were badly damaged when the fires spread. By June 1945, the prime targets on LeMay's list had been bombed out, and he began targeting smaller cities. Several were placed off-limits to his 20th Air Force. One was Kyoto, which was spared because of its historic significance. No reason was given to airmen for setting aside four other cities, including Hiroshima and Nagasaki. Nor were they told the purpose of a new unit called the 509th Composite Group, which arrived on Tinian in June and trained in B-29s for a secret mission. Only the commander of that group, Col. Paul W. Tibbets, and a few other officers knew that their mission was to deliver an atomic bomb. Tibbets was told that it would detonate with the destructive force of 20,000 tons of TNT—roughly twice the tonnage of all the bombs dropped by hundreds of B-29s on Tokyo on that catastrophic night in March. "That's going to be a damn big explosion," he replied.

The atomic bomb was six years in the making. In August 1939, renowned physicist Albert Einstein sent a letter to President Roosevelt warning that German scientists were seeking ways of triggering "a nuclear chain reaction in a large mass of uranium," a process that could result in "extremely powerful bombs." Roosevelt decided that something must be done "to see that the Nazis don't blow us up." If a superbomb was indeed possible, America would have to build one before its enemies did. A government committee was established to fund nuclear research, much of it conducted initially at Columbia University in New York. That inspired the code name Manhattan Project for what became a huge, nationwide effort after the United States entered the war. The top-secret program, supervised by Gen. Leslie Groves, involved processing uranium to produce two isotopes: uranium-235 and plutonium-239. Both were highly fissionable, meaning that they could be used to fuel nuclear chain reactions, during which atoms would split apart and release vast amounts of energy. A team of scientists at Los Alamos, New Mexico, led by physicist Robert Oppenheimer designed a bomb that would compress nuclear fuel and trigger an explosive chain reaction.

As Oppenheimer's team prepared to test that bomb in July 1945, President Harry S. Truman—who had learned about the Manhattan Project only after being sworn in following Roosevelt's death in April—debated with advisers whether to issue a warning and urge Japan to surrender before deploying the weapon. Some officials believed that Japan would soon yield without being subjected to a nuclear attack if the United States modified its demand for unconditional surrender to allow Hirohito to remain as emperor. Before Truman met with other Allied leaders at Potsdam, Germany, in mid-July, Assistant Secretary of War John McCloy drafted a proclamation that laid out strict terms for Japan's surrender, including complete disarmament, war crimes trials, and military occupation, but he promised that the occupying forces would be "withdrawn as soon as there has been

NUCLEAR PHYSICIST ROBERT CARTER
CENSORSHIP AND ROBERT OPPENHEIMER

When the professors Bob Carter had been assisting at Purdue University left to work at the Manhattan Project at Los Alamos, they recruited him away from his job teaching Navy recruits to help with the development of a nuclear reactor that could run on enriched uranium. Here's how he first met Robert Oppenheimer, as he told it to students of the Story Quest Project at Washington College's Starr Center for the Study of the American Experience.

We weren't allowed to tell anyone what we were doing, and all of our mail, we were allowed to exchange mail, but all of our mail was kind of censored. What was done was that there was an office at Los Alamos, and all incoming mail went through that office. Military officers opened up everybody's mail and incoming mail. They scanned and looked through it for any comments or questions or difficulties that might release, in some way, or might indicate that someone outside knew what was going on at the project. Then the outgoing mail, all the mail that we sent out, we were not allowed to seal the envelopes. We would post it into a special mailbox, which would go through that same office, and they would look through it to make sure we weren't releasing some kind of classified information. So my mother and I exchanged information letters, I guess not very frequently. I wasn't a very good corre-

Los Alamos physicists Limon Perrot, Robert Carter, Enrico Fermi, and David Inglis

spondent. Well, I was kind of lazy as far as correspondence was concerned, but we exchanged mail.

A letter that my mother sent to me, when it went through the security people, they cut out a few words that were in my mother's letter. When I got it then, I remember I opened it and held it up. There were three or four of us sitting in an office, and I held it up and said, "Look what they did to my letter." One of the professor-level people was there with us, and he looked at it and said, "Bob, come on!" And he grabbed me by the hand, and we ran to Robert Oppenheimer's office. Now, he was the director of the Los Alamos laboratory program, and we ran to his office. And I remember he had an inner office and secretary in an outer part of his office, and this man and I came running in. She looked up and said, "can I help you?" This man, who had me by my hand, said, "no." And we burst right into Oppenheimer's office, and my friend held my letter up and said, "Look what they did to Bob's letter." And Oppenheimer jumped up. The three of us went over to the office—it was in a different building—where the censor people were, and I remember Oppenheimer pointed to the officer who was in charge of that office and said, "Don't you dare ever do something like this again!" Then he said, "Find all the pieces you cut out of this letter." The poor man. He was a major, or lieutenant colonel; I forget exactly what his rank was in the army. And he said, "I'm sorry, the pieces were probably put in the trash, and I have no way of locating them now." So I never did find what was cut out of my letter. But I was not much of a historian. Over the next several months, I threw the letter away, whereas, if I had kept it, these days it would probably be a priceless relic from the war. ∎

> "Oppenheimer pointed to the officer who was in charge of that office and said, 'Don't you dare ever do something like this again!'"

407

established a peacefully inclined and responsible government," which could include "a constitutional monarchy under the present dynasty."

Truman preserved the pledge to withdraw forces from Japan when a peaceful government was in place, but he eliminated any reference to a constitutional monarchy under Hirohito, who had approved Japanese aggression and would be allowed to remain on the throne after his country was defeated only as a ceremonial figure with no real power. The official proclamation that Truman and other Allied leaders issued at Potsdam concluded with a stern warning: "We call upon the government of Japan to proclaim now the unconditional surrender of all Japanese armed forces . . . The alternative for Japan is prompt and utter destruction."

"We call upon the government of Japan to proclaim now the unconditional surrender of all Japanese armed forces . . .
The alternative for Japan is prompt and utter destruction."

Proclamation issued at Potsdam by President Harry Truman and other Allied leaders

Truman was at Potsdam when a veiled message arrived there signaling that an atomic bomb had been tested successfully in the desert near Alamogordo, New Mexico, before dawn on July 16: "Operated on this morning, diagnosis not yet complete but results seem satisfactory and already exceed expectations . . . Dr. Groves pleased." A week later, Truman told Stalin that the United States had "perfected a very powerful explosive which we are going to use against the Japanese, and we think it will end the war." Stalin replied that he hoped America would "make good use of it against Japan." In fact, he already knew of the Manhattan Project, which had been penetrated by Soviet spies whose disclosures would help the U.S.S.R. produce its own nuclear weapons.

By the time the conference ended on August 2, Japan had dismissed the surrender terms and Truman had authorized the 20th Air Force to deliver its "first special bomb." As he wrote later: "I regarded the bomb as a military weapon and never had any doubt that it should be used." No alternative means of ending the war other than easing the surrender terms appeared less horrific. LeMay predicted that six more months of conventional strategic bombing would force Japan to surrender, but that meant destruction on a scale that might rival, if not surpass, the use of the two nuclear weapons that were ready for delivery. An invasion of Japan's home islands threatened to be costlier in lives on both sides than any punishment inflicted on that country from the air.

Several hours before dawn on August 6, 1945, Colonel Tibbets and his crew took off from Tinian in his B-29. Christened *Enola Gay* for his mother, it carried a single 9,000-pound bomb dubbed "Little Boy," fueled with uranium-235. Capt. William Parsons of the U.S. Navy armed the bomb after takeoff to avoid a catastrophe if the plane crashed on Tinian. Hiroshima was the primary target, and clear skies there ensured that the city and its 245,000 inhabitants would not be spared in favor of a secondary target. Japan's air defenses were now negligible, allowing Tibbets to approach Hiroshima unchallenged at 31,600 feet and target the city in broad daylight. At 8:15 a.m., Little Boy plummeted from the plane's bomb bay and exploded a minute later in a blinding flash 2,000 feet above the city. Wearing dark goggles to shield their eyes, Tibbets and his crew saw a mushroom cloud billow from the lurid fireball and felt a violent shock wave rock their plane. "The city we had seen so clearly in the sunlight a few minutes before was now an ugly smudge," recalled

*A mushroom cloud rises nearly 30,000 feet above Hiroshima in a photograph
taken from the* Enola Gay *when it circled back to record the impact
of the atomic bomb dropped there on August 6, 1945.*

Tibbets. "My God," said his copilot, Capt. Robert Lewis, "what have we done?"

In Hiroshima, a thermal blast hotter than the surface of the sun, followed seconds later by a supersonic shock wave, killed nearly everyone within a half mile of ground zero and leveled most buildings within a mile or two. Kinue Tomoyasu, a 44-year-old widow who lived three miles from where the bomb fell, saw a dazzling light, which she described as "a thousand times brighter than a camera flash bulb," and was knocked to the floor unconscious. When she came to, she went in search of her daughter—who had gone to work that morning in downtown Hiroshima—and came upon a stricken girl who was naked and whose skin was peeling off. She was calling for her mother and begging for water. "I thought she might be my daughter, but she wasn't," said Tomoyasu. "I didn't give her any water. I am sorry that I didn't, but my mind was full, worrying about my daughter."

Prevented from crossing a bridge into downtown Hiroshima, Tomoyasu was returning home when "the black rain started falling from the sky." That radioactive fallout burned her exposed skin as she ran for shelter. Late that night, she learned of her daughter's whereabouts and found her near death, so disfigured that she was recognizable only by her voice. "Her face looked terrible," her mother recalled. "She still appears in my dreams like that sometimes." She was one of more than 100,000 people who perished in the explosion or soon after. Tens of thousands fell ill later from exposure to radiation, as Tomoyasu did, many of whom died or never fully recovered.

On August 9, a second atomic bomb, fueled with plutonium-239, was dropped on Nagasaki, which had about 200,000 inhabitants but suffered roughly half as many casualties as Hiro-shima because the bomb did not explode over the most densely populated area. Most of the victims in both cities were civilians—as were at least 25 million of the 50 million or more people killed in World War II. On the same day Nagasaki was bombed, Soviet forces entered the conflict against Japan. Its fate was sealed, but some war leaders in Tokyo remained defiant. When Prime Minister Kantaro Suzuki proposed accepting the terms laid out at Potsdam, Japan's war minister, Gen. Korechika Anami, protested. "Who can be 100 percent sure of defeat?" he said. "We certainly can't swallow this proclamation."

Finally, Emperor Hirohito overruled the militants who sought to prolong Japan's hopeless struggle and prevailed on the cabinet to accept defeat. "I cannot bear to see my innocent people suffer any longer," he said. On August 15, following a failed coup attempt against Suzuki by militants who hoped to pressure the emperor into backing down, Hirohito announced that the government was surrendering to prevent the "ultimate collapse and obliteration of the Japanese nation."

The end of the largest and most destructive war ever waged was a joyous moment for some people and a somber one for others. Soldiers on Okinawa who were preparing to invade Japan received the news "with quiet disbelief coupled with an indescribable sense of relief," recalled Eugene Sledge of the First Marine Division. "Except for a few widely scattered shouts of joy, the survivors of the abyss sat hollow eyed and silent, trying to comprehend a world without war."

General MacArthur, who joined Admiral Nimitz in accepting Japan's formal surrender on September 2, spoke for millions when he expressed his hope that "a better world shall emerge out of the blood and carnage of the past." Afterward, he warned that rival powers could no longer afford to resort to armed conflict as the ultimate solution to their disputes. "The utter destructiveness of war now blots out this alternative," he declared. "We have had our last chance. If we do not devise some greater and more equitable system, Armageddon will be upon us."

CONTRIBUTORS

Neil Kagan, editor, heads Kagan & Associates, a firm specializing in designing and producing innovative illustrated books. Formerly publisher/managing editor and director of new product development at Time-Life Books, he created numerous book series, including the award-winning *Voices of the Civil War, Our American Century,* and *What Life Was Like*. Recently he edited *Great Battles of the Civil War, Great Photographs of World War II,* and for National Geographic the best-selling *Concise History of the World, Eyewitness to the Civil War, Atlas of the Civil War,* and *The Secret History of World War II*.

Stephen G. Hyslop, author, has written several books on American history, including National Geographic's *Eyewitness to the Civil War* and *Atlas of the Civil War*. A former writer and editor at Time-Life Books, he contributed to many books on World War II, including *Great Photographs of World War II, Lightning War,* and *Barbarossa*. His articles have appeared in *American History, World War II,* and the *History Channel Magazine*.

Harris J. Andrews, military historian and consultant, specializes in American military history and material culture. He is a historian and artifact consultant for the National Museum of the United States Army Project and has extensive experience researching historical artifacts and military maps for numerous publications. He has contributed to many military history projects, including Time-Life Books' landmark series *World War II* and the arms and equipment volumes of *Echoes of Glory*. He was a contributing editor to National Geographic's *From the Front: The Story of War*, by Michael S. Sweeney; *Eyewitness to the Civil War*; and *Atlas of the Civil War*.

TEXT RIGHTS AND PERMISSIONS

CHAPTER 1

Louise Whatley | credit: Originally published on the website WWII Experience *(www.wwiiexperience.com).* Used by permission of Frances B. North.

George D. Phraner | credit: The words of George D. Phraner, Jr.

CHAPTER 2

Major Roesler | credit: *Documents on the Holocaust* by the University of Nebraska Press, Lincoln and London and Yad Vashem, 1996 edition, pp. 430–32, *www.yadvashem.org.*

Buddy Howe | credit: Copyright © 2017 William K. Howe, used by permission.

John Marote | credit: Copyright © John Marote, originally published on the website WWII Experience *(www.wwiiexperience .com).* Used with permission.

CHAPTER 5

Oreste Maina | credit: Excerpt courtesy of Rosanna Del Buono's "Diary of an Italian Deportee," *http://anitaliandeportee.org/.* ·

CHAPTER 6

James Donahue | credit: Pfc. James Donahue, USMC, First Marine Division H Company, Second Battalion, First Regiment, *www .guadal.com.*

Neal Hook | credit: Copyright © Neal Hook, originally published on the website WWII Experience *(www.wwiiexperience.com)*. Used with permission.

Julia Conner | credit: Originally published on the website WWII Experience *(www.wwiiexperience.com)*. Used by permission of Peggy Walker-Conner.

CHAPTER 7

Margaret Latimer Straight | credit: Copyright © 2017 Margaret Latimer Straight. Used by permission.

Janice Benario | credit: The National WWII Museum, *http://www .ww2online.org/view/janice-benario/segment-1,* August 21, 2009.

CHAPTER 8

James Jochen | credit: From 89th Infantry Division of WWII website *(www.89infdivww2.org)*. Used by permission of Mark Kitchell.

Gerda Drews | credit: From *My Favourite Veterans: True Stories From World War Two's Hometown Heroes,* copyright © 2016 Elinor Florence, used with permission. For more information, visit *elinorflorence.com.*

CHAPTER 9

Francis T. Kleber | credit: Originally published by U.S.S. *West Virginia* website *(http://usswestvirginia.org)*. Used by permission of Mike Mullins.

Robert Carter | credit: Originally published by the Story Quest Project at Washington College's Starr Center for the Study of the American Experience *(storyquestproject.com)* made possible by Iron Mountain's Living Legacy Initiative, used by permission.

ILLUSTRATIONS CREDITS

Cover, Hulton Archive/Getty Images; Back cover (LE), U.S. National Archives, 111-SC-194399; (CT), Roger Viollet/Getty Images; (RT), Margaret Bourke-White//Time Life Pictures/Getty Images; 2, W. Eugene Smith/The LIFE Picture Collection/Getty Images; 6, W. Eugene Smith/The LIFE Picture Collection/Getty Images; 10, Hulton Archive/Getty Images; 15, AP Photo/H.S. Wong; 18, U.S. National Archives, 208-PP-10A-2; 23, AP Photo; 24, Three Lions/Hulton Archive/Getty Images; 28, Keystone-France/Gamma-Keystone via Getty Images; 32, Popperfoto/Getty Images; 39, Bettmann/Getty Images; 46, Naval History and Heritage Command, Washington, D.C., NH-50930; 48, Courtesy of Frances B. North; 50, Official U.S. Navy Photograph/U.S. National Archives, 80-G-019948; 54, Franklin D. Roosevelt Library Public Domain Photographs/U.S. National Archives, 195617; 58, MPI/Getty Images; 60, Laski Diffusion/Getty Images; 66, United States Holocaust Memorial Museum, courtesy Library of Congress; 68, Serge Plantureux/Corbis via Getty Images; 72, Keystone/Getty Images; 75, Slava Katamidze Collection/Getty Images; 78, Roger Viollet/Getty Images; 82, George Strock/The LIFE Picture Collection/Getty Images; 84, Courtesy William L. Howe; 87, Alfred Eisenstaedt/The LIFE Picture Collection/Getty Images; 88, Courtesy John Marote; 91, Copyright © Boeing; 95, U.S. National Archives, NWDNS-44-PA-124; 97, George Karger/Pix Inc./The LIFE Picture Collection/Getty Images; 100, Dorothea Lange/U.S. National Archives, 210-GC-839; 103 (UP), Dorothea Lange/Library of Congress Prints and Photographs Division, LC-USZ62-23602; 103 (LO), Toyo Miyatake; 106, Library of Congress Prints and Photographs Division, LC-USZC4-1663; 112, U.S. National Archives, 208-AA-80B-1; 120, U.S. National Archives, 208-AA-288BB-2; 129, Official U.S. Navy Photograph/U.S. National Archives, 80-G- 007398; 133, U.S. National Archives, 80-G-215398, image courtesy Naval History and Heritage Command, Washington, D.C.; 135, NG Maps; 139, U.S. Naval History and Heritage Command Photograph NH-93595, courtesy of the U.S. Naval Institute, Annapolis, MD; 140, Official U.S. Navy Photograph/U.S. National Archives, 80-G-017054; 142, Official U.S. Navy Photograph/U.S. National Archives, 80-G-14384; 146, AP Photo; 154, AFP/Getty Images; 158, Albert Harlingue/Roger Viollet/Getty Images; 161, Time Life Pictures/U.S. Army/The LIFE Picture Collection/Getty Images; 165, AP Photo; 172, U.S. National Archives, 111-SC-179564; 174, IPC Magazines/Picture Post/Getty Images; 176, NG Maps; 180, National Archives of the U.K., #WO 106/5921/23; 185, U.S. National Archives, 111-SC-178198; 186, U.S. Army/Getty Images; 190, Hulton Archive/Getty Images; 197, NG Maps; 199, Marty Katz/National Archives/The LIFE Picture Collection/Getty Images; 206, © CORBIS/Corbis via Getty Images; 209, U.S. National Archives, 208-NP-6XXX-1; 212, Galerie Bilderwelt/Getty Images; 214, Carl Mydans/The LIFE Picture Collection/Getty Images; 216, Howard Brodie Collection, Library of Congress, Prints & Photographs Division, LC-DIG-ppmsca-22659; 219, Official U.S. Navy Photograph/U.S. National Archives, 80-G-17080; 224, Time Life Pictures/U.S. Marine Corps/The LIFE Picture Collection/Getty Images; 226, Courtesy of www.GuadalcanalJournal.com; 232, Alinari Archives/Getty Images; 236, Courtesy Neal Hook; 239, George Silk/The LIFE Picture Collection/

INDEX

GREAT BOOKS ON WORLD HISTORY

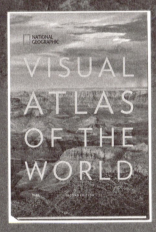

Winston Groom's gifted storytelling sends us soaring with three brave daredevil pilots who became American heroes during the epic era of flight—Eddie Rickenbacker, Jimmy Doolittle, and Charles Lindbergh.

Groom tells the intertwined and uniquely American tales of George Patton, Douglas MacArthur, and George Marshall—from the World War I battle that shaped them to the World War II victory they sealed.

Graphic journalism at its best from the world's leading authority on geo-news and cartography. This must-have, award-winning reference for families, students, and travelers is filled with maps, charts, country facts, and more than 600 photos, satellite images, and illustrations.

ALSO AVAILABLE
National Geographic Maps offer elegant and classic world maps that will help you chart world events, historical happenings, and your own travel. Visit natgeomaps.com for more information.